# AN ARCHAEOLOGICAL ASSESSMENT
# OF THE MIDDLE SANTA CRUZ RIVER BASIN,
# RILLITO TO GREEN VALLEY, ARIZONA,
# FOR THE PROPOSED TUCSON AQUEDUCT PHASE B,
# CENTRAL ARIZONA PROJECT

Prepared for

Arizona Projects Office
U.S. Bureau of Reclamation
Contract No. 0-07-30-X0091

by

Jon S. Czaplicki
and
James D. Mayberry

with contributions by

James E. Ayres
and
Lyle M. Stone

Submitted by

Cultural Resource Management Division
Arizona State Museum
University of Arizona

May 1983

Archaeological Series No. 164

# CONTENTS

# LIST OF FIGURES

# LIST OF TABLES

Table B.2 (pages 105 through 121) contains sensitive information and has been omitted from some copies of this report.

# ACKNOWLEDGMENTS

This report has benefited from the assistance and interest of a number of people. Rich Lange, John Madsen, Paul Fish, David Wilcox, Sharon Urban, and Henry Wallace willingly shared unpublished survey data with the authors. Discussions with Lynn Teague, Arthur Vokes, Phil Jacome, Charles Miksicek, Dave Gregory, Bill Deaver, Allen Dart, Earl Sires, Mike Bartlett, Ken Rozen, and Bruce Huckell provided valuable insights on a variety of topics dealing with Tucson Basin prehistory and history. Don Formby shared his time, collections, and knowledge about the archaeology of the Avra Valley. Keith Kintigh and Carol McCarthy assembled important computer data on pertinent sites and surveys. Julio Betancourt took time from his busy schedule to act as guide to several archaeological and paleontological sites, and to provide important information and insight on the Santa Cruz River and past riverine environments. Daphne Scott and Madelyn Cook of the Arizona State Museum Library helped us locate archival materials.

Brian Byrd and Michael Faught drafted the maps, and Maria Abdin not only entered (and re-entered) our handwritten copies into the computer, but also provided thoughtful observations about report format. Carolyn Niethammer edited the report and prepared it for printing.

Special thanks go to Gene Rogge and Tom Lincoln of the Bureau of Reclamation, Arizona Projects Office, for their patience in waiting for us to complete the report.

Jon S. Czaplicki
James D. Mayberry

A number of institution and agency staff members assisted the historical and cultural resources study by providing access to map collections, document collections, mining claim records and maps, and homestead records. Individuals in the Hayden Library, Arizona State University; Main Library, University of Arizona; Library, Arizona Heritage Center (Arizona Historical Society); and the State Office of the Bureau of Land Management provided access to research materials and answered numerous questions. Sharon Urban, Arizona State Museum; Susie Sato, Arizona Heritage Foundation; Bill Perreault, State Preservation Office, and Don Bufkin, Arizona Heritage Center, were especially helpful in providing assistance and answering questions.

James Scordato, Bernard Fontana, Jay Stock, David Stephen, James Hewitt, and Mr. Reichardt all contributed site specific information. Their assistance is gratefully acknowledged.

Jon Czaplicki of the Arizona State Museum provided advice and assistance that helped make the project a smooth operation throughout.

Finally, John Clonts, of the National Park Service, provided a guided tour of a number of mining sites south of Ajo Road. John's knowledge of the sites and his unselfish sharing of information has made this a better project.

James E. Ayres
Lyle M. Stone

# ABSTRACT

This report presents the results of an intensive archaeological assessment of Phase B of the Tucson Division, Central Arizona Project. Because of the relatively large amount of survey data available for the Phase B area, the Bureau of Reclamation and the Arizona State Museum decided that in lieu of the additional field investigations usually expected at the class 2 level survey, an in-depth review and assessment of existing data in terms of Phase B alternatives would be more appropriate. The survey data were used to discuss the Paleo-Indian, Archaic, Hohokam, Protohistoric, and Historic periods in the Phase B area. Settlement patterning and subsistence strategies for these periods were studied, as were various models for prehistoric cultural development in the area.

Against this background, the three proposed canal-pipeline alternatives and the two reservoir and two sump site alternatives were assesed in terms of their impacts on known and expected cultural resources. Routes B-1 and B-2, the Twin Hills Reservoir, and the Bopp Road sump site were determined to be the best choices because they would have fewer impacts on the cultural resource base.

Finally, to help determine a research orientation for future Phase B cultural resource studies, various research problems were discussed for each of the above-mentioned periods.

# MANAGEMENT SUMMARY

This report presents the results of an intensive review and assessment of existing cultural resource survey data for Phase B of the Tucson Aqueduct of the Central Arizona Project (CAP). Because of the large body of survey data available for the Phase B area, Bureau of Reclamation (USBR) and Arizona State Museum (ASM) archaeologists recommended that in lieu of a Class 2 sample survey, a more thorough study of existing survey data would be more appropriate for future Phase B cultural resource studies.

The main purpose of this study was to assess the various Phase B canal, pipeline, and reservoir alternatives in terms of their impacts on known and expected cultural resources. Because canal-pipeline routes were tentative, one-mile-wide corridors, one-half mile on either side of the proposed centerline of each route, were outlined and all cultural resources in them identified. Assessments of the cultural resources in areas immediately adjacent to the proposed alignments will provide USBR planners with data on cultural resource sensitivity in the event that portions of an alignment change. These data will also be useful to archaeologists investigating cultural resource distribution along the Phase B alternatives. Although an assessment could be done relatively quickly and reliably given the amount of cultural resource information available, it was felt that the prehistory and history of the Phase B area deserved more detailed discussion, and that the existing site data should be reviewed and put into both a local Tucson Basin perspective and a broader Southwestern perspective. Such a review would provide a research orientation for future Phase B cultural resource studies and generate specific research problems that could be addressed by these studies.

An important aspect of cultural development in the Phase B area was the Santa Cruz River and the microenvironment it created in the adjacent floodplain. The river, which supplied precious water, made the land arable and supported abundant and varied flora and fauna in the semiarid Tucson Basin. Consequently, it was the focus of prehistoric and historic development in the basin and played a crucial role in basin prehistory. Using available site data, prehistoric settlement patterning and cultural development in the project area were studied and the influence of the Santa Cruz River on this patterning and development is discussed in this report.

At least 20 percent of the Phase B area had been previously surveyed (surveys ranged from very informal to intensive), and over 300 sites had been recorded. However, a large part of this survey data base had been accumulated over the past several decades and the quality of the recorded information—including descriptions of the survey boundaries—varied considerably. The most serious problem this study confronted was the lack of adequate site function-site type information. Discussions of settlement patterning and subsistence strategies rely on this kind of information; unfortunately, it was often not available or, if present, was too general. All available site survey information, including site function and type information, no matter how brief or general, was used; however, the authors are aware that some of this information is problematical and that future studies will probably necessitate changes in some of our interpretations based on these data.

The report is divided into seven chapters. Chapter 1 sets this report in perspective by briefly discussing previous Tucson Division cultural resource studies. Chapter 2 focuses on the paleoenvironment of the project area. Using historical references and limited paleoenvironmental data, the Santa Cruz River is discussed in terms of what it and its floodplain environment may have been like when Archaic period hunter-gatherers and the later Hohokam farmers lived in the basin. Chapters 3, 4, and 5 provide detailed discussions of the Paleo-Indian—Archaic; Hohokam—Prehistoric; and Historic periods, respectively. Chapter 6 discusses each Phase B canal alternative, ranking them according to the predicted magnitude of their impacts on known and expected cultural resources. Chapter 7 concludes the report with a discussion of potential research problems for each occupational period.

Settlement and subsistence studies indicate, not surprisingly, that the primary focus of prehistoric and early historic occupation in the Phase B area was in, or adjacent to, the Santa Cruz River floodplain. Although the numbers and locations of sites in the floodplain have shifted over the centuries in response to different factors, this area remained the focus of occupation. This fact is reflected today by the number of sites recorded in and along the floodplain.

Areas marginal to the Santa Cruz floodplain were occupied with varying degrees of intensity by Archaic,

Hohokam, and Historic groups, although never with the intensity exhibited along the Santa Cruz River itself.

In assessing the three Phase B alternate routes and their corridors, it was readily apparent that route B-5, running down the Santa Cruz River Valley, was the least favorable in terms of the number and kinds of cultural resources that would be impacted by aqueduct construction. This route runs through the area of greatest prehistoric and historic occupation, and in addition to the numerous recorded sites, the potential for buried sites in floodplain alluvium is very high. Either route B-1 or B-2 offers a much better choice, impacting fewer known and expected sites. While buried and surface sites can be expected along either of these corridors, the overall number of these sites and, to a lesser degree, their size and significance, is expected to be *generally* less than for sites along the B-5 alternative (Table 6.1).

The two potential reservoir sites, Cat Mountain and Twin Hills, are essentially identical in terms of their known and expected cultural resources. The Twin Hills site is slightly more favorable because it will impact fewer sites and because no Archaic period sites are known in the area. Of the two potential sump sites, Bopp Road and Marana, the former would impact no known sites, while the latter would impact seven sites.

Potential research problems for future Phase B cultural resource studies are numerous. Some of the more important ones that may be addressed are the nature of prehistoric occupation in Avra Valley, and the extent of the late Archaic occupation in the Phase B area, including its influence on early experimentation with agriculture, and its relationship to the early Pioneer period Hohokam occupation in the northern part of the project area. The question of the presence and abundance of Hohokam irrigation canals in the Tucson Basin remains to be adequately resolved, as do the social and political implications for Hohokam society of the canals that were present in relatively extensive networks. The Hohokam Classic and Postclassic periods in the basin present several important questions that may be addressed by future Phase B investigators.

# Chapter 1

# PROJECT DESIGN AND RESEARCH METHOD

## Jon S. Czaplicki

This report discusses the results of archaeological assessment of Phase B of the Tucson Aqueduct, a feature of the Central Arizona Project (CAP-TA). The study, initiated 4 January 1982 and completed 30 April 1982, focused on existing survey data for the project area and involved only minimal fieldwork. The amount of previous survey in the Phase B area was such that Bureau of Reclamation and Arizona State Museum (ASM) archaeologists recommended that, in lieu of a class 2 sample survey, a research strategy focusing on recorded sites would be more appropriate and cost effective.

The Phase B assessment will provide the Bureau with additional, detailed cultural resource information needed for project planning. Two of the major goals of the study were an assessment and ranking of the various alternate canal or pipeline routes, and a discussion of the prehistoric and historic occupation of the Phase B area, in terms of particular research problems or themes that could be the focus of the future class 3 intensive survey of the preferred aqueduct route and the resulting data recovery program.

## Project History

The Tucson Aqueduct will provide Colorado River water to eastern Pima County, Arizona, for Indian and non-Indian agricultural, municipal, and industrial use. Prior to actual aqueduct construction the Bureau of Reclamation must identify cultural resources in the project area that may be affected by aqueduct construction. Specific regulations for dealing with cultural resources are defined by the 1966 Historic Preservation Act and subsequent regulations (36 CFR 200 and 43 CFR 422).

Three phases of research are required during project planning and evaluation. A class 1 survey provides basic environmental, cultural resource, and ethnographic information on the project area and is basically a literature search of existing pertinent cultural resource data. The class

2 survey is an on-the-ground sample survey using information from the class 1 survey as well as field checks of selected areas. It is used to further evaluate potential project impacts or to develop predictive models. The last phase, the class 3 survey, is an intensive on-the-ground examination of the preferred project route(s). It will provide the final cultural resource inventory and provide the Bureau with specific information necessary for mitigation planning.

In 1979, the Cultural Resource Management Division (CRMD) of the Arizona State Museum undertook a class 1 (overview) survey of the entire Tucson Aqueduct project area as it was then defined (Westfall 1979). Westfall summarized and assessed previous archaeological research in the project area and identified all known cultural resource sites. She also developed a predictive model of cultural resource sensitivity, based on correlations between site types and environmental zones, and ranked the various aqueduct alternatives by their known and predicted cultural resource sensitivity.

During the spring of 1980, CRMD conducted a class 2 (sample) survey of Phase A of the Tucson Aqueduct, which encompassed an area of about 240 square miles extending from Picacho Reservoir to the community of Rillito, north of Tucson. The sample survey covered approximately 9.7 square miles and recorded 30 sites (McCarthy 1982). Analysis of the survey data provided a ranking of the Phase A aqueduct alternatives in terms of cultural resource sensitivity. It also indicated that Westfall's model was not especially successful in predicting cultural resource sensitivity of environmentally defined areas.

Also in 1980, the Bureau of Reclamation increased the size of the Tucson Aqueduct project area by extending the aqueduct alternatives south of Tucson to Green Valley. The Cultural Resource Management Division undertook a supplemental class 1 overview of the new project area, which identified and evaluated all known cultural resources (McCarthy and Sires 1981). During the summer and fall of

1982, the Arizona State Museum conducted a class 3 survey of Phase A of the Tucson Aqueduct; a similar intensive survey of Phase B is scheduled early in 1983.

## Phase B Project Area

Phase B covers about 392 square miles from the Pima-Pinal county line to Green Valley; it is roughly defined by Brawley Wash and the Avra Valley on the west and by the Santa Cruz River floodplain on the east (Figure 1.1). It encompasses the Santa Cruz River from Green Valley north to Rillito and includes the western portion of the Tucson Basin. Phase B includes all or parts of the following Arizona State Museum archaeological grids: AZ AA:12, AZ AA:16, AZ BB:13, AZ DD:4, and AZ EE:1.

The amount and intensity of previous archaeological research in the Phase B area is substantially greater than for Phase A, primarily because of the greater prehistoric and historic occupation centered along the Santa Cruz River and the extensive urban and commercial development in the area. In contrast, the Phase A area remains essentially undeveloped desert with some agricultural and only minor urban development. Until recently this area was beyond the scope of interest of archaeologists focusing on Tucson Basin prehistory and history.

Westfall (1979) and McCarthy and Sires (1981) discuss and evaluate previous archaeological research in the Phase B area, and the reader is referred to their reports. Because substantial survey and excavation data are available for the area, the class 2 survey (assessment) focuses on these data rather than on new survey data that most likely would duplicate the data already available.

Arizona State Museum site survey project files show that at least 71.25 square miles (about 18 percent) of the Phase B area have already been surveyed. This figure does not include approximately 8 square miles of Saguaro National Monument West surveyed in 1964 by the Arizona State Museum (Figure 1.2); the survey of Saguaro National Monument is poorly described and the survey area not well defined, making assessment of those portions of the Monument that were investigated difficult. However, when this survey is included, the previously surveyed area comprises about 79 square miles (or 20 percent of the Phase B area), a figure almost six times greater than the sample survey coverage of the Phase A area. More than 30 sites have been recorded in the Phase B area.

## Research Method

Recorded sites present a continuum of information on the prehistoric and historic occupation of the Phase B area.

Distributed over time from at least 50 years ago up to the first quarter of the twentieth century, they include the middle and late Archaic, Hohokam, Piman, Spanish, Mexican, and Anglo occupations of the area. This report will emphasize interpretation of these data in terms of prehistoric and historic settlement patterns. One very important aspect of these settlement patterns is the Santa Cruz River, the major focus of prehistoric and—until the advent of the electric pump for tapping ground water—historic occupation in the Tucson Basin. To better understand prehistoric settlement patterns, this study will review the paleoenvironment of the Santa Cruz River (and to a lesser extent that of Brawley Wash in Avra Valley) and its impact on prehistoric occupation of the area. In a semiarid land where water was (and still is) a scarce and often uncertain resource, the river played a crucial role in determining the extent and intensity of human occupation in the Tucson Basin.

Analysis of settlement patterns will be of predictive value in determining where sites can be expected in less well-known parts of the project area, such as Brawley Wash and the bajadas bordering the western slopes of the Tucson Mountains. When coupled with stratigraphic data, the analysis may provide useful predictive information on buried sites.

A better understanding of stream dynamics may help archaeologists interpret existing site data and may provide predictive information needed to define areas of prehistoric occupation. The problem of canal irrigation and its importance to, and impact on, Hohokam occupation along the Santa Cruz River also can be better addressed given a clearer understanding of river dynamics and hydrology.

The majority of data used for this report came from Arizona State Museum site survey files and from the computerized AZSITE files. Site survey collections were not used for this study, all specific site information coming from that available in the files. Limited field checking was done on several Archaic and Hohokam sites recorded in Avra Valley, and two previously unrecorded sites in this areas were added to Arizona State Museum site survey files. Although not directly related to this study, archaeological survey of 31 auger pit sites, each covering about 900 square meters, was undertaken as a part of the project. Two archaeological sites were identified during this ancillary survey.

The historic occupation of the project area was extensive and is reasonably well documented. Archaeological Research Service, Inc. (ARS), whose staff is familiar with Tucson Basin historic archaeology, subcontracted to provide both an assessment of the known historic cultural resources and a predictive model for the presence of these resources in canal corridors of the Phase B area. Data for this study came from Arizona State Museum site survey files

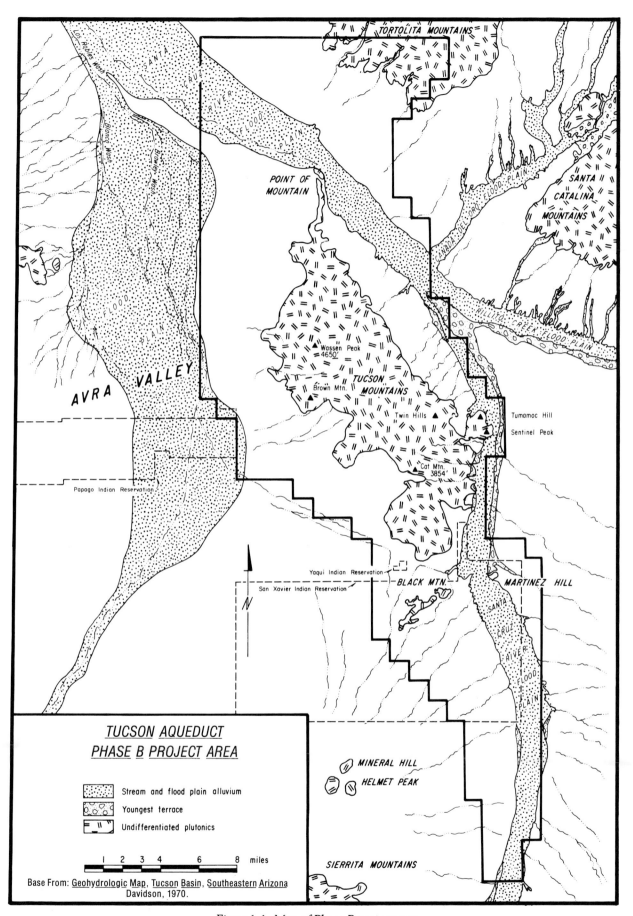

*Figure 1.1.* Map of Phase B project area

[ 3 ]

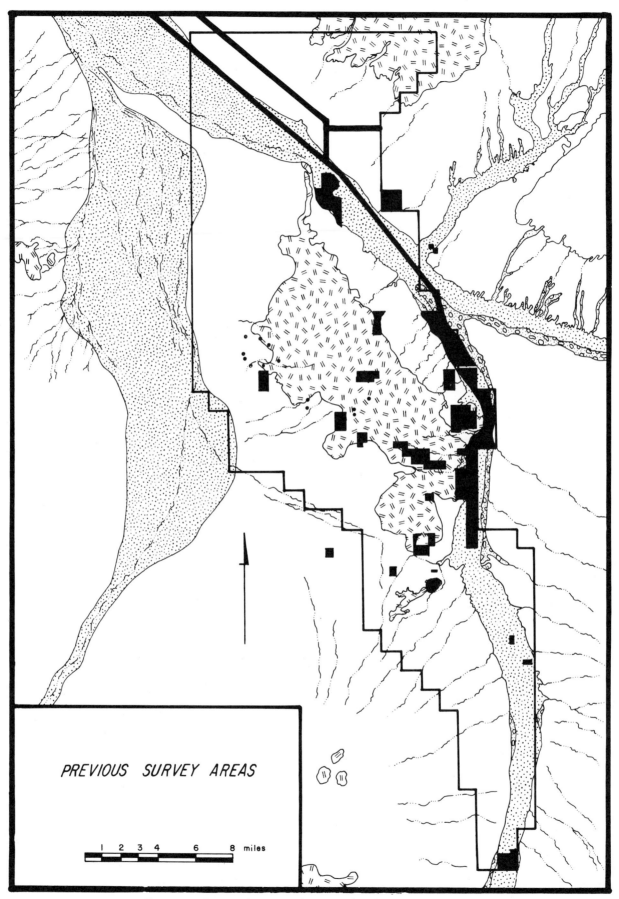

*Figure 1.2.* Previously surveyed areas in the Phase B project area

PREVIOUS SURVEY AREAS

1 2 3 4   6   8 miles

and various records and land survey notes on file with the Arizona Heritage Center, the Bureau of Land Management, and other institutions.

The study by Archaeological Research Service Inc., comprises Chapter 5. Their research method varied from that described for Chapters 3 and 4; consequently, their approach in discussing the historic cultural resources in the Phase B area also varies. The end result, however, is basically the same and provides the assessment of known and expected historic cultural resources necessary in evaluating the potential construction impact of each canal corridor.

# Chapter 2

# EFFECTIVE ENVIRONMENT: PAST AND PRESENT

## Jon S. Czaplicki

Westfall (1979) and Betancourt (1978a, b) discuss the current environment of the project area at some length, and the reader is referred to these reports for specific details. The following synthesis from these reports should provide a general view of the current environment and serve as a background for a discussion of the past environment.

Betancourt (1978b: 31) also points out that there have been few attempts to correlate past environmental conditions with the basin's archaeological and historical record. One of the goals of this study is to look at the past environment of the Phase B area and relate this information to prehistoric occupation in the area. The major problem in doing this is the scarcity of data required to assess past climatic conditions. Such data would include pollen and macrofloral studies, pack rat midden analyses, faunal analyses, alluvial stratigraphy, paleohydrology, and radiocarbon dating. More work is being done today to supply these kinds of data, but much remains to be done. Some areas, such as paleohydrology, are only now coming under consideration in terms of their impact on the prehistoric occupation of the basin.

## Present Environmental Background

The Tucson Basin, of which Phase B encompasses the western part, is a typical Basin-and-Range intermontane trough resulting from uplifting of surrounding mountain masses. The Phase B area includes the north-south trending Tucson Mountain Range and is flanked by alluvial valleys: the broad Avra Valley and Brawley Wash drainage on the west, and the Santa Cruz River Valley on the east.

The northward trending basin is bounded on the east by the Santa Rita, Empire, Rincon, and Tanque Verde mountains, on the north by the Santa Catalina and Tortolita mountains, and on the west by the Sierrita, Black, and Tucson mountains. These ranges were formed in the late Tertiary and early Quaternary by block-faulting and

were accompanied by volcanic extrusions that formed "A" Mountain (Sentinel Peak), Tumamoc Hill, Martinez Hill, and the Black Mountains, all of which lie in the Phase B area.

## Hydrology and Climate

The Santa Cruz River and its tributaries constitute the primary drainage system in the study area. The river heads in the San Raphael Valley of southern Arizona and drains some 8990 square miles (Bowden 1981) on its northward journey through the basin and on to the Gila River. All drainages in the basin are intermittent, flowing only after heavy rains. The Santa Cruz channel today is a dry, broad trench filled with gravel, sand and twentieth century rubble and landfill garbage. The river's banks are bare dirt walls; mesquite trees, which grow along portions of the trench, are so thick in some areas that they are impassable. At irregular intervals dry gullies—the river's tributaries—intersect the trench wall (Sheridan 1981:60).

The Tucson Basin lies in a semiarid climatic zone where potential evaporation is eight times greater than the average annual precipitation of 11 inches (Burkham 1970: 34). Precipitation varies with altitude and occurs in two distinct rainy seasons: a summer rainy season from late June through September, and a winter rainy season from November through March. The summer rainy season is associated with warm tropical air coming into southern Arizona from the Gulf of Mexico and from the west coast of Mexico. These storms are usually localized, and brief but intense, in contrast to winter storms, which come in from the Pacific and are less intense but of longer duration and more widespread.

Temperature, like precipitation, varies with elevation. The mean low January temperature in Tucson is 1.67 degrees C (32.2 degrees F), while mean July temperatures range from 40 degrees C (105 degrees F) in the valleys to 21 degrees C (70 degrees F) in the higher mountains. The average growing season is 245 days, sufficient for planting and harvesting two crops annually.

## Flora and Fauna

The Phase B area lies in the Lower Sonoran lifezone and is characterized by two biotic communities: creosote-bur sage, and mixed palo verde-cacti, which contains numerous important plant resources used by the Pima and Papago. The Santa Cruz River and Brawley Wash floodplains form the major riparian zones, supplemented by numerous smaller tributary drainages originating in the Tucson and Tortolita mountains. These drainages also contain important plant resources: mesquite, ironwood, blue palo verde, catclaw acacia, desert willow, and desert hackberry.

The diversity and local variation of these biotic communities support a large number of wildlife species including mule deer, jack rabbits, cottontail rabbits, mountain sheep, ground squirrels, rodents, and quail.

## Past Environment, Or Don't Judge a Book by Its Cover

Climate is the single most important determinant of the plant life of an arid region (Hastings and Turner 1965: 10). For a prehistoric population directly and indirectly dependent on plant life, climate is a critical factor influencing how well a population adapts. The Santa Cruz River of the twentieth century is a far cry from the Santa Cruz River of 200 years ago when Tucson was founded, or of 800 years ago when Hohokam settlements along the river reached their peak density. The drastic changes in the Santa Cruz River and, to a lesser degree, along Brawley Wash in the Avra Valley, are not due solely to changes in climate, however. Man's tampering with the hydrology of the river over the past 100 years has contributed significantly to these changes. Looking at the dry, deep channel of the Santa Cruz River of 1982, it is difficult to visualize what the valley was like several hundred or thousand years ago, when the river and its tributaries provided the semiarid Tucson Basin with adequate, if not abundant, water and a riverine habitat rich in plant and animal resources.

## Post-Pleistocene Climate

The Tucson Basin-Avra Valley area has been a semiarid region for at least the past 8000 years. Several lines of evidence indicate a cool, moist climate in the Southwest at the end of the Pleistocene, followed first by warmer, drier conditions, and then by a return to a somewhat cooler and wetter climate. These climatic divisions of the Holocene were postulated by Antevs (1948) and are known, respectively, as the Anathermal (from about 7000 to 5000 B.C.), the Altithermal (from about 5000 to 2000 B.C.), and the Medithermal (2000 B.C. to some time during the first century A.D.).

While Antevs's tripartite division of Holocene climates is still generally accepted (see Baumhoff and Heizer 1965: 697), additional environmental studies have provided new data and contradictory interpretations.

Martin's analysis of Southwestern pollen samples (Martin 1963) was the basis for a Holocene climatic reconstruction that proposed an arid period from 8500 to 6000 B.C., during which climatic conditions were similar to those of today; a period from about 6000 B.C. to 2000 B.C. (corresponding to Antevs's Altithermal), when conditions were wetter but no warmer than at present; and a period from 2000 B.C. to the present, with climatic conditions similar to those in the Southwest today. Martin's climate reconstruction has been questioned on grounds that his pollen samples were taken from desert floodplains where pollen preservation is usually poor and that, because he did not recover the whole Holocene stratigraphic sequence at any one site, the sequence had to be reconstructed piecemeal (McGuire 1982). What is important in terms of human occupation, however, is that the Southwest has been semiarid for the last 10,000 years.

The most recent and perhaps the most promising climatic reconstruction is based on analyses of fossil pack rat (*Neotoma*) middens colleted from Southwestern mountains. Van Devender (1977; Van Devender and Spaulding 1979) believes the present Sonoran Desert climatic and vegetational regimes were established after 6000 B.C. Prior to that, woodland trees and shrubs were present in the Sonoran Desert of southern Arizona: single-needle pinyon (*Pinus monophylla*) was present as low as 510 m, while a more xeric juniper woodland was found at an altitude of only 240 m. About 8000 years ago, previously heavy winter precipitation began to diminish, initiating a vegetation shift in which Sonoran desertscrub communities replaced low elevation juniper and pinyon woodlands in southern Arizona. Areas where summer monsoons are now characteristic probably received more summer precipitation during the Altithermal, because warmer global temperatures favored development of the Bermuda High. Consequently, Van Devender (Van Devender and Spaulding 1979: 709) favors restricting use of the term Altithermal to areas where warm, dry, middle Holocene climate is documented: the northern Mohave Desert and Great Basin. Again, a semiarid environment is postulated for much of southern Arizona for the last 8000 years.

Late Holocene time in the Southwest is represented by epicycles of erosion and alluviation along stream courses. The number, magnitude, and duration of these events varied from basin to basin as well as along reaches of the same stream. These differences are indirectly indicated by the depth to which streams cut below the floodplain, and by areas of alluviation along present drainage ways (Kottlowski and others 1965: 289).

Recent attempts to reconstruct the late paleoclimatic record of the Southwest have focused on the Colorado Plateau (Euler and others 1979), where special efforts have been made to obtain refined climatic resolution through more precise dating of alluvial records. Using the results of a variety of research techniques including dendrochronology, palynology, analysis of pack rat middens, independently dated alluvial stratigraphy, and radiocarbon dating, Euler and his colleagues conclude that the period A.D. 950 to 1100 brought increased effective moisture in the Colorado Plateau and a noticeable increase in human population and spatial density, resulting in part from increased carrying capacity (Euler and others 1979: 1096). McGuire (1982: 43) warns, however, that because of the extensive variability in intensity and range of the various episodes of climatic fluctuation identified on the Colorado Plateau, it is not advisable to apply these reconstructions directly to the Sonoran Desert. Until more data from desert regions are available, the issue of synchrony must remain unresolved.

While a semiarid, Sonoran Desert environment apparently has existed in southern Arizona since about 6000 B.C., available data are far from complete and different interpretations of the causes and nature of the Holocene environments have been proposed. One important fact to remember when considering paleoenvironmental conditions in the Southwest is aptly stated by Malde (1964: 123): "Although environment is not the only factor controlling man's destiny, its influence is particularly evident in the Southwest, where small climatic changes have noticeably altered the landscape, the plants and animals, and man's way of life." This appears to have been the case on the Colorado Plateau, where population movements and changes in population densities seem to reflect changes in the length of growing seasons, in seasonal distribution of precipitation in soil nutrients that affect distribution of precipitation, or in soil nutrients that affect crops (Euler and others 1979: 1095). It was also undoubtedly true of the semiarid Sonoran Desert region of southern Arizona.

## Hydrology

Changes in stream regimes in southern Arizona are reflections of an arid and semiarid area (Hastings and Turner 1965: 4). Until the latest episode of severe arroyo cutting beginning in the 1890s and the dramatic lowering of the water table which began several decades ago and continues today, climate was the major factor affecting water availability in the Tucson Basin. Water was—and remains—the critical factor in man's use of the region.

Study of the behavior of water—in the atmosphere, on the surface of the land, and underground—is known as hydrology; paleohydrology studies these phenomena

with reference to the past (Schumm 1965: 183). The paleohydrology of the Tucson Basin is not well known and a discussion of past water availability and its role in the prehistory of the area will have to depend on extrapolation of recent hydrologic data and historic accounts.

Streams and drainages found in the basin today are typical of arid and semiarid lands where channels are dry for long periods of time. Surface flow occurs only after heavy precipitation and lasts for only a day or two (Davidson 1970: E54). Floods are generally confined to the channels, but frequently inundate floodplains where channels are not deeply cut. Flooding in bottomland results mainly from summer thunderstorms, while streams near the mountains have more evenly distributed flows because the drainages extend into mountain areas where precipitation is greater and is complemented by snowmelt (Davidson 1970: E55). Although summer precipitation is often very intense, it does not penetrate deeply into the soil, the majority being lost through evaporation from the heat and low humidity of the semiarid climate (Harshbarger and others 1966: 2, 5; Hastings and Turner 1965: 15).

Floods in the desert region in and around the basin are documented well back into the Spanish period, and have most likely been part of the natural scene for as long as arid and semiarid conditions have existed. The climate is a major reason for their existence because the sparse, intermittent precipitation does not promote the dense ground cover which is necessary to impede runoff and promote infiltration. Floods were apparently frequent, but, prior to 1890, floodwaters spread out in a shallow layer over the floodplains, causing little damage (Hastings and Turner 1965: 41-42).

Desert streams behave differently from streams in more humid areas. Sparse rainfall and vegetation inhibit formation of the clay products of chemical weathering, and the low clay content and negligible anchoring effect of the sparse vegetation result in friable riverbanks that are vulnerable to erosion. In wide bottomlands containing shallow channels and covered with dense vegetation, a desert stream may develop and maintain meanders, cutting off these same meanders during periods of flooding, thus taking on a braided appearance. Without anchoring vegetation, a channel can become entrenched, with overbank flooding less likely as the channel adjusts itself to accommodate flood waters. Within the last 100 years the Santa Cruz River changed rapidly from a meandering and perhaps braided river to a deep, dry arroyo. While arroyo cutting has been a factor in arid and semiarid lands, this recent historic entrenchment was abetted by man's attempts to control and alter the river, and has had severe effects on the available water supply (Betancourt 1978b: 33; see also Cooke and Reeves 1976).

Numerous changes have occurred in the basin landscape since the Indians and early Spanish explorers first settled along the Santa Cruz and found its flow to be adequate for their needs. The river's flow south of the Pima village of

Bac (located in the vicinity of the present Mission San Xavier del Bac) to the confluence with Rillito Creek was dependable, if not truly perennial, prior to 1890. The water table was higher, resulting in cienegas and perhaps an increased surface flow (Betancourt 1978a: 4). Hinton (1970: 178, 270) points out that while the Santa Cruz was small compared to streams in the northern and eastern states, and ran underground for a portion of its length, there was nonetheless a good deal of water in it "...sufficient to irrigate a small valley." Wells were not difficult to sink in the river bottom and water was readily obtainable (Hinton 1970: 180).

Thus it appears that prior to the start of extensive arroyo cutting, but even after channeling began, surface and subsurface water was present—adequate for most needs but not necessarily abundant. With the initiation of groundwater mining, surface flow ceased as the water table began to drop. The loss of floodplain vegetation coupled with high evaporation rates prevents infiltration from replenishing dwindling ground water supplies.

Never abundant (except during flooding when there was too much), and susceptible to fluctuations in precipitation, water was present in the Santa Cruz River and its tributaries into the early twentieth century, both as surface flow and as groundwater at generally shallow depths. With water available along most of its course, except where it disappeared underground (Bowden 1981; Browne 1950: 144; Dobyns 1981: 60; Smith 1938: 46), the Santa Cruz River Valley was the focal point of human occupation in the Tucson Basin. It was a dynamic river reflecting vagaries of climatic change over the centuries. In contrast to conditions today:

> ...the valleys were wetter and more open than today, and relatively unchanneled. But the precise conditions varied from place to place and probably from time to time. As tributary washes dumped greater or less amounts of debris, depending upon where heavy summer rains may have struck, the rivers had to transport varying loads of sediment at different points along their course. Channeling and filling, aggradation and degradation—all may have been going on simultaneously, in various stages of development along various parts of the stream. If this dynamic situation existed, one can be sure that the vegetation reflected it. At a given time there may have been mesquite invading, where a temporary trench had sliced through the old flood plain, draining it; mesquite dying where the plain was aggrading and marshes being developed. The old accounts present a picture that is neither homogeneous, nor static. By postulating a dynamic situation one can reconcile the variety of conditions that evidently existed (Hastings and Turner 1965: 37).

## Avra Valley and Brawley Wash

On the west side of the Tucson Mountains lies Avra Valley and its primary drainage system, Brawley Wash.

Considerably less is known about the former appearance of this valley. It is not mentioned in Spanish records, and only cursorily mentioned in later documents with the exception of one or two twentieth century hydrologic studies (Andrews 1937; Turner and others 1943). A tributary of the Santa Cruz River, the valley extends northward from a point near the Mexican border, paralleling the Santa Cruz Valley. It joins the Santa Cruz some 30 miles north of Tucson, where Blanco and Brawley washes join to form Los Robles Wash. The northern portion of Avra Valley expands to a wide, flat area, and consists of a number of braided channels several feet deep and spread out over a mile in width. A few miles before reaching the Santa Cruz River, several channels merge into two or three main channels. The large size of the channel indicates that it carries heavy floods at times (Andrews 1937; Turner and others 1943).

Groundwater in the valley was considerably deeper than in the Tucson Basin, even before heavy pumping in the 1960s. Today—and probably in the past—water in Avra Valley was primarily surface runoff, and was not as readily available as in the Santa Cruz River and other basin drainages. This undoubtedly contributed to the neglect of the valley by Spanish and later settlers.

Avra Valley has not undergone the deep downcutting in its main stream channel so noticeable in the Santa Cruz (Gelderman 1972: 60), and is subject to heavy flooding, including sheet flooding. Prior to the arrival of the white man, the floodplain and wash flats probably supported stands of sacaton grass (Wilson 1980: 9), and cottonwoods and other trees may have dotted the stream margins. Today mesquite bosques choke much of the floodplain where they have not been cleared for fields.

With no consistent surface flow and a deep water table, floodwater farming was used both by Indians and a few Anglo ranchers. By 1943, the stream channels of Brawley Wash were too deep for floodwater farming (Turner and others 1943: 12), and pumps were required to tap the deep groundwater.

## Early Views of the Santa Cruz River

In 1864 J. Ross Browne viewed the Santa Cruz River upstream from San Xavier Mission:

> The valley of the Santa Cruz is one of the richest and most beautiful grazing and agricultural regions I have ever seen. Occasionally the river sinks, but even at these points the grass is abundant and luxuriant...Mesquit and cotton-wood are abundant and there is no lack of water most of the way to Santa Cruz (Browne 1950: 144).

Such accounts are not uncommon and can be found in the writings of the first Spanish explorers and missionaries to visit the valley (Bolton 1936, 1948; Karns 1954). Father Eusebio Kino, while laying the foundation for a mission at

Bac, noted that it was not necessary to carry water to make mortar because irrigation ditches carried water wherever it was needed (Bolton 1936: 507). The Indian fields along the river north of Bac were extensive and amply supplied with water via irrigation canals (Bolton 1948: 205; Karns 1954: 135).

Early American accounts of the river and its tributaries compare very favorably to Spanish accounts of the late seventeenth and early eighteenth centuries. They agree that grass was plentiful and the landscape open; mesquite, although widespread, was not as dense as in twentieth century accounts; and streams at both times were open, marshy and unchanneled (Hastings and Turner 1965: 34). Prior to 1860 the Santa Cruz and other major rivers of southern Arizona such as the San Pedro in the valley east of the Tucson Basin, were sluggish streams running most of the year along much of their course through grass-covered valleys with numerous cienegas and pools. Beaver dams were numerous as late as 1882, and fish were plentiful (Hastings and Turner 1965: 35; Martin 1963: 3) (Figure 2.1). Clotts (1917: 60) reports two springs along the Santa Cruz—Agua de la Mission near San Xavier del Bac and Acequia de la Punta de Agua several miles upstream from there—that supplied water to Papago Indian farmers during the last half of the nineteenth century.

Extensive marshes or cienegas were present in the basin of the Santa Cruz, and along the Rillito and Pantano creeks, as well as on other streams in southern Arizona, and probably offered year-round water, even if the creeks were not perennial (Betancourt 1978a: 4). Along the Santa Cruz, cienegas occurred south of Martinez Hill, at the foot of Sentinel Peak, and near the confluence of Rillito Creek further downstream. These were fed from the shallow water table and were a continuous problem in historic times because of the mosquitos they harbored and the malaria these insects transmitted (Bowden 1981: Bryan 1928: 475; Dobyns 1981: 61; Hastings and Turner 1965: 37; Thornber 1910: 334). Hastings and Turner (1965: 37) and Hastings (1958-1959: 28) mention malaria as a major problem for Army personnel stationed along the Santa Cruz at Tucson, at Camp Grant at the confluence of Aravaipa Creek and the San Pedro, and along Babocomari and Sonoita creeks. The swampy areas on the Santa Cruz contained extensive stands of bulrushes, and the valley was covered with sacaton grass (Bryan 1928: 475; Spalding 1909: 9; Wilson 1963: 484).

Sayles (1958: 13-14) describes a cienega near the head of San Simon Creek along the Arizona-New Mexico border that probably closely resembled past marshy conditions along the Santa Cruz and other rivers in southern Arizona.

> Here the vegetation is in marked contrast to that of the adjoining slopes which are covered with typical desert plants, such as creosote bush, yucca, cacti, and mesquite. The San Simon Cienega, half a mile or more wide and nearly 5 miles in length, is heavily grassed.

The meandering channel of the stream usually contains water, and is filled with cattails (*Typha*) and other water-loving plants. Cottonwood, willow, sycamore, and other trees requiring constant water are found in great numbers. The rich plant environment attracts both birds and animals. Similar cienegas are reported to have been present in former times in many Arizona river valleys.

Sayles (1958: 17) goes on to mention that main streams as well as many minor tributaries were in earlier days lined with groves of cottonwood, willow, ash, walnut, sycamore, and some live oak (see Figure 2.1). Scrub oak was present away from valley bottoms, while mesquite, desert hackberry, and blackbush occurred in thickets along sides of valleys.

The bottomlands of the Santa Cruz were fertile and easily irrigated by canals in historic times. The soil was 8 to 20 feet thick and without caliche (Rothrock 1875: 126; Smith 1938: 51), and the water table was within reach of crop and tree root systems (Thornber 1910: 334; Wilson 1963: 484). The first Spanish visitors in the late seventeenth century encountered Northern-Piman speaking Indians living along the river and cultivating alluvial fields near the stream, irrigating them from canals carrying water from valley margin springs as well as with water diverted from the river (Dobyns 1981: 60).

## Flora and Fauna

The relatively abundant water supply during the last 300 years enabled a variety of trees, shrubs and grasses to thrive in and along the Santa Cruz River floodplain. Fauna, including beaver, fish, and ducks, were found in the riparian conditions along the Santa Cruz, and along Brawley Wash, although probably to a lesser extent. This has likely been the case since the early Holocene, with the numbers and kinds of fauna changing as local climatic changes affected the water supply and flora.

The historical descriptions of the river valley provide an idea of what the semiarid riverine environment in the Tucson Basin was probably like during middle Holocene and late prehistoric times. Obviously this picture is tentative and requires considerable research before it is accurately documented. While the Sonoran Desert vegetation common to the area today has been present since about 600 B.C. (Van Devender 1977; Van Devender and Spaulding 1979), prior to that time a more mesic vegetation was evidently present and conditions were more favorable for grasslands away from the rivers and streams. What effect this had on fauna in the area is uncertain, but it is not unlikely that pronghorn and perhaps bison may have been present, in addition to deer. Mammoth remains—many associated with evidence of man—are abundant in the San Pedro Valley east of the Tucson Basin (Haury and others 1959; Huckell 1982a). At Ventana Cave

*Figure 2.1* Two views of the Santa Cruz River: upper photograph shows extensive vegetation and marsh conditions once characteristic of the river; photograph probably taken sometime before 1900; lower photograph is a 1904 view of the river looking northeast from Sentinel Peak and shows secondary vegetation. The river may have looked similar to this in prehistoric times. (Photographs courtesy of the Arizona Heritage Center)

75 miles west of the basin, extinct ground sloth was found associated with evidence of early hunters (Haury and others 1975). The discovery in 1981 of a mammoth scapula by USGS geologists in the channel of the Santa Cruz River near Green Valley and an earlier report by Hay (1927) of mammoth remains from Tucson are the only evidence to date for the presence of mammoth in the basin. Since then, according to Julio Betancourt of the University of Arizona Geosciences Department, more Pleistocene faunal material, including bison and tortoise, has been found eroding out of deeply buried alluvium in the river. None of this material has been dated, and no evidence of man is associated with it. Its significance lies in the fact that late Pleistocene fauna have been found in the basin portion of the Santa Cruz River Valley, and that an association of Pleistocene fauna and man in the valley may be likely.

With the presence of Pleistocene fauna now documented for the Santa Cruz Valley, and at least one instance of its presence being reported in the Avra Valley by Bruce Huckell of the Arizona State Museum, a picture of the late Pleistocene and early post-Pleistocene environment of the Tucson Basin-Avra Valley area, compatible with that elsewhere in southern Arizona (Haynes and Mehringer 1965; Huckell 1982a), is emerging. The pack rat midden studies of Van Devender and others, coupled with better pollen analyses and alluvial stratigraphic studies, should begin to provide an accurate picture of the early Holocene and late prehistoric environment of the region.

## Environment and Man

Water was the limiting factor to prehistoric man's occupation of the semiarid and arid deserts of southern Arizona. Where water was available, either seasonally or year-round, man was present. The previous discussions have reviewed some of the available historical documentation and the scanty but increasing environmental data from pollen, pack rat midden, faunal and hydrologic analyses, and provide an approximate picture of what the Tucson Basin and Avra Valley drainages were like during the past 300 years and what they probably were like during the long span of prehistoric occupation in the area. The following chapters will look at the long record of man's occupation in the basin, specifically the Phase B area, from the Paleo-Indian period to recent historic times,

in reference to the probable environmental conditons previously discussed.

The Santa Cruz River—and to a still undetermined extent Brawley Wash—has been the primary focal point for both prehistoric hunter-gatherers and farmers, and historic settlers. Water was available on the surface or just beneath it, and the river valley contained abundant trees, shrubs, grass and a variety of game animals including fish. In the late Pleistocene, mammoth and other now-extinct animals probably roamed the valley (camel and horse remains are known from one locale in Avra Valley), while later Archaic hunter-gatherers undoubtedly found deer and smaller game animals available in addition to a wide variety of plant foods. Hohokam and later Piman farmers planted extensive fields in the fertile floodplains, using canals and the shallow water table to irrigate them. Spanish, Mexican, and Anglo settlers likewise settled along the river and cultivated fields that were watered by a system of canals and ditches. In the early twentieth century, after arroyo cutting and the lowering of the water table, pumps were used to provide water to meet the needs of expanding agricultural and urban development of the valley, lowering the water table even more.

Viewing the deep, desolate channel of the Santa Cruz today, it is difficult to imagine a flowing stream meandering in a floodplain covered with sacaton grass, trees, and shrubs and dotted with swampy cienegas where bulrushes and cattails grew thick. Yet there was a long period when the river was a dynamic force in shaping the local riverine environment and prehistoric man's use of it. Climate was the critical factor, and as Hastings and Turner (1965: 4, 25) note, changes in stream regime in southern Arizona reflect the climate context in which they occur:

> Because Arizona was arid—its plant life exhibited marked vulnerability to what would have been relatively minor fluctuations any place else, say two or three inches of rainfall in the annual total. At the same time that plants were unusually susceptible to variation...much greater variation could be expected. An arid climate experiences greater variability than a humid one.

Prehistoric man was dependent on the water resource of the Santa Cruz River and other streams in southern Arizona and the plant and animal resources associated with them. Where and how he lived were tied to these resources, and changes in their availability affected prehistoric man's ability to live in this semiarid area.

# Chapter 3

# PALEO-INDIAN AND ARCHAIC PERIOD CULTURAL RESOURCES

## Jon S. Czaplicki

In lieu of a synopsis of the project area's culture history, which has been presented by Westfall (1979), this chapter and the following two chapters will present more detailed discussions of the prehistoric and historic occupation of the Phase B area, providing an expanded review of the culture history, while discussing the recorded data in terms of settlement patterns and expected site distribution.

As previously mentioned, data on the prehistoric occupation came from the Arizona State Museum site survey files; no field survey was undertaken to acquire new data specifically for this report. However, limited field checks of several recorded sites were made. Interpretations, based on survey data collected over a number of decades and varying considerably in the quantity and quality of specific site information, will be somewhat biased and subject to revisions as new data become available. It is the intention of this report, however, to accept the basic survey data at face value, aware that inconsistencies and biases exist, in order to study general settlement trends and patterns through time. Future class 3 intensive survey and testing and eventual data recovery will refine portions of this data base.

This chapter will begin with an overview of Paleo-Indian (Clovis) and Archaic occupation in the Southwest, which will provide a background for more specific discussions of these occupations in the areas adjacent to the Tucson Basin, and in the Phase B area. While a pre-Clovis stage has been postulated (Bryan 1965; MacNeish 1976), arguments in favor of such a stage do not focus on southern Arizona. Therefore, discussion of a pre-Clovis stage will be limited to noting that evidence for it has yet to be identified in southern Arizona.

## Late Pleistocene and Early Holocene Human Occupation in the Southwest

As the Pleistocene drew to a close about 12,000 years ago, the Clovis complex appeared in the Southwest. A sudden and short-lived (9500 to 9000 B.C.) Paleo-Indian complex, Clovis big game hunters nonetheless represent a considerable population increase, probably resulting from their successful adaptation to big game hunting centered primarily, but not exclusively, on the mammoth. Bison, horse, camel, and sloth were also taken occasionally (Irwin-Williams and Haynes 1970:61).

Mammoth, camel, horse and other Pleistocene fauna began to decline at the end of the Pleistocene, and eventually became extinct. Loss of these game resources and other environmental changes brought about by a climatic transition towards drier conditions with less effective moisture, resulted in a shift to bison hunting by late Paleo-Indian hunters such as Folsom and other Plano groups. Continued changes in effective moisture in the Southwest eventually forced these bison-hunting cultures to move out of the Southwest and focus on the short-grass plains of the central United States. Remains of extinct bison and evidence of Folsom and other Plano cultures are rare in Arizona and are confined primarily to the northeast part of the state. Apparently, early Holocene bison-hunting cultures were unwilling or unable to adapt to the mixed foraging subsistence patterns needed to survive in marginal areas and withdrew to areas where optimal hunting conditions prevailed (Irwin-Williams and Haynes 1970: 63-64).

Following the Paleo-Indian big game hunters in the Southwest were the Archaic hunter-gathers. Continuing climatic changes during the Holocene resulted in environmental conditions that forced Archaic hunter-gatherers to reorganize in order to survive. Increasing aridity and decreasing surface water tended to restrict these groups to relatively small areas where water was available (Haury 1958: 71).

Irwin-Williams and Haynes (1970: 65) see a continuum of related Archaic materials stretching from southern California north and east into Arizona and north-central New Mexico. With the abandonment of the Southwest by Plains-based Paleo-Indian cultures, western-based groups of hunter-gatherers (for example, Lake Mohave-Silver Lake and Jay complexes) penetrated eastward into the northern Southwest. The character of the artifact inventories and site locations of these groups suggest some dependence on hunting, but with a subsistence pattern more adaptable to changing conditions.

From about 5500 to 3000 B.C. environmental conditions gradually became drier, and Archaic groups, while not abandoning the Southwest, were sparsely distributed and probably concentrated around remaining resources, leaving large areas subject to marginal or temporary occupation (Irwin-Williams and Haynes 1970: 66). By 3000 B.C., as climatic conditions ameliorated, Chiricahua Cochise, Pinto Basin, and other hunter-gatherer groups increased and expanded rapidly with the increase in available resources. During this period, Archaic occupation in the Southwest again seems to have been a broad continuum of related cultures: a Pinto Basin complex in southern California and adjacent Arizona, and a southern Cochise complex in southeastern Arizona and southwestern New Mexico. The basic economy throughout the area was based on plant gathering and foraging with incipient horticulture appearing in the Cochise by 2000 to 1500 B.C. (Irwin-Williams and Haynes 1970: 67).

The fundamental subsistence pattern in the Southwest throughout the Archaic period was extensive exploitation of local resources. While there was undoubtedly local variation in the emphasis on hunting or gathering, both pursuits were apparently universal. Subsistence patterning was geared to seasonal movements based on maturation and availability of plant and animal resources, and also on the increasing importance of horticulture beginning roughly around 1500 B.C. (Irwin-Williams 1967: 441–443).

## Paleo-Indian Occupation Adjacent to and in the Tucson Basin

The Sulphur Spring Valley has been a center of Paleo-Indian research in Arizona since 1926 when Byron Cummings uncovered a mammoth skull and artifacts, the latter in a geologic bed underneath the skull. Since then, the upper San Pedro Valley has yielded numerous Paleo-Indian remains. Six buried Clovis kill sites and several isolated Clovis projectile points have been found in addition to 31 mammoth locales without associated human artifacts (Huckell 1982a: 2-3). The Naco, Lehner, and Murray Springs sites have been excavated (Haury 1953; Haury and others 1959; Hemmings 1970, respectively) and have provided important data on the Clovis occupation and early Holocene environment in southern Arizona. The San Pedro River Valley of the late Pleistocene and early Holocene was characterized by more abundant surface water than is available today, and a desert grassland environment which would have been an attractive habitat for Clovis hunters. The apparent concentration of Clovis remains in this valley may be due in part to the exposure of late Pleistocene-early Holocene sediments both as arroyo cuts and extensive land surfaces. (Huckell 1982a: 26).

North and west of the Tucson Basin, Paleo-Indian remains are represented by several isolated Clovis points (Huckell 1982a). Isolated points may be indicative of the potential range of Clovis hunters, or may represent points picked up by later peoples, then lost or discarded. Clovis point fragments from one site in the Avra Valley may represent Clovis occupation of the site, which also contains Cochise and Hohokam components (Huckell 1982a: 15).

Ventana Cave in the Castle Mountains west of the basin has produced the only stratified sequence of preceramic remains in southern Arizona, but there is no general agreement on the depositional history of these units. The earliest occupation at Ventana Cave is dated at 11,000 ± 1200 B.P. and may be a regional variant of the Clovis culture (Huckell 1979: 18). Further west, in Organ Pipe National Monument, Ezell (1954) found an isolated Clovis point. Apparently there was some Clovis occupation of south central and southwestern Arizona, but the evidence is scanty and the intensity of occupation unknown.

San Dieguito remains, also considered to be Paleo-Indian and related to big game hunting (Warren 1967: 181-182), are known primarily from southern California and the Lower Colorado River Valley (Rogers 1966). However, a San Dieguito occupation associated with extinct fauna was identified at Ventana Cave (Haury and others 1975), and Rogers (1958) identified San Dieguito I material on river terraces in the Tucson Basin.

## Paleo-Indian Remains in the Phase B Area

No Paleo-Indian sites are known in the Phase B area, or in the Tucson Basin. Evidence for possible Clovis occupation in the basin is restricted to an area between the Santa Cruz River and Avra Valley, and is limited to three surface finds of Clovis projectile points (Figure 3.1).

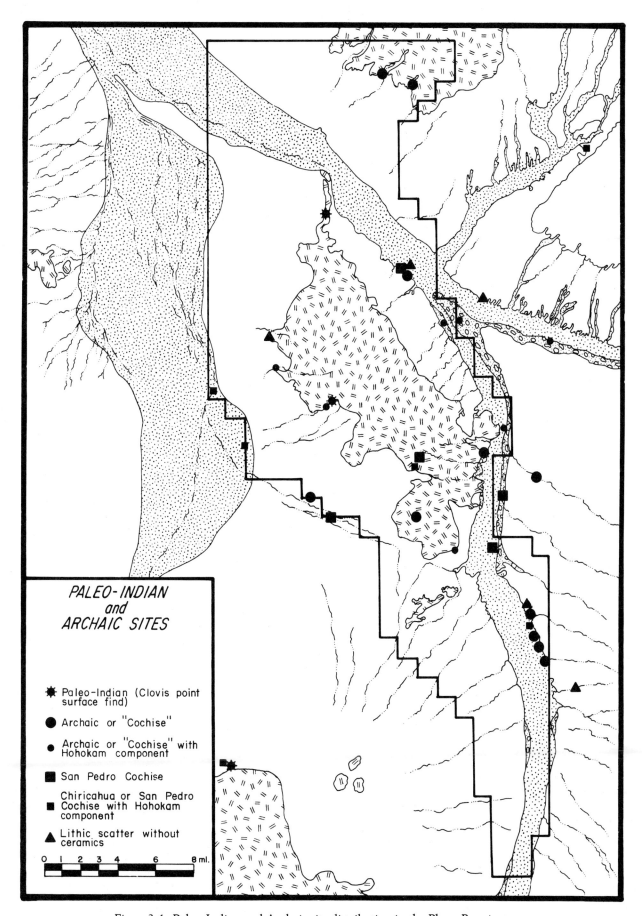

### PALEO-INDIAN and ARCHAIC SITES

✳ Paleo-Indian (Clovis point surface find)

● Archaic or "Cochise"

• Archaic or "Cochise" with Hohokam component

■ San Pedro Cochise

▪ Chiricahua or San Pedro Cochise with Hohokam component

▲ Lithic scatter without ceramics

0 1 2 3 4 6 8 ml.

*Figure 3.1.* Paleo-Indian and Archaic site distribution in the Phase B project area

Isolated projectile points have been found in Avra Valley on an unnamed tributary of Brawley Wash (AZ AA:16:34, Ayers 1970a), and at Rattlesnake Pass in the Tucson Mountains (Agenbroad 1967). The former were found in association with Tucson Basin Hohokam plain brown ware sherds and flaked stone debris, while the latter is a fluted point labeled "Clovis-Folsom?" by Agenbroad. Two Clovis point basal fragments were found in Avra Valley at AZ DD:4:79 just outside the southwest corner of the San Xavier Indian Reservation (also outside the Phase B area), in a mixed ceramic and preceramic context. Huckell (1982a: 15) notes, however, that while no other typical Clovis artifacts were found at the site, the presence of two Clovis point basal fragments suggests that there may have been an actual Clovis occupation at the site.

Along the terraces of Rillito Creek and Pantano Creek on the east side of the basin, Rogers (1958) identified San Dieguito I artifacts. Warren (1967) has equated similar artifacts from southern California with big game hunting. No San Dieguito artifacts are known in the Phase B area, although they may be present on the terraces along the Santa Cruz River and Brawley Wash.

Absence of definite *in situ* evidence for a Clovis occupation in the basin and Phase B area is most likely a factor of the depositional history of the area. Neither the Santa Cruz nor its tributaries have cut deep enough to expose late Pleistocene-early Holocene deposits that might contain this material (Betancourt 1978b; Gregonis and Huckell 1980: 11; McCarthy and Sires 1981: 11–12). A second factor may be that in the absence of diagnostic projectile points, these sites have not been recognized. Subsistence activities other than big game hunting may have been practiced. Since they may not have required diagnostic artifacts, their remains are not easily identifiable (McCarthy and Sires 1981: 11–12). While *in situ* Clovis sites are probably buried under floodplain alluvium, scarcity of surface finds is puzzling. As Huckell notes, landforms of Pleistocene age are present in the basin, and yet, despite a large urban population that has been present for many years, no sites of this period have been recorded.

> Perhaps discoveries of such sites have gone unrecognized or unreported, or the intensive later prehistoric occupation of the area has obscured or removed them. In any case, the lack of evidence for this earliest Classic Paleo-Indian industry in the Tucson Basin is probably not an accurate indication that these people were not in residence (Huckell 1982b: 3).

With the presence of five Clovis kill sites, one hunting camp site (Murray Springs), several isolated Clovis projectile points in the San Pedro Valley, and many mammoth sites lacking artifacts, it seems likely that Clovis hunters and mammoth and other game animals occupied the Santa Cruz Valley and perhaps Avra Valley

as well. Environmental conditions similar to those in the San Pedro Valley were undoubtedly present along the Santa Cruz River and perhaps in Avra Valley. Faunal evidence from the volcanic debris level at Ventana Cave indicates that extinct animals were hunted by man in an environment "...of a savannah or plains, with persistent, shaded streams, rather than desert..." (Haury and other 1975: 148). The recent discovery of a mammoth scapula in the Santa Cruz River near Green Valley and an earlier report of mammoth remains from an unknown location in Tucson (Hay 1927) provide the only solid—if undated—evidence for mammoth in the basin.

Clovis sites in the San Pedro Valley are primarily kill sites located in channel fill of tributary drainages of the San Pedro River in a stratum corresponding to Haynes' depositional unit B1 (Haynes 1966; Hemmings 1970). Given that the environmenttal settings of the San Pedro, Santa Cruz, and Avra valleys were similar, Clovis sites, if present in the latter two valleys, probably will be found in similar gemorphological settings and in a stratum corresponding to Haynes' B1 depositional unit. They are likely to be kill sites representing either recurrent kills or single one-time kills (Hemmings 1970: 175).

Stratigraphic studies comparable to those done in the San Pedro Valley are lacking for the Santa Cruz. C. Vance Haynes of the Department of Anthropology, University of Arizona, has been formulating a stratigraphic sequence for the Santa Cruz over the two past decades, but his data remain unpublished and it is not known how complete the sequence is in comparison to that for the San Pedro Valley. (Haynes was overseas when this report was being researched, and the author was not able to discuss the status of his alluvial studies in the Santa Cruz. Haynes has the basis for such a stratigraphic record and will hopefully publish his data soon.)

Although the Santa Cruz River Valley would appear to be the primary area where buried Clovis sites may be expected, it is interesting that the only evidence for a Clovis occupation in the area has been found in Avra Valley. Perhaps this valley presented more of the open, grassy plains environment favored by mammoth. AZ DD:4:79 provides a good view of Avra Valley and could have been a vantage point from which Clovis hunters watched for game activity. Unfortunately, the site has apparently been so badly disturbed by artifact collectors and erosion that it may not be possible to definitely identify a Clovis component, if one is present.

Stratigraphic study of Avra Valley is lacking, but is a prerequisite for determining the possibility of buried Clovis sites. Downcutting here is substantially less than for the Santa Cruz, and the identification of late Pleistocene-early Holocene deposits has yet to be made, although some exposures are known.

One site in the valley, AZ AA:16:85, is located in a tributary of Brawley Wash and contains horse and camel bone associated with cienega deposits, but no Paleo-Indian material (ASM site survey files). (Archaic artifacts are also present here and are discussed below.) It is possible that late Pleistocene deposits are not deeply buried in Avra Valley, but until stratigraphic studies are done, this cannot be substantiated. Identification of strata comparable to Haynes' B1 and B2 depositional units would at least indicate that the depositional units known to contain extinct fauna and associated Paleo-Indian artifacts elsewhere in the Southwest (see Haynes 1966) are present in Avra Valley and may have the same potential.

Another slightly younger (about 10,000 to 9500 B.P.) Paleo-Indian occupation may have been present in or near the basin. Fragments of two projectile points very similar to the Plainview type have been found (Huckell 1982b). Agenbroad (1970) mentions two basal fragments from the Lone Hill Site, on an eastern flank of the Santa Catalina Mountains, while Hewitt and Stephen (1981) mention a basal fragment from an Archaic site in the Tortolita Mountains.

## Archaic Occupation Adjacent to the Phase B Area

The Archaic period in southern Arizona is generally better understood than the preceding Paleo-Indian period, although numerous questions remain unanswered and gaps in the data are large. Archaic cultures in southern Arizona are represented by the Cochise culture (Sayles and Antevs 1941; Sayles 1958), and the Amargosa complex (Rogers 1966, Haury and others 1975; Hayden 1970) (see Table 3.1).

The Cochise culture was identified from lithic and ground stone material found in the Sulphur Spring Valley of southern Arizona (Sayles and Antevs 1941). It was divided into four stages: Sulphur Spring (10,500 to 9,000 B.C.; early Archaic), Cazador (9000 to 6000 B.C.), Chiricahua (6000 to 2500 B.C.; middle Archaic), and San Pedro (2500 B.C. to about A.D. 200; late Archaic) (Sayles 1958). The Sulphur Spring stage lacked projectile points but was represented by large numbers of slab milling stones and one-hand manos, and a few percussion-flaked lithic tools for cutting, scraping, and chopping (Sayles and Antevs 1941: 8). The Cazador stage included projectile points and appears to represent a hunting orientation. Whalen (1971: 81) views Cazador as the hunting aspect of the Sulphur Spring stage. Westfall (1979: 34), however, notes that Cazador may not be a real stage. Following Sulphur Spring-Cazador, the Chiricahua stage is characterized by large, shallow basin milling stones, ovoid one-hand manos, unifacial and bifacial percussion and pressure-flaked tools, and some pressure-flaked projectile points. By the San Pedro stage, deep basin metates, well-developed mortar and pestle, and a complex chipped stone tool assemblage with numerous projectile points are

characteristic. This stage is also characterized by developing sedentism reflected by the appearance of pit houses and experimentation with agriculture (Westfall 1979: 34; Whalen 1973).

At Ventana Cave, Haury (and others 1975) found stratified Archaic material that represents a mixture of eastern Cochise and western Amargosan cultures. The cultural sequence at Ventana Cave has lent itself to several different and confusing interpretations. Huckell (1979: 19) reviewed these and tried to place them in perspective. Briefly, Hayden (1976) sees a San Dieguito I occupation until 7000 B.C., followed by the Altithermal and abandonment of the Papagueria until about 3000 B.C. when Amargosa hunter-gatherers entered the area. Antevs (in Haury and others 1975: 528) sees Amargosa people occupying the region from 8000 B.C. through the Altithermal until around 3000 B.C. when climatic conditions moderated. Bryan (in Haury and others 1975: 528) sees the period between 8000 B.C. and 3000 B.C. as unknown, while Hack (in Haury and others 1975: 528) sees the Ventana (Clovis) complex occupation lasting until 6000 B.C. when an Amargosa I occupation begins. Obviously, there is a great need to better define Archaic relationships and periods of occupation in southwestern Arizona.

The Amargosa complex is the characteristic Archaic tradition of the Lower Colorado River Basin and consists of three stages: Amargosa I, II, and III. Amargosa II occurs in Ventana Cave with Chiricahua Cochise material. In terms of artifact typology and technology and geographic position, it is apparently more closely affiliated with the "Pinto Basin" complex of southwestern Arizona and southeastern California (Irwin-Williams 1967: 447). Amargosa III material, while not present at Ventana Cave, is probably coeval with San Pedro Cochise, which is strongly represented in the higher levels at Ventana Cave. Apparently, western Archaic influence represented by Amargosa, weakened substantially at the end of the middle Archaic and was replaced by eastern Archaic groups of San Pedro Cochise (Haury and others 1975: 533). Hayden (1970) feels that Amargosa-Cochise may be aspects of a single cultural tradition, Cochise being distinguished from Amargosa by ground stone tools and probably representing an adaptation to the desert grasslands of southeastern Arizona, while Amargosa was geared towards hunting.

The Sulphur Spring stage is poorly understood and only a handful of sites have been identified (Sayles and Antevs 1941). Haury (1960: 609-610) discussed the apparent contemporaneity of mammoth and other extinct animals with Sulphur Spring stage material, and concluded that "...the oldest Cochise gatherers not only knew the late Pleistocene fauna but they also relished balancing their diet with mammoth protein."

More is known about the Chiricahua and San Pedro stages, but as Wilcox (1979a: 80) points out, the late Archaic is still poorly understood. Work by Agenbroad

TABLE 3.1

## Postulated correlation of southern Arizona and southern Great Basin cultural sequences (from Marmaduke and Berry, 1980)

| Time Years B.P. | Papagueria-Ventana (Antevs Model) (Haury 1975)[1] | Papagueria-Ventana (Bryan Model) (Haury 1975)[2] | Southeast Ariz Cochise Culture (Antevs) (Haury 1975)[1] | Southeast Ariz Cochise Culture (Bryan) (Haury 1975)[2] | Lower Colorado River Basin-Antevs (Haury 1975)[1] | Lower Colorado River Basin-Bryan (Haury 1975)[2] | Lower Colorado River Basin (Rogers 1939) | Southern Great Basin Series (Bettinger & Taylor 1974) | Great Basin Point Types |
|---|---|---|---|---|---|---|---|---|---|
| 500- | Papago ? | Papago ? | | | Yuma III | Yuma III | Yuman-Shoshonean | Marana / Haiwee | Cottonwood Series and Desert Side-Notched |
| 1,000- | Hohokam | Hohokam | Hohokam | Hohokam | Yuma II | Yuma II | | | |
| 2,000- | | | Mogollon | Mogollon | Yuma I / BM III-P II | Yuma I / BM III-P II | ? | Newberry | Rose Spring Series and Eastgate Expanding Stem |
| 3,000- | San Pedro | San Pedro | San Pedro | San Pedro | Amargosa III | Amargosa III | | | |
| 4,000- | Chiricahua-Amargosa II | Chiricahua-Amargosa II | Chiricahua | Chiricahua | Amargosa II | Amargosa II | | | Little Lake Series and Pinto Basin Series |
| 5,000- | Ventana-Amargosa I / Ventana Complex | Ventana-Amargosa I ? | | | Amargosa I | Amargosa I | Pinto Basin | Little Lake | |
| 6,000- | | Erosion | | ? | San Dieguito II-III / San Dieguito I | San Dieguito II-III | | | |
| 7,000- | | | Chiricahua | | | | | Mohave | Silver Lake and Lake Mohave |
| 8,000- | | | | | | San Dieguito I | | | |
| 9,000- | | Ventana Complex | Sulphur Spring | Sulphur Spring | San Dieguito I | | | | |
| 10,000- | | | | | | | | | |

[1] Correlations based on Antevs' dates for the Cochise Culture.
[2] Correlations worked out with M.J. Rogers, based on Kirk Bryan's dates.

(1966), Huckell (1973), Whalen (1971, 1973, 1975), and Windmiller (1973) has provided new information on and interpretations of the middle and late Archaic periods.

In the San Pedro Valley, Whalen (1971, 1975) identified Cochise sites occurring in three areas: mountain pediment (1448 to 1493 m), bajada terrace (1166 to 1207 m), and riverine. Seasonal movement between these areas by small family bands (microbands) has been postulated (Huckell 1979; Whalen 1971; Windmiller 1971). Whalen (1971) sees the mountain sites occupied during late summer-early fall and the lower elevation sites occupied during winter and spring. Small family groups moved into each area as certain plant foods matured and ripened, perhaps coming together into larger camps during seasonal periods when certain plant and animal resources were abundant.

Whalen (1975: 205) noted that Chiricahua and San Pedro stage sites were fairly equally distributed on the bajada terrace and pediment. Sites in the pediment are located very close to the mountains and cluster at the mouths of canyons, providing easy access into the mountains. Other sites were located on terraces overlooking tributary arroyos draining into the San Pedro River. Of the Archaic sites he recorded, 56 were on the pediment near mountains, 27 on terraces, and five in the floodplain. Two sites were located between the terraces and pediment; no sites were found in the area between the tributary stream channels.

The Cochise sites Whalen recorded ranged from small "use" areas to large habitation or camp sites. Base camps differed from use camps by the presence of food processing implements and hearths. Ground stone tools and a wide range of cutting, chopping, and scraping tools were typical of these large habitation sites. Use or work sites were geared to the exploitation of one or two resources and lacked the wide range of tool types, having only specialized tools needed for the particular resource being processed. Hearths were not present at work sites (Whalen 1971: 190-191).

The densest and largest sites were located in the pediment and may have been the focus of seasonal amalgamation by Archaic bands for communal hunting (Whalen 1975: 207). These sites had three times as many finished tools per unit as terrace sites, and more than eight times as much lithic manufacturing debris. The pediment zone evidently saw more intensive production and use of stone tools than terrace or riverine sites, suggesting that sites in this area were favored for stone tool production (Whalen 1975: 208-209).

The lack of sites in the San Pedro floodplain is more a reflection of alluvial processes than an actual lack of Archaic occupation (Whalen 1975: 205). Buried Archaic sites found eroding out of floodplain arroyos indicate that Cochise groups visited and exploited this resource area. Linear exposures in arroyo walls show that remnants of sizable camps exist in the floodplain.

Other Cochise sites have been excavated in the San Pedro Valley and provide additional information on the middle and late Archaic occupation. The Fairchild Site (Windmiller 1971, 1973) on Whitewater Draw covered 50,000 square meters and had at least 45 cm of cultural depth. Large quantities of stone artifacts were recovered in addition to 91 hearths and 2 storage pits. Windmiller (1973: 136, 161) interpreted the site as a seasonally occupied base camp where a hunter-gatherer group (or groups) exploited the local microenvironment. Apparently a cienega existed nearby with a narrow forest gallery of ash and willow. Chiricahua and San Pedro artifacts were present, and this site may be transitional between the two stages.

Further downstream on the eastern flanks of the Santa Catalina Mountains, Agenbroad (1966) recorded a large Chiricahua stage site, the Lone Hill Site. Located 5 to 6 miles away from the river, it is situated between two large canyons. Excavation at this large base camp or village yielded 23 hearths, large quantities of ground stone, and over 100 projectile points.

## Archaic Occupation in the Empire Valley and Santa Rita Mountains

Closer to the Tucson Basin are the Empire Valley, located to the southeast between the Empire and Whetstone mountains, and the northern part of the Santa Rita Mountains. Archaic period material is abundant in both areas. Eddy (1958) reported several Archaic sites in Matty Canyon in the northern end of the Empire Valley. Here sites containing many pits, some of which may be house depressions, suggest that San Pedro Cochise people were occupying the alluvial flats along Cienega Creek, constructing temporary and semipermanent base camps, and exploiting the rich plant and animal resources along the cienega. Sorties from the base camps into the surrounding plains and mountains for additional resources were probably made seasonally. Perhaps these San Pedro Cochise people gathered for communal rabbit or pronghorn hunts when these animals were plentiful. At other times when game was not as plentiful, the people stayed in smaller family units to forage and hunt (Eddy 1958: 58-59, 104).

The Archaic—and Hohokam—sites in Matty Canyon were buried under at least two meters of alluvium, only to be exposed by lateral stripping of the alluvial overburden by the currently incised arroyo.

Several miles west of Matty Canyon more than 20 Archaic sites were recently recorded in the Barrel and Upper Davidson canyon drainages of the Santa Rita Mountains (Huckell 1982c). These sites are located on relatively flat ridge termini on terraces that are old, stable landforms and tend to be situated towards the head of the drainages at elevations between 1493 m and 1585 m. This is an oak-juniper and oak-grassland community, crosscut by drainages with associated riparian communities. These sites appear to date from the middle and late Archaic (5000 to 2500 B.C.) on the basis of the projectile points recovered during survey. Several of the points were stylistically similar to those reported by Haury (and others 1975) from the Red Sand layer at Ventana Cave, and could be as old as 8000 to 7000 B.C. or as young as 2500 to 2000 B.C. based on geologic estimates. The style seems to predate the Chiricahua-Amargosa II and San Pedro (Huckell 1982c: 7).

Test excavations revealed that these mountain sites were probably camps where tool use rather than tool manufacture occurred. Cores were generally rare, and unifacially retouched tools, particularly scrapers, were common. Ground stone was rare, making up 3 percent of the total artifact assemblage. The sites appear to have been occupied briefly, but on a recurrent—probably seasonal—basis by small bands of people (Huckell 1982c: 6-7).

The areas bordering the Tucson Basin, particularly the San Pedro Valley, had large Archaic occupations with sites located in a variety of environmental and topographic areas. The alluvial floodplains of major and minor drainages, river and arroyo terraces, upper and lower bajadas, and intermediate elevation mountain areas all witnessed various aspects of this occupation.

## Archaic Occupation of the Tucson Basin and Phase B Area

### Eastern Tucson Basin

Although Cochise and Amargosa sites have been recorded in the basin, little is actually known about these occupations—how extensive they are, how old or how late, or how they fit into the regional picture of the Southwestern Archaic.

Drainages on the eastern side of the basin—the Rillito, Pantano and Tanque Verde—contain varying amounts of Archaic materials, usually surface lithic scatters, isolated projectile points, and occasionally a buried hearth eroding out of a river or arroyo bank (Gregonis and Huckell 1980). Rogers (1958) surveyed stretches of the terrace along the Rillito and Pantano creeks and found considerable evidence for Archaic occupation. This included what he considered San Dieguito I material, in addition to trails, sleeping circles, and stone tools of Amargosa I and II, some of which were found in lateral canyons up to 2 km away from the main stream beds (Rogers 1958; Stacy and Hayden 1975). Dates of these occupations are not known, however. The absence of a reliable chronology is one of the major prob-

lems that plague archaeologists trying to interpret the Archaic occupation in the basin.

No Archaic sites in the basin have been systematically excavated. Hemmings and others (1968) conducted limited excavations at the Pantano Site (AZ EE:2:50) on Pantano Creek. This site was buried under 5 m of alluvium, and a good portion of it had already been lost to erosion by the time a cultural layer identifying the site was found eroding out of the arroyo wall. This buried layer was up to 1.5 m thick and 150 m long, and represented a San Pedro Cochise camp that was occupied during the first centuries of the Christian era. It may have been between 2 and 5 acres in size, based on the length of the exposed cultural material (Hemmings and others 1968: 8–9, 22). This site appears to be particularly significant for several reasons: 1) its apparently late date; 2) the presence of corn (Zea) in a cultural layer; and, 3) the unusual degree of sedentism and intensity of occupation suggested by the size of the site, the density of lithic debris, and the heavy-duty nature of the ground stone assemblage. It may have been a base camp occupied during the summer when cultivation in the floodplain was possible (Hemmings and others 1968: 22).

### Santa Cruz River Valley

The Archaic occupation in the western part of the basin along the Santa Cruz River and its major tributaries, Rillito Creek and Cañada del Oro, has been recognized for several decades. Many of these sites have been found eroding out of arroyo channels in the floodplain and are usually covered by several meters of alluvium. A few Archaic sites have been found on the terraces along the floodplain.

Figure 3.1 shows the distribution of recorded Archaic and possible Archaic sites in the Phase B area. Eighteen sites have been recorded in or adjacent to the Santa Cruz River floodplain, and five sites have been recorded on tributary drainages, including two sites along washes near canyon mouths on the west side of the Tortolita Mountains. Like the Archaic occupation on the eastern side of the basin, little is really known about these sites.

The most extensively studied Santa Cruz River sites are those clustering along Brickyard Arroyo on the east side of the floodplain south of Sahuarita Butte (Martinez Hill). Stratigraphic studies of the Quaternary alluvium revealed Archaic sites located in a distinctive stratum, designated Unit B, that is buried beneath two bedded units of variable thickness. Red-brown in color, Unit B is a calcic, hard, silty, clayey, medium-coarse sand with dispersed pebbles and cobbles. Some lenses of subrounded to subrectangular gravels also occur sporadically (Gregonis and Huckell 1980: 38). Bruce Huckell of the Arizona State Museum has investigated these sites with C. Vance Haynes and reports that a piece of charred root or log from Unit B at AZ BB: 13:70 was radiocarbon dated near 3980 ± 100 B.P.

(A1783), while a similar piece of material from the overlying Unit C level at AZ BB:13:73 was radiocarbon dated at 2290 ± 80 B.P. (A1782). Unit C is stratigraphically above Unit B which also contained a grinding slab.

The Joe Ben Site (AZ BB:13:11), also in Brickyard Arroyo, was buried under some 6 or 7 m of alluvium and was eroding out of an 8-m high arroyo wall. Hohokam ceramics were present 1.5 m below the surface, while Cochise artifacts were found 5 m beneath these on a yellowish, indurated sand layer. Three pit hearths, a burial, and numerous chipped and ground stone artifacts have been excavated from this layer over the years. The lithic artifacts were considered to be almost identical to other late Chiricahua-early San Pedro stage artifacts from southeastern Arizona (Fontana 1956). This site has been destroyed by continued erosion of the arroyo.

Betancourt (1978b: 97-98) discusses two other buried Cochise sites (AZ BB:13:107 and 108) located downstream from Brickyard Arroyo. Both sites are situated along small tributary arroyos cut into the floodplain. AZ BB:13:107 is buried under 1.5 m to 2.5 m of alluvium, and has flakes and other lithic debris eroding out of a yellow-brown indurated sand layer (Unit B). AZ BB:13:108, possibly dating to the San Pedro stage, has lithic artifacts eroding out of a pinkish indurated sand layer about 4 m below the surface.

Salvage operations in 1949 in the Santa Cruz River floodplain near downtown Tucson uncovered a number of burials at the Brickyard Site (AZ BB:13:6) which were suggested as being Archaic (Smiley and others 1953: 179). Additional excavation at the Tucson site of San Agustín, immediately south of the Brickyard Site, revealed a burned structure 20 cm below the deepest of several historic mission period burials. A 3 m by 4 m floor area was excavated, and nine artifacts and some unworked stones were found associated with it (Smiley and others 1953). The artifacts—three manos, a metate, a pestle, a hammerstone, two choppers, and a possible palette—were identified by Sayles as typical of the Cochise culture, possibly San Pedro Cochise (Huckell 1982b: 11).

Other floodplain sites occur downstream near the confluence with Rillito Creek and Cañada del Oro (see Figure 3.1), and in the floodplains of these tributary drainages. One site, AZ AA:12:111, is buried under 2 m of alluvium on the western side of the Santa Cruz River floodplain opposite the mouth of the Cañada del Oro. A probable campsite, it contained numerous hearths and, according to Bruce Huckell of the Arizona State Museum, yielded two radiocarbon dates: an upper occupational unit, 50 cm to 90 cm deep, dated at 2820 ± 280 B.P. (A2237) and a lower occupational unit, 1.5 m to 2 m deep, at 4260 ± 140 B.P. No diagnostic artifacts were found; however, if the dates are accurate, the site would fall into the late Archaic, probably representing a San Pedro stage camp site (Gregonis and Huckell 1980: 44).

Another site, AZ AA:12:130, was located nearby and contained at least 86 firepits ranging in size from 0.5 m to 1.5 m in diameter, which were ringed with fist-sized cobbles. Powdered charcoal and a few pieces of charcoal were recovered from the pits; several lithic artifacts were also found. Site size was estimated at some 20,000 square meters, and the hearths were located at the bottom of a pit that was excavated to between 12 m and 14 m below the surface (ASM site survey files). The age of the site is not known, but the charcoal samples may provide that information when they are radiocarbon dated. This particular site has been destroyed, but other hearths are likely to be present in the area.

Buried Archaic sites are common in the Santa Cruz River floodplain. That more have not been found is likely due to past periods of aggradation and degradation which have buried the sites with alluvium, only to destroy all or parts of them during periods of downcutting. The sites that have been found were identified either by careful examination of exposed arroyo walls, or by chance excavations into the alluvium during construction or mining of sand and gravel. The lack of Archaic and Paleo-Indian sites upstream from Tucson in the Continental-Green Valley area is probably due to their being deeply buried in the floodplain (Gregonis and Huckell 1980: 20).

Archaic sites are not confined to the floodplain; several are located along the terrace of the Santa Cruz River. The largest and potentially most significant is AZ AA:12:86 which is on the first terrace on the west side of the river, opposite its confluence with the Cañada del Oro. According to Ed Roland of the University of Arizona, who has surface collected and mapped the site (including point proveniencing all artifacts), it covers about 10 acres and contains a large amount of lithic tools and debris, hearths, some ground stone, and a little shell. It was probably a large San Pedro stage camp that was seasonally occupied. It also contains a Chiricahua stage component. No radiocarbon dates are available.

Two other nonfloodplain sites are located near the mouths of drainages in the Tortolita Mountains, and appear to date from the middle Archaic or Chiricahua stage. They were recently recorded by the Arizona State Museum's Tucson Basin Survey, and have not yet been fully reported. According to John Madsen of the Arizona State Museum, this survey has also found at least 30 isolated projectile points in the upper bajada of the Tortolita Mountains. These appear to range in age from early to late Archaic, based on point styles, indicating extensive Archaic occupation of the northern portion of the Phase B area—an occupation which may go back to the early Chiricahua or possibly Sulphur Spring stages of the Cochise culture. Rogers (1958) noted San Dieguito I and Amargosa artifacts along the Santa Cruz River terraces south of its confluence with Rillito Creek.

## Avra Valley

Four Archaic sites are known in the Brawley Wash floodplain in the Avra Valley (see Figure 3.1). Very little survey has been done here, and this has been limited primarily to narrow transmission line rights-of-way outside the Phase B area (Wilson 1980, 1981; see also Hartmann 1981). Consequently, the prehistoric occupation of the valley is not well known, and is generally considered to have been sparse, especially when compared to that in the Santa Cruz River Valley. However, this does not appear to be the case; Avra Valley may have seen heavier use by prehistoric groups—Archaic and Hohokam—than previously expected. Undoubtedly, this misconception is due largely to the lack of systematic archaeological survey in the valley.

Archaic sites are located along the eastern edge of the Brawley Wash floodplain. One of these, not yet officially recorded by the Arizona State Museum, is located in a dune area and appears to be a camp. No hearths were noted during a brief reconnaissance, but some ground stone and much lithic debitage were seen. One projectile point and a biface were recovered. The point is similar to other late Archaic styles found in southern Arizona. An interesting feature of the site is the high density of small flaking and retouch debitage, indicating that lithic tool manufacture or heavy lithic tool use and reworking, or a combination of these activities, were occurring on the site.

Two other Archaic camp sites are located downstream (north) of the dune site. AZ AA:16:39 (the Werner Site) is buried under at least 0.5 m of sheetwash alluvium; lithic material and ground stone, possibly belonging to the San Pedro stage, can be seen eroding out of several shallow gullies running across the site. Hohokam ceramics are present on and just below the surface (Arizona State Museum site survey files). North of the Werner Site is AZ AA:16:85, a Chiricahua and San Pedro stage site that appears to be a series of short-term campsites occupied sporadically during the middle and late Archaic. Fire-cracked rock is abundant, as are projectile points, scrapers, debitage, and ground stone. This site is also buried under up to 1 m of alluvium and is being exposed by continuing bank erosion of the wash that cuts through the site. Hohokam ceramics are also present on the surface. Some late Pleistocene faunal remains (camel and horse) are present in the bank. They are not associated with the Archaic material, but appear to be associated with a cienega deposit (ASM site survey files).

Wilson (1980, 1981) reported fire-cracked rock concentrations in the valley without any associated diagnostic artifacts. While these may be deflating hearths or pits, no charcoal or ash was noticed. These may represent Archaic features; however, in the absence of diagnostic artifacts or radiocarbon dates, no definite cultural affiliation or age can be given them.

Additional evidence for a potentially heavy Archaic occupation of the Avra Valley comes from Don Formby, a local collector, who has over 300 "Pinto" style projectile points from sites he has found in the valley. Most of these sites are not in the Phase B area, but their abundance and the quantity of chipped stone they contain argue strongly for a more intensive middle and late Archaic occuption of the valley than was anticipated.

## Tucson Mountains

Five or six Archaic sites have been located in the Tucson Mountains which separate the Santa Cruz and Avra valleys. Several surveys in the mountains and adjacent bajadas (Hartman 1981; Masse 1979; Stacy and Hayden 1975) have also reported isolated Archaic artifacts. Stacy and Hayden's (1975: 26) survey of the Tucson Mountain portion of Saguaro National Monument identified San Dieguito I artifacts, and Amargosa artifacts, trails, shrines, and sleeping circles. Amargosa tools were particularly common on the bajadas. Hartmann's survey (Hartmann 1981) located two Archaic sites in the Cat Mountain area near the southern end of the Tucson Mountains. These sites are identified as long-term camps probably belonging to San Pedro Cochise hunter-gathers. In addition to several projectile points, scrapers, and other lithic debris, there were several pieces of ground stone including mano fragments, pestles, metates, and a hammerstone. Hartmann (1981: 69, 71) believes the larger of the two sites (AZ AA:16:2) was a small base camp, while the other site (AZ AA:16:82) may have been contemporaneous with the larger one, serving as an outlier. The tool assemblage indicates a variety of resource-related activities occurred at the sites, probably on a seasonal basis. The larger site was also reused at a much later date by the Hohokam, who left pieces of brown ware ceramic vessels.

Another large campsite (AZ AA:16:70) was reported by Hartmann (1981: 52-54) on the west side of the Tucson Mountains north of Brown Mountain. Located on the upper bajada, this site is an extensive lithic scatter with large numbers of primary and secondary flakes and cores, five hearths, and four rock alignments (small structures?). A small number of Hohokam sherds and three incised brown ware sherds, identified as a Tucson variant of Sweetwater Red-on-gray, were also found. Several heavily patinated flakes suggest use of the site during Archaic times, but it is not clear whether the bulk of the lithic material represents an Archaic or Hohokam camp.

The remaining two Archaic sites are labeled as "lithic scatters" and do not appear to have evidence indicating their use as camps. These, however, have no diagnostic artifacts and it is not clear whether they represent Archaic or Hohokam sites.

Hewitt and Stephen (1981: 69) reported a Chiricahua Cochise site in the Tortolita Mountains. Located in an oak-juniper-mixed cactus zone around 1219 m in elevation, the site consists of a dense surface scatter of chipped stone debitage, projectile points, cores, scrapers, cobble manos, choppers, and utilized flakes. They believe the artifacts represent a mixed hunting-gathering site.

Masse's (1979: 149-151) survey of the bajada on the west side of Tumamoc Hill yielded nine lithic tools assignable to the Archaic period: three Chiricahua stage and one San Pedro stage projectile points and five heavily patinated flakes. Like the upper bajada on the west side of the Tortolita Mountains, these isolated projectile points are indicative of an Archaic occupation in the mountains along the western portion of the Tucson Basin.

# Discussion

Virtually nothing is known about the Paleo-Indian occupation of the Phase B area, and no definite *in situ* sites have been identified. Assuming that the late Pleistocene-early Holocene environment of the Santa Cruz and Avra valleys was similar to that known for the San Pedro Valley with its abundant and reasonably well documented mammoth and Clovis sites, these sites should be present in the Phase B area. That none have been found is most likely due to their being buried in floodplain deposits which have yet to be exposed to the degree present in the San Pedro Valley. It is puzzling that more surface evidence for Clovis occupation has not been found. However, much of the Phase B has been intensively occupied or developed for over 100 years, resulting in severe changes along much of the Santa Cruz floodplain and adjacent terraces and bajadas. Surface evidence that may have been present 50 or 100 years ago has been destroyed by this intensive and extensive development. In contrast, the upper San Pedro Valley has not undergone this prolonged, intensive development; the area was, and remains, primarily ranching country.

As noted above, evidence for Paleo-Indian occupation in the Phase B area is restricted to Avra Valley. Development here has been much slower than along the Santa Cruz River, and it has been only in the past several decades that farming, and more recently, urban development, have impacted portions of the valley. Also, archaeological survey has been limited, and most of the valley's cultural resource potential remains unknown. It appears that if surface evidence, and perhaps buried sites, are to be found, Avra Valley may present a better opportunity than the highly developed Santa Cruz River and western Tucson Basin.

Although Avra Valley has undergone considerably less development, it apparently has not escaped the attention of artifact collectors; as a result many sites have been stripped of diagnostic artifacts, making identification of cultural affiliation difficult—if not impossible—without excavation. Evidence for Paleo-Indian occupation of the valley may be in the hands of collectors, and has gone unreported.

Floodplain arroyos and tributary drainages offer the most likely locales of buried Paleo-Indian remains. One buried site (AZ AA:16:85, discussed above), exposed in a tributary arroyo of Brawley Wash, has yielded horse and camel remains, although not in any apparent association with cultural materials. This site is in the Phase B area, and it is possible that other sites are present in the project area in similar geomorphological contexts.

Despite the number of Archaic sites known in the Phase B area, almost no work has been done to define and interpret this occupation. As previously mentioned there has been no intensive, systematic excavation of an Archaic site anywhere in the basin. Consequently, current views and interpretations of the Archaic period are based on survey data and extrapolation from excavated Archaic sites elsewhere in southern Arizona.

The Archaic occupation in the basin does not appear to differ from similar occupations in the San Pedro Valley or elsewhere in southern Arizona. Site distribution is similar to that described by Whalen (1971, 1975) and others (Huckell 1973; Windmiller 1971, 1973) (see Table 3.2). Base camps and smaller campsites are common in the Santa Cruz and Brawley Wash floodplains and on the terraces along these floodplains. Recalling the discussion of the likely paleoenvironmental conditions of these riverine areas, location of camps adjacent to reliable and plentiful water sources is expected in a semiarid desert region, and follows the pattern of site location elsewhere in the Southwest. The rich plant and animal resources available in the riverine zone would have supplied Archaic families with a varied larder during most of the year. Seasonal trips to nearby bajadas and mountains would have provided addi-

---

TABLE 3.2

**Paleo-Indian and Archaic Site Distribution**

| Cultural Affiliation | Topographic Setting | | |
| --- | --- | --- | --- |
| | Floodplain | Terrace/ Lower Bajada | Upper Bajada/ Mountain |
| Paleo-Indian (isolated artifact) | | | 3 |
| Archaic or Cochise | 4 | 4 | 3 |
| Archaic or Cochise with Hohokam component | 4 | | 3 |
| San Pedro Cochise | 3 | 1 | 1 |
| Chiricahua or San Pedro Cochise with Hohokam component | 3 | 1 | 2 |
| Aceramic lithic scatter | 1 | 3 | 1 |

tional and varied plant and animal resources as they became available.

Most of the Archaic sites located in and along the floodplain have been identified as campsites, with a few labeled base camps, primarily on the basis of size and the presence of hearths, manos, metates and other ground stone grinding or crushing implements, and a variety of chipped stone artifacts. This artifact assemblage suggests some degree of temporary or semipermanent habitation, consistent with the assemblage that Whalen (1971: 190-191) associates with base or camp sites. No evidence of structures has been found, with the exception of the rectangular structure from San Agustin Mission that may be Archaic. It is possible that structures of some sort exist, but have yet to be identified. Other buried sites are most likely to be campsites and will contain hearths or roasting pits, chipped and ground stone artifacts, and perhaps structures and burials.

Buried Archaic sites in the Santa Cruz and Brawley Wash floodplains are covered by at least a meter, usually more, of alluvium. Locating floodplain sites remains a problem, and except where downcutting has exposed them, excavation by developers has provided the only other opportunity for locating these sites. Since the sites are often deeply buried, even areas that have undergone intensive agricultural development, which has destroyed more recent and shallower Hohokam sites, probably has not impacted deeply buried sites.

Although some buried sites have undoubtedly been destroyed by erosion and development, others can be expected anywhere in the floodplain. Identification of old cienega deposits can aid in the location of buried sites since many of the recorded sites in southeastern Arizona are in close proximity to, if not direct association with, cienega deposits. Such deposits are also likely areas for Paleo-Indian and Pleistocene fauna remains. Likewise, identification of the locally defined B Unit which has been directly associated with Archaic material elsewhere in the floodplain, will aid in detecting Archaic sites.

Four Archaic sites are located on the terraces along the Santa Cruz River and Rillito Creek floodplains, and others are likely to be present. These terraces have not been systematically surveyed, and very little is known about the number and kinds of sites present on them. Most of the river terraces have been disturbed or destroyed by housing construction, and what resource base may have been present is now gone. Rogers (1958) apparently surveyed a portion of the Santa Cruz River terraces south of the confluence with Rillito Creek and found the same kinds of San Dieguito I and Amargosan material that occurred on the terraces of Rillito and Pantano creeks.

Archaic sites have been recorded on the upper bajada adjacent to the Tucson Mountains as well as in the mountains. However, the only upper bajada-mountain areas scheduled to be affected by canal construction are at the southern end of the Tucson Mountains at the Cat Mountain and Twin Hills reservoir sites. Two San Pedro stage campsites are located near Cat Mountain, indicating that this area was occupied during the late Archaic. Survey here has been limited, but other Archaic sites are probably present. A local collector recently showed the author a small, shouldered, tapering-stemmed projectile point similar to a type known as Lake Mohave, that was found at the base of Cat Mountain. Isolated projectile points are common throughout the Phase B area suggesting a relatively intensive Archaic occupation. This same collector has found several hundred Pinto-type projectile points in Avra Valley.

The upper bajada and mountain areas of Phase B can be expected to contain Archaic sites, although not as many as the floodplain and river terraces. Both camp and "use" sites will be present, the former most likely along drainages (see Whalen 1975). Use sites should contain a more restricted artifact assemblage reflecting the procuring or processing of one or two specific resources such as lithic raw material. Isolated artifacts (projectile points) and hearths or roasting pits (see Wilson 1980, 1981) can also be expected.

# Chapter 4

# THE HOHOKAM AND PROTOHISTORIC PERIODS

## James D. Mayberry

The following survey of Hohokam settlement patterns in the Tucson Aqueduct Phase B project area relies solely on existing survey data, supplemented by data from excavations in the project area, including the Tucson Basin. Its goals will be to establish a predictive model for the distribution of Hohokam sites in the project area and, by analogy, for the rest of the middle Santa Cruz River Basin.

All recorded ceramic sites, prehistoric and historic, in Arizona State Museum site survey quads AZ AA:11, AZ AA:12, AZ AA:16, AZ BB:9, AZ BB:13, AZ DD:4 and AZ EE:1, an area encompassing the project area and its immediate environs, were classified by the following typology (see Table 4.1):

Class I sites: all those with either trash mounds or visible architecture, other than trincheras;

Class II sites: those with surface artifact scatters but no domestic architecture or mounds; and

Class III sites: sites without artifact scatters, visible architecture or mounds. Class III sites consist of rock art locales, isolated burials, caches and cemeteries.

TABLE 4.1

**Site Typology**

| Site Type | Frequency | Percentage | Function |
|---|---|---|---|
| Class I | 139 | 25.5 | town-village |
| Class II | 389 | 71.0 | artifact scatter |
| Class III | 20 | 3.5 | rock art, caches, burials |
| | | | |
| Totals | 548 | 100.0 | |

All Class I sites will be interpreted as areas occupied on a permanent basis; architecture and localized trash deposits have been previously associated with sedentism in the area (Westfall 1979: 64). Class I sites will be interpreted as habitation sites, including town-villages and isolated structures. Within the study area 139 Class I sites, 25.4 percent of the total, have been recorded in Arizona State Museum site survey files. The majority of these are within the Phase B project area. Features within recorded Class I sites include hearths, canals, cremation and inhumation burials, pits, platform mounds, ballcourts, bedrock mortars, wells, rock art, stone features, terraces and middens.

Class II sites, artifact scatters without structures or trash mounds, comprise the majority of recorded sites in the area: 389 Class II sites, 71.1 percent of the total, have been recorded, many within the project area. Excavations in southern Arizona, including the Tucson Basin, have revealed a high incidence of subsurface architecture at sites whose surface features are limited to artifact scatters (Masse 1980a; Rosenthal and others 1978; Teague 1982). Functional identification of such sites is therefore difficult (and frequently unreliable) in the absence of subsurface testing and has often necessitated use of generalized site typologies (McCarthy 1982) such as the one used in this report.

In light of this, many Class II sites probably do contain subsurface architecture. Consequently, this class of sites is ambiguous with respect to function. In southern Arizona many Class II sites have been associated with specialized resource procurement and processing activities involving agricultural exploitation of wild biotic resources (Ackerly and Rieger 1975; Westfall 1979). Nevertheless, the class can be assumed to include nonhabitation and habitation sites, some of which were occupied on a short-term basis, and others on a more permanent basis.

In order to test the assumption that the majority of Class II sites were functionally distinct from Class I sites (definite habitation sites) the distribution of both site types was plotted among several landforms. A chi-square test was then performed to determine the significance of the differences of the distributions (Appendix C). In every case, significant differences in the distribution of the two site types were established. This indicates that the distribution of specialized sites and habitation sites lacking visible architecture or trash mounds differs from that of habitation sites having surface architecture or trash mounds. The relative distributions suggest that Class II sites are more likely to be situated away from sources of permanent surface water than are Class I sites. Specialized Class II sites were probably not permanently occupied.

Recorded features at Class II sites include: artifact scatters, stone features, fire-cracked rock, hearths, rock shelters, pits, bedrock mortars, rock art, field gardens, cerros de trincheras, trails, and "water control" features.

Class III sites are limited to those few sites without either architecture or artifact scatters. The majority of Class III sites are rock art locales; other Class III sites include caches, isolated burials, and a cemetery. Class III sites are interpreted as nonhabitation sites that, unlike Class II sites, are not likely to contain subsurface architecture. Only 20 Class III sites, 3.4 percent of the total, have been recorded in the study area, most of them within the Phase B project area (Appendix A).

## The Landform-Site Type Model

Previous work (McCarthy 1982; McCarthy and Sires 1981) has indicated serious flaws in the vegetation zone-site type association model prepared for the project area (Westfall 1979). Potential sources of error in the model include the possibility of fluctuation in the spatial distribution of the zones over time (Martin and Turner 1977: 68; Masse 1980a: 252; McCarthy 1982: 40), the ambiguous nature of some zones, especially the desert riparian zone (McCarthy 1982: 22), and the differential preservation of artifacts, rendering classification of most sites into Westfall's categories difficult at best (Masse 1980a: 45; Rosenthal and others 1978: 218; Withers 1973: 71).

A fallacy basic to any model predicated on a presumed one-to-one correspondence between site types and environmental zones involves the assumption that human populations are adapted to specific vegetation zones or individual species. Human populations can best be viewed as being adapted to a limited number of critical resources, not specific plant communities or species (Hole and others 1969; Whalen 1971: 202). Since archaeological sites are the products of past human adaptations, the distribution of sites should be determined by the availability and location of resources critical to the adaptive strategies used by the populations of those sites (Gasser 1980: 72). In the study area the two resources most critical to sedentary populations are arable land and available water. In contrast

with some models (McGuire and Schiffer 1982) ethnographic evidence points to arable land, as well as available water, as the principal resources of sedentary agriculturalists in southern Arizona (Doyel 1980: 21; Smith, Kessel, and Fox 1966: 43; Wilson 1980: 13).

The model used in this study, adapted from models developed by others (Marmaduke and Berry 1980: 210; Teague and Baldwin 1978) is based on landform rather than vegetation zones. Figure 1.1 illustrates these land form zones, which include:

Zone 1. Alluvial floodplains of major streams - Such areas contain optimum levels of both arable land and water. Floodplains of secondary drainages, such as Brawley Wash, contain arable land but little available water. Past periods of more moist climatic conditions may, however, have provided such areas with water sources no longer present.

Zone 2. Bajadas - These areas have primarily localized water sources, many of them presently impermanent. Areas of arable land would also be more limited and localized than in Zone 1.

Zone 3. Mountain - These areas, while containing some water sources, would have relatively limited areas of arable land.

Transitional zones, such as those between the alluvial floodplain and surrounding nonriverine areas, afforded ready access to the biotic and abiotic resources of two microenvironments, enabling prehistoric populations to procure resources with relatively little expenditure of energy (Hewitt and Stephen 1981: 33). These areas, primarily the elevated terraces of major streams, were not only immediately adjacent to the resources of both floodplain and bajada areas, but were also elevated above areas susceptible to seasonal flooding.

Many Hohokam village sites in the Santa Cruz Valley south of the project area have been recorded in this transition zone (Frick 1954: 35). Ethnographic evidence (Di Peso 1956: 486; Betancourt 1978b: 61) suggests that such areas were also preferred by historic agricultural groups as locales for villages. A similar preference for ecotonal areas has been proposed for large Hohokam sites during the Classic period in the Salt River Valley (Wilcox, McGuire and Sternberg 1981: 99). The advantages of ecotonal areas to sedentary populations by virtue of their proximity to two distinct environments has been recognized as a major determinant in the distribution of sites in prehistoric systems (Doyel 1972; Flannery 1968; Hole and others 1969). According to Paul Fish of the Arizona State Musuem, the transition between the upper bajada and mountainous areas has also been identified as a favored locale for site locations (see also Hewitt and Stephen 1981). Unlike the transition between riverine and bajada environments, these are primarily Class II, rather than Class I, sites.    The landform-site type and frequency model involves three predictive assumptions:

Class I sites will occur in all three zones. The majority of such sites including most of the large sites will occur either in the floodplains of axial streams or in the transitional zone along the margins of floodplains. Class I sites in the bajada (Zone 2), will be primarily located near localized water sources or arable land; however, the incidence of such sites will be much lower in Zone 2 than in Zone 1. Zone 3, the mountains, will have the lowest frequency of Class I sites and the majority of these will be relatively smaller in size than those in Zones 1 and 2.

Class II sites will also occur in all three zones. The incidence of these sites in Zones 1 and 2 will be about the same; the number of sites in Zone 3 will be lower than in either Zones 1 and 2. The transitional ecotone will not be a determining factor in locating Class II sites; therefore the incidence of Class II sites in transition areas will be lower than that of Class I sites. The distribution of Class II sites, most of which are assumed to be related to the extraction of resources during both agricultural and nonagricultural activities, will be determined primarily by the subsistence strategies of the occupants of those sites.

Class III sites will occur in all three zones; however, as the majority of Class III sites are rock art locales, most will occur in or near Zone 3. Previous survey, both in the Tucson Basin (White 1966) and elsewhere in southern Arizona (Ferg 1979; Westfall 1979:66), has shown a tendency for rock art sites to be located in volcanic rock outcrops, often isolated from permanent occupation sites. Zone 3 should contain the majority of such formations. Most Class III sites are interpreted as relating to ceremonial or funerary traditions, not subsistence pursuits.

The distribution of Class I sites through time among the three landforms will be determined primarily by two independent variables — the subsistence strategy of the population and climatic conditions. Some data have indicated that paleoclimatological conditions in southern Arizona may parallel those in the Colorado Plateau, at least for portions of the past 2000 years (Bryan 1941: 231; Euler and others 1979: 1097; Miksicek 1982; Weaver 1972: 41). The similarities in the climatic fluctuations of the last century in southern and northern Arizona (Bryan 1941: 231, 236; Humphreys 1958: 39) support the validity of this association. Although this correlation has been challenged (McGuire 1982), dendrochronological and palynological data from both areas is discussed later in the chapter when relevant to the dynamics of prehistoric subsistence systems.

Excavation data on subsistence practices will also be discussed, supplemented by inferences based on the distribution of sites. The following assumptions are incorporated into the landform-site type frequency model: Evidence of subsistence strategies featuring a broad-based mixed economy with equal emphasis on agriculture and the use of wild biotic resources will occur in Class II sites in both floodplain and bajada environments. A majority of Class I sites in primarily agricultural systems will occur in, or adjacent to, the floodplains of major streams. Systems relying more on hunting and gathering will have a higher incidence of Class I and II sites in nonriverine environments.

Recorded sites were divided by estimated surface area into the following categories: small Class I and II sites (less than 30,000 square meters in area), and large Class I and II sites (greater than 30,000 square meters in area), based on an examination of Arizona State Museum site survey files. Site distributions based on this typological hierarchy are shown on Figures 4.2 through 4.9. The size of another 102 sites was unknown or indeterminate. Most of the maps illustrate the distribution of a single decorated ceramic type. Since the relative chronologies of the Salt-Gila Basin, Tucson Basin, and the Papaguería are based on an assumed one-to-one correlation between named decorated ceramic types and their corresponding phases (Haury and others 1975, 1976; Kelly 1978), the distribution of sites whose ceramic assemblages include a particular decorated type corresponds to the distribution of all sites occupied during the phase associated with that type. Thus Figure 4.2, showing the distribution of sites whose ceramic assemblages included sherds of Snaketown Red-on-buff, is also the distribution of sites assumed to contain Snaketown phase loci. Figure 4.9 shows the distribution of sites whose ceramic assemblages did not contain named decorated types; such sites are known only to contain prehistoric ceramics and may represent Hohokam or Piman occupations.

Previous work in the Hohokam area has demonstrated the likelihood of early components being buried under later occupations (Haury 1976; Kelly 1978), especially at Class I sites. Thus the distribution of recorded sites, especially those dating to the Preclassic, may include many early components inaccessible without subsurface testing. Interpretive implications presented by such biases are discussed in Chapter 7.

Most Class I sites in the project area have several phase components. Without excavation it is impossible to isolate the specific occupations associated with the habitation features; therefore unexcavated, multiphase habitation sites cannot be assumed to have been permanently occupied during any particular phase to which that site is dated. The maps then, show habitation sites with ceramics of a particular phase, not sites known to have been permanently occupied in that phase.

Although site distributions can be used to interpret settlement patterns during individual phases, they should be used in estimating relative populations only on a most general level. Several potential sources of error in deriving population estimates from site frequencies have been identified. One problem is that sites with similar ceramic assemblages cannot be assumed to be absolutely contemporary (Doyel 1977a: 201; Greenleaf 1975b: 275; Plog 1980: 14; Wilcox, McGuire and Sternberg 1981: 152). Given a transhumant residence pattern similar to that of the historic Papago, a number of sites could have been occupied by a single group during one yearly round, resulting in over-inflated population estimates (Doyel 1980: 27). The duration of most prehistoric archaeological periods, 200 years or more, is of sufficient length to allow for significant population shifts (Doelle 1980: 233), resulting in a single group occupying more than one site. If successive phases exhibit changes in site frequencies, particularly in the frequency of Class I sites, limited inferences on relative population sizes are valid. At best though, site frequencies can be used only as very general indices of demographic processes (Rice and others 1979).

# The Hohokam

## Definitions

Probably the most singular process in the prehistory of southern Arizona is the crystallization, florescence and ultimate decline of the Hohokam. The term "Hohokam" has been differentially defined through time. First derived from a Pima Indian word meaning "all used up" (Russell 1908), "Hohokam" was later used to refer to the aboriginal population presumed to be associated with the Precolumbian ruins of the desert regions of Arizona (Huntington 1914). The term first appeared in the archaeological literature as denoting a prehistoric ethnic group (Gladwin and others 1937), who were later theorized as having migrated to the American Southwest before the time of Christ from an unspecified region of Mesoamerica (Haury 1976). From a "core" area, the Salt-Gila Basin, the Hohokam were envisaged as colonizing much of Arizona, including the Tucson Basin and the Papaguería, by filling an environmental niche, the alluvial floodplains, not intensively occupied by the indigenous Cochise culture population (Doyel 1977b: 108; Haury 1978). Other models have called for the Hohokam entering the area a millennium later and subjugating the "Ootam," an indigenous population that had already incorporated many Mesoamerican cultural complexes (Di Peso 1956; Hayden 1970).

While the ultimate Mesoamerican derivation for much of the material culture and subsistence practices of the Hohokam cannot be argued, the mechanism behind the spread of ceramic technology, domestic architecture and the corn-beans-squash agricultural triad from Mesoamerica to the American Southwest remains problematic (Schroeder 1965, 1966; Teague 1974: 10; Winter 1976: 424). Several publications have diverged from more traditional models by viewing the Hohokam, not as an ethnically distinct group of Mesoamerican emigrants, but rather as a regional socioeconomic system of interaction. This "interaction sphere" encompassed, to varying degrees,

several distinct populations (Doyel 1977a: 247; Wilcox 1979b: 78; Wilcox and Sternberg 1981: 35). This systemic definition of the Hohokam is associated with recent reevaluations of assumptions basic to archaeology, principally the affiliation of material culture assemblages with presumed ethnic groups (Doyel 1972: 59; Masse 1980a: 37). Most traditional models have associated changes in the geographic distribution of artifacts with migrations of populations (Di Peso 1956; Haury 1945, 1976). A primary objection to this centers on the view that a group's material culture is more the result of their adaptation than of an identity system defining group membership (Doyel 1972: 13; McGuire and Schiffer 1982). Thus material cultures reflect differing adaptations, not different populations. This contradicts traditional associations of material culture assemblages and ethnic groups. "Material culture traits are reflective of a group's level of sociocultural integration and…of the adaptive requirements of the social systems involved" (Doyel 1977b: 107); they do not denote ethnic identity.

An ethnographic example illustrating a possible source of error in the assumption of a one to one correspondence involves the Areñenos, the Sand Papago. A nomadic group inhabiting what is now southwestern Arizona, the Sand Papago were regarded as fellow Pima by the Papago and Gila Pima, their cousins to the east (Ezell 1955: 371). Traditional archaeological interpretations, however, would tend to affiliate the Sand Papago with the Yuma of the lower Colorado River Valley to the west on the basis of a shared material culture, especially the use of Lower Colorado buff ware by the Areñenos (Bowen 1972: 37; Ezell 1954: 23, 1955; Rosenthal and others 1978: 121). This use of what is considered Yuman material culture did not affect the Areñenos' sociocultural integration with other Pima, despite differing ceramic traditions and subsistence practices. Similarly, the Historic Papago and Pima regarded themselves as a single ethnic and cultural entity, despite different material cultures and adaptations (Coe 1978: 37). At the time of contact the major distinctions between the Pima, Sobaipuri, and Papago were economic, not ethnic (Rosenthal and others 1978: 15).

Archaeological data suggest similar conditions may have existed in prehistoric southern Arizona. The traits traditionally used to define the Hohokam, primarily red-on-buff and red-on-brown ceramics, cremation burials, distinctive traditions in lithics, and worked shell, rarely occur as a homogenous assemblage outside of the Salt-Gila Basin. Hybridization of Hohokam artistic, architectural, and funerary traditions has been noted in the Tucson Basin (Greenleaf 1975a; Kelly 1978), as well as in the San Pedro Valley (Franklin 1978; Tuthill 1947: 84), and the Verde Valley (Fish and others 1980). If the Hohokam entered Arizona as a distinct ethnic group, they maintained their identity only in the Salt-Gila Basin while readily adopting local traditions everywhere else.

Less traditional models have defined the Hohokam as a dynamic behavioral system without any particular ethnic affiliation, rather than a set of shared "typical material culture traits" distinctive to one group (Doyel 1977b: 247). Thus the cultural traditions associated with the Hohokam were adopted in varying degrees by several distinct groups across southern Arizona. Systemic models view the relative degree of incorporation of Hohokam traditions (for example, the use of red-on-buff ceramics) by local groups as indicative of the degree of participation by those groups in a "Hohokam interaction sphere." This Hohokam system, after originating in the Salt-Gila Basin, was to encompass much of Arizona (Wilcox 1979b: 78; Wilcox and Sternberg 1981: 35).

## Origins

Although the origins of the Hohokam are beyond the scope of this discussion, possible relationships between the ceramic and preceramic occupations of southern Arizona may aid interpretation of the initial Pioneer period. One model calls for the Hohokam occupying an environmental niche, the alluvial floodplain, not intensively exploited by Archaic populations (Doyel 1977b: 108). Data from the Tucson Basin and San Pedro Valley (see Figure 4.1 for location of sites discussed below), however, indicate a late Archaic presence in riverine environments at a number of sites attributed to the San Pedro stage of the Cochise culture (2000 B.C. to 500 B.C.—A.D. 200?). Similarities between the area's ceramic and preceramic horizons include such Hohokam traditions as: pit house architecture (Eddy 1958: 42; Sayles 1941: 24), palettes (Hemmings and others 1968: 14), basin and trough metates (Betancourt 1978a: 65; Hemmings and others 1968: 10), cremation burials (Gladwin and others 1937: 251; Haury 1957) and undecorated brown ware ceramics (Breternitz 1978: 16; Fritz 1972: 3; Walker and Polk 1973: 12).

Several San Pedro stage sites excavated outside of the project area have yielded radiocarbon dates suggesting the persistence of the San Pedro stage after the time of Christ (Hemmings and others 1968; Masse 1980a: 10, 306). This establishes approximate contemporaneity of the terminal Archaic with the Pioneer period Hohokam. Settlement data illustrate the presence of a considerable number of late Cochise sites in, or adjacent to, alluvial floodplains of major streams, an environmental niche not vacant prior to the appearance of the Hohokam (see Chapter 3 this volume; Eddy 1958: 55; Whalen 1971a: 105; Wilcox and Sternberg 1981: 34).

The terminal Archaic population in the Tucson Basin and adjacent areas may have had a growing reliance on agriculture, perhaps encouraging settlement in areas containing arable land and available water. The San Pedro stage was marked by increasing use of cultigens, including pumpkins, corn, squash and beans (Lensink 1976: 7; Whalen 1971: 92), which enabled a semisedentary lifeway as early as 2000 B.C. (Whalen 1973), a process associated with the introduction and hybridization of cultigens derived from Mesoamerica (Whalen 1971: 214).

Accompanying the adoption of agriculture in favored locales was a growing trend toward sedentism, indicated by the presence of small, shallow pit houses at a number of sites (Breternitz 1978: 16; Rogers 1958: 21; Sayles 1945). The adoption of a developed ceramic tradition from an unknown source (Breternitz 1978: 16, Walker and Polk 1973: 12) suggests that the terminal Archaic period may have been a time of transition between the aceramic Cochise culture and the Hohokam, a time when many traditions basic to the latter were first established. One such transitional site in the project area may be AZ BB:13:11, the Joe Ben Site, buried in the floodplain of the Santa Cruz River. Consisting of several hearths containing San Pedro stage lithics, this site also yielded a cremation, and a single sherd of plain brown ware deemed "unlikely to have washed in" (ASM site survey files). A larger assemblage of "pre-Hohokam brown ware" in direct association with San Pedro stage lithics and middens has also been recorded at AZ BB:14:79 in the eastern Tucson Basin (ASM site survey files).

Available data from the project area and elsewhere indicate that the alluvial floodplains of southern Arizona, prior to the Pioneer period, were not empty niches. A late Cochise culture population centered on the major drainages may well have persisted until after the time of Christ, and this population may have possessed a material culture, subsistence practices, and settlement pattern similar to the subsequent Pioneer period Hohokam. The proliferation of ceramics may well be the only major difference between the late Archaic and the earliest Hohokam in the area. The adoption of ceramics occurred without further change in material culture at several sites excavated in southern Arizona: Ventana Cave in the Papaguería (Haury and others 1975; Doyel 1979: 262), Matty Canyon in the Empire Valley (Eddy 1958: 67) and Red Mountain in the Salt River Valley (Morris 1969: 10, 50).

# The Pioneer Period
# (A.D. 100 to 500)

## Recorded Sites

The earliest recorded Hohokam sites are primarily in the Salt-Gila Basin; no remains attributed to the early Pioneer period, the Vahki or Estrella phases, are recorded in the project area. The earliest recorded ceramics from sites in the Tucson Basin and the Avra Valley date to the

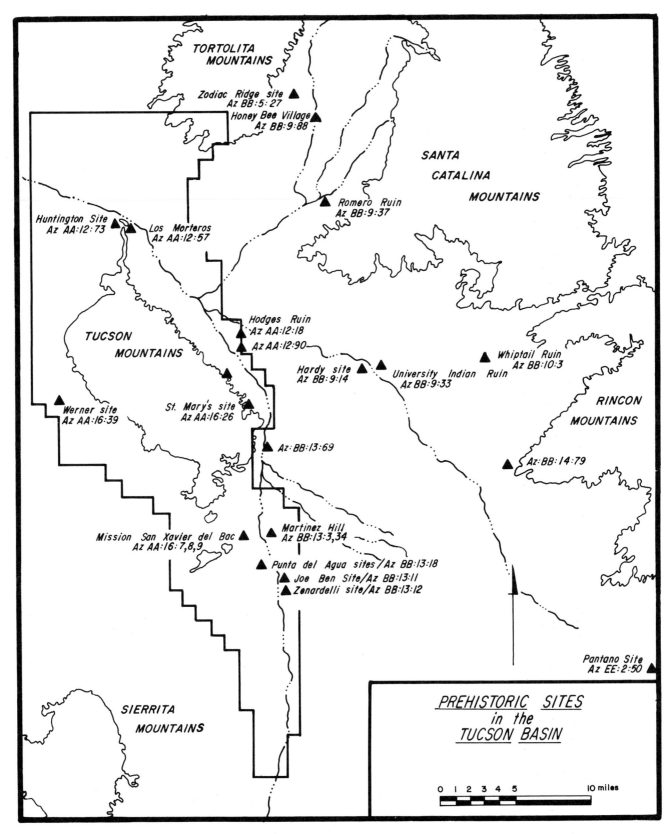

TORTOLITA
MOUNTAINS

Zodiac Ridge site ▲
Az BB:5:27

Honey Bee Village ▲
Az BB:9:88

SANTA
CATALINA
MOUNTAINS

Romero Ruin ▲
Az BB:9:37

Huntington Site ▲ ▲
Az AA:12:73   Los Morteros
              Az AA:12:57

TUCSON
MOUNTAINS

Hodges Ruin ▲
Az AA:12:18

▲ Az AA:12:90

Hardy site ▲ ▲ University Indian Ruin
Az BB:9:14      Az BB:9:33

▲ Whiptail Ruin
  Az BB:10:3

RINCON
MOUNTAINS

Werner site ▲
Az AA:16:39

St. Mary's site ▲
Az AA:16:26

▲ Az:BB:13:69

▲ Az:BB:14:79

Mission San Xavier del Bac ▲
Az AA:16:7,8,9

Martinez Hill ▲
Az BB:13:3,34

▲ Punta del Agua sites / Az BB:13:18

▲ Joe Ben Site/Az BB:13:11

▲ Zenardelli site/Az BB:13:12

Pantano Site ▲
Az EE:2:50

SIERRITA
MOUNTAINS

*PREHISTORIC SITES*
*in the*
*TUCSON BASIN*

0 1 2 3 4 5          10 miles

*Figure 4.1.* Some major sites in and adjacent to the Phase B project area

[ 32 ]

Sweetwater phase (A.D. 100 to 300). Two such sites are within the project area. One, AZ AA:16:70, located in the eastern Avra Valley in the bajada of the Tucson Mountains, consists of a lithic scatter some 140,000 square meters in area containing several sherds of Sweetwater-incised plain ware as well as San Pedro stage lithics. Though the sherds have not been shown to be in direct association with the Archaic artifacts, their occurrence in the same biotic environment suggests that the earliest Hohokam in the area may have had a subsistence base similar to that of late Archaic groups. A second project area site with Sweetwater phase ceramics has recently been recorded by the Arizona State Museum in the ecotone along the edge of the floodplain of the Santa Cruz River northwest of its confluence with the Cañada del Oro.

The Hodges Site (AZ AA:12:18) located less than one-half kilometer to the east of the project area in the Tucson Basin has yielded the only excavated material dated to the Sweetwater phase in the Tucson Basin: 24 sherds and four restorable vessels of Sweetwater Red-on-gray (Kelly 1978: 20). Since no architectural features have yet been found in association with Sweetwater phase artifacts, the initial Hohokam occupation of the Santa Cruz Valley may have been on an impermanent or seasonal basis similar to that of the San Pedro stage Cochise in the project area. Similar occupations have been proposed for the Pioneer period in the Papaguería (Haury and others 1975; Masse 1980a: 13) and the upper Santa Cruz Valley (Di Peso 1956: 226; Grebinger and Adam 1978: 33).

The Snaketown phase (A.D. 300 to 500) of the late Pioneer period is better represented. A total of 10 sites with late Pioneer period materials has been recorded in the project area; another six such sites are known in the immediate vicinity (Figure 4.2). Among the latter is the Hodges Site; excavation here has revealed the only architectural feature attributed to the Pioneer period in the Tucson Basin, a wall-less house floor (Kelley 1978: 15). While the degree of sedentism of the earliest Hohokam in the area remains problematic, the distribution of sites points to agriculture as a principal means of subsistence during the Snaketown phase (Betancourt 1978b: 41). All of the late Pioneer period sites in the project area are located either in, or overlooking, the floodplain of the Santa Cruz. The six Snaketown phase sites recorded outside of the Phase B area are also to be found in, or immediately adjacent to, the floodplain of the Santa Cruz or its major tributaries, Cañada del Oro and Rillito Creek. Sites in the project area occur in several areas; three are in the floodplain of the Santa Cruz, one is on the margin of the bajada of the eastern slope of the Tucson Mountains, and the remaining six Snaketown phase sites are located in the area of transition between the Santa Cruz floodplain and surrounding terrace or bajada areas (see Tables 4.2A and B below).

TABLE 4.2

**Pioneer and Early Colonial Periods**
**Site Distributions and Frequencies**

A. Site Frequency in the Project Area

| Phase | Floodplain | Transition | Bajada | Mountain | Avra Valley | Total |
|---|---|---|---|---|---|---|
| Sweetwater | 0 | 1 | 0 | 0 | 1 | 2 |
| Snaketown | 3 | 6 | 1 | 0 | 0 | 10 |
| Cañada del Oro | 2 | 10 | 2 | 1 | 0 | 15 |

B. Site Distribution in the Project Area

| Phase | Floodplain | Transition | Bajada | Mountain | Avra Valley | Total |
|---|---|---|---|---|---|---|
| Sweetwater | 0 | 50% | 0 | 0 | 0% | 100% |
| Snaketown | 30% | 60% | 10% | 0 | 0 | 100% |
| Cañada del Oro | 13% | 67% | 13% | 7% | 0% | 100% |

C. Site Frequency in the General Area

| Phase | Floodplain | Transition | Bajada | Mountain | Avra Valley | Total |
|---|---|---|---|---|---|---|
| Sweetwater | 0 | 2 | 0 | 0 | 1 | 3 |
| Snaketown | 3 | 12 | 2 | 0 | 0 | 19 |
| Cañada del Oro | 4 | 17 | 3 | 1 | 0 | 25 |

D. Site Distribution in the General Area

| Phase | Floodplain | Transition | Bajada | Mountain | Avra Valley | Total |
|---|---|---|---|---|---|---|
| Sweetwater | 0 | 67% | 0 | 0 | 33% | 100% |
| Snaketown | 18% | 70% | 12% | 0 | 0 | 100% |
| Cañada del Oro | 16% | 68% | 12% | 4% | 0 | 100% |

## Models

The proximity of every recorded site with Snaketown phase components to the floodplains of major streams can best be interpreted as indicating that such areas contained resources critical to the populations of those sites. The limited floral assemblage from Snaketown phase loci at AZ AA:12:18, consisting exclusively of charred corn and beans (Kelly 1978: 122), indicates that agriculture was a principal means of subsistence during the Pioneer period. Though some archaeologists have called for a primary emphasis on the hunting and gathering of wild resources during the Pioneer period (Plog 1980: 16), data from the majority of Pioneer period sites excavated in southern Arizona suggest that agriculture was the primary subsistence strategy in even

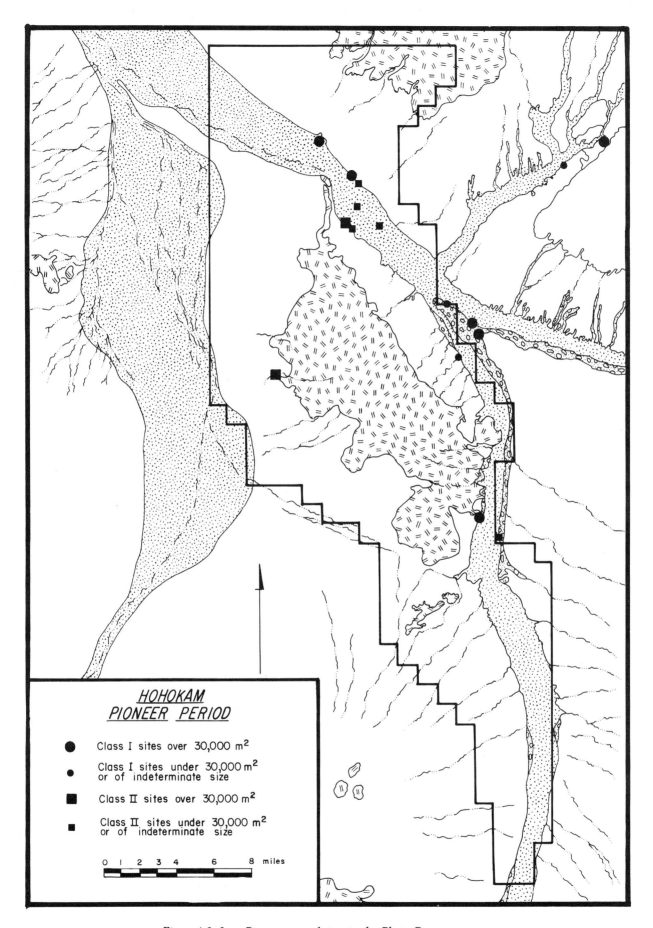

*Figure 4.2.* Late Pioneer period sites in the Phase B project area

[ 34 ]

the earliest Hohokam periods (Gasser 1976: 7; Haury 1976; 118, 147; Masse 1980a: 66, 191). The absence of Snaketown phase sites in nonriverine environments in the study area tends to contradict models postulating the relative importance of hunting and gathering over agriculture in the early Hohokam period (this, however, may be due to sampling biases). At present, evidence for irrigation agriculture in the Pioneer period is limited to the Salt-Gila Basin (Haury 1976: 132); the distribution of the majority of early Hohokam sites implies, however, that floodwater or irrigation farming played a primary role in early Hohokam subsistence in the Tucson Basin (Betancourt 1978b: 14; Gasser 1976; Masse 1979: 139).

The nature of the initial Hohokam occupation in the Tucson Basin has inspired several models, based mainly on the striking similarities between the material culture of the area and that of the Salt-Gila Basin. Decorated ceramics from the two basins, dating to the Snaketown and Sweetwater phases, have been called "indistinguishable" (Kelly 1978: 20). This, as well as closely related traditions in lithic artifacts, worked shell, and bone, has inspired models calling for the colonization of the Tucson Basin and Papaguería by groups from the Salt-Gila Basin (Haury 1976; Masse 1979; 1980b: 208; Stacy and Hayden 1975). Others have associated the spread of red-on-buff ceramics, formal palettes, and distinctive Hohokam lithic forms to the project area with the adoption of Hohokam cultural traditions by the indigenous Cochise culture population of the Tucson Basin (Greenleaf 1975a; McCarthy and Sires 1981: 150; Wilcox 1979a).

One line of evidence supporting the latter interpretation is the similarity between the decorated ceramics of the two basins. Although surface attributes and raw material types have long been assumed to have cultural significance (Di Peso 1956; Gladwin and others 1937; Kelly 1978), some data suggest that raw materials, not cultural norms, are often the principal determinants for surface finish in ceramics. Specifically, the buff color of ceramics from the Salt-Gila Basin results not from cultural selection, but rather from the formation of a buff-colored "false slip" of scum and salts on vessel surfaces during firing. The presence of salts in either clays or water sources localized in the Salt-Gila Basin may be the sole determinant of the distinctive buff-colored finish of that area's prehistoric ceramics (Rosenthal and others 1978: 117). The differences between the buff ware of the Salt-Gila Basin and the brown ware of the San Pedro, Verde, and Santa Cruz valleys may reflect the use of different raw materials, not ethnic or cultural differences (Doyel 1977a: 105; Greenleaf 1975a: 58). Geographic variation in raw materials has also been associated with variation in the ceramics of the prehistoric Sells phase (Rosenthal 1978: 91) and the Historic Papago (Fontana and others 1962: 135).

If this is correct, then the fact that the earliest Hohokam ceramics from the study area are buff wares suggests that they were not locally made, at least not by using local clay sources. Given the ready availability of clay sources in the project area, the importation of raw materials in the necessary volume from as far afield as the Salt-Gila Basin seems improbable. The emergence of an unnamed Tucson Basin plain ware in the Snaketown phase (Kelly 1978: 73), distinct from Vahki or Gila Plain, indicates that the manufacture of plain ware in the Tucson Basin may predate the local manufacture of decorated ceramics by as much as 200 years. If the population of the Tucson Basin in the Pioneer period did indeed import decorated ceramics while producing local plain wares, their identification as "colonists" from the Salt-Gila Basin becomes rather tenuous. A more probable interpretation is that the population of the Tucson Basin was participating in the Hohokam interaction sphere by producing plain ware for their own use while relying on the potters of the Salt-Gila Basin for decorated ceramics.

## Local Origins of the Tucson Basin Hohokam

Two bodies of evidence lend credibility to models calling for local origins of much of the Hohokam culture: the overall similarity of the material culture and subsistence practices of the early Hohokam and early Mogollon; and, in contrast, the general dissimilarity between Pioneer period and contemporary Mesoamerican traditions. Areas of dissimilarity between Hohokam and Mesoamerican traditions include domestic architecture (Haury 1976: 351; Kelley 1966: 104), the absence of canals and cremations in northern Mesoamerica (Kelley 1966: 99-102; Pailes 1978), the lack of palettes among any Mesoamerican culture (Gladwin and others 1937: 125; Kelley 1966: 103) and the absence of figurines, present in the earliest Hohokam periods, in northwestern Mesoamerica until the Huatabampo culture (A.D. 1000 to 1250) (Haury 1976: 267; Johnson 1966: 37).

Although the concept of ceramic production may have diffused out of Mesoamerica, no contemporary ceramic tradition in northwest Mexico comparable to Pioneer period Hohokam has yet been identified, nor are there any intermediate Hohokam sites in northern Mexico. The ceramic horizon in northwestern Mesoamerica occurs long after the earliest Hohokam ceramics (Pailes 1978: 48). Assumptions for a strong Mesoamerican-Hohokam connection are belied by the Trincheras and Rio San Miguel cultures of Sonora which, from their beginnings, are more integrated with Southwestern traditions than with Mesoamerican cultures (Bowen 1972; Johnson 1966: 34; Kelley 1980: 65). Of several Mesoamerican imports in the Pioneer period detailed in one major migration model (Haury 1976: 347), only irrigation agriculture, censers, figurines, shaped metates, and shell mosaics have not been found in the material culture of the San Pedro Cochise. A number of Hohokam traditions are, as previously cited, to be found in late Archaic assemblages, including: domestic cultigens, pit house architecture, plain brown wares, palettes, cremation burials, and traditions in the working of turquoise, shell, bone and mica. As noted elsewhere (Haury 1976: 352), a standard set of archaeological criteria for the validation of prehistoric migrations (Rouse 1958: 64ff) cannot be satisfied by current models of Hohokam migration out of Mesoamerica.

In contrast to the general dissimilarity between early Hohokam material culture and that of Mesoamerica, is the relatively close association between the early Hohokam and the contemporary Mogollon. This includes close similarities in vessel morphology and repertoire (Gladwin 1942: 12; Wheat 1955: 199), as well as in decorative techniques. Early Mogollon ceramics and contemporary Hohokam wares also exhibit similarities in finish, paste, polish, and decorative styles (Kelly 1978).

Although the Hohokam have been seen as the source for Mogollon ceramic traditions (Haury 1976: 193), early Hohokam ceramics have also been termed "technically inferior to their counterparts from the Mogollon", implying that Hohokam ceramic traditions may not predate those of the Mogollon (Gladwin 1948: 620; Wheat 1955: 199). The basic similarity in lithics, ceramics, and architecture between the Pioneer period and early Mogollon suggests that…"both Hohokam and Mogollon grew out of a late Cochise horizon by the addition of pottery to a continuing lithic complex" (Wheat 1955: 231).

The general picture that emerges for the Pioneer Hohokam is one of a small, apparently sedentary, population with a primary reliance on agriculture for subsistence, dwelling in non-nucleated *rancheria* settlements along major watercourses (Doyel 1977a: 20; Wilcox, McGuire and Sternberg 1981: 11). The small size of most Pioneer period sites may have encouraged the relatively rapid spread of Hohokam traditions due to a need for village exogamy. The movement of individuals in a marriage system has been proposed as a primary mechanism behind the diffusion of material culture traditions throughout southern Arizona, resulting in a fairly homogenous village culture in the Pioneer period, encompassing the Salt-Gila Basin, the lower San Pedro Valley, the Papaguería, and the Santa Cruz Valley, including the Tucson Basin (Wilcox 1979b: 101).

External contacts in the Tucson Basin during the Pioneer period were primarily limited to the Salt-Gila Basin (Kelly 1978: 18), but the presence of worked marine shell from Snaketown phase loci at the Hodges Site (Kelly 1978: 114) points to the existence of some type of shell procurement system, involving either trips by individuals or down-the-line trade, from the Tucson Basin to the Gulf of California. The limited number of sites in Sonora with Pioneer period ceramics indicates that such contacts by the

Hohokam were infrequent (Bowen 1972: 162), implying that local populations may have played a part in supplying the Hohokam with marine shell.

# The Colonial Period
# (A.D. 500 to 900)

## The Cañada del Oro Phase
## (A.D. 500 to 700)

### Recorded Sites

The subsequent Cañada del Oro phase of the early Colonial period is marked by the initiation of a number of trends in site distribution and subsistence practices that continued until the early Classic. One such trend was a significant increase in the frequency of sites over preceding periods. A total of 15 sites with early Colonial ceramics, either Gila Butte Red-on-buff or Cañada del Oro Red-on-brown, have been recorded in the project area, an increase of 50 percent over the preceding period (Table 4.2A). In the surrounding area, the number of sites increases from 17 to 25; similar rises in site frequency have been noted for the early Colonial period in the Papaguería (Masse 1980a: 166), the San Pedro Valley (Masse 1980b), and the Salt-Gila Basin (Wilcox, McGuire and Sternberg 1981: 200).

There were also changes in the topographic distribution of sites in the early Colonial period (Figure 4.3). In the project area, the incidence of sites on the upper terraces of the Santa Cruz River and in bajada and mountain areas increases. In contrast, the number of sites in the floodplains of major streams is stable. The percentage of sites in the ecotone along the margins of the major floodplains also increases (Table 4.2B). Sites are somewhat uniformly distributed along the Santa Cruz River north of Martinez Hill, but only one early Colonial site has been recorded south of that point. No sites dating to either the early Colonial period or the previous Snaketown phase have been recorded in Avra Valley.

The incidence of sites in bajada and mountain areas in the project area rises from 10 percent in the Pioneer period to 23 percent in the Cañada del Oro phase (Table 4.2B). This may be the prelude to an emphasis on dry farming practices evident in later Hohokam periods (Crown 1982; Doyel 1977b: Masse 1979). One sherd and lithic scatter with Cañada del Oro phase ceramics, AZ AA:16:1, has been recorded at the summit of Cat Mountain in the Tucson Mountains; it offers the first instance for exploitation by the Tucson Basin Hohokam of an area totally unsuited for agriculture.

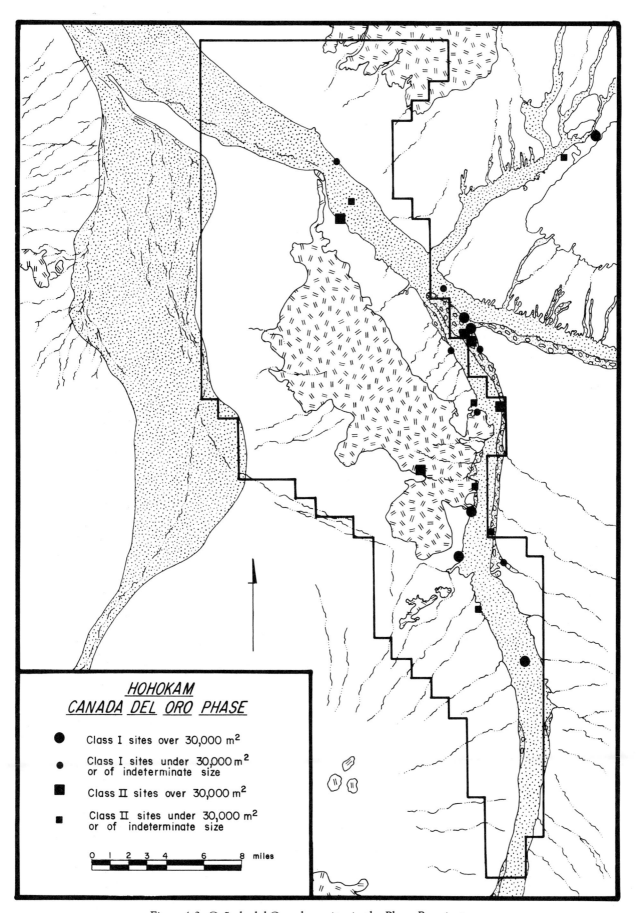

*Figure 4.3.* Cañada del Oro phase sites in the Phase B project area

The continued clustering of sites around riverine enviroments, together with limited excavation data from Cañada del Oro phase loci at the Hodges Site, support the view that agriculture remained a principal means of subsistence during the period. The excavation of four wall-less house floors attributed to the Cañada del Oro phase, as well as a transitional Cañada del Oro-Rillito phase structure at AZ AA:12:18, offers the only evidence for sedentism in the area during the period.

## Models

The most significant development in the material culture of the Tucson Basin during the Cañada del Oro phase is the divergence of locally made decorated ceramics from traditions of the Salt-Gila Basin. During the early Colonial period the first locally made decorated ceramic ware, Cañada del Oro Red-on-brown, emerges in numbers comparable to Gila Butte Red-on-buff from the Salt-Gila Basin. Of the 25 early Colonial sites recorded in the general area, 10 contain Cañada del Oro Red-on-brown as the sole decorated type; 10 have assemblages with only Gila Butte Red-on-buff; and 5 sites have both types. Though many of the differences between the two types may relate to the use of different raw materials, the polish, surface finish, slip, and paste of Cañada del Oro Red-on-brown indicate that the ceramics of the Tucson Basin were, from their beginning, influenced by ceramic traditions of the Mogollon and San Simon areas to the east (Greenleaf 1975a: 45; Kelly 1978: 22). The continued close correspondence in the material culture of the Tucson and Salt-Gila Basins, however, suggests the existence of a well-integrated Hohokam system encompassing both areas.

Models calling for colonization of the Tucson Basin by groups out of the Salt-Gila Basin are similar to those for the Pioneer period. Given the marked increases in site frequencies during the Colonial period in the Salt-Gila Basin as well as in such outlying areas as the Tucson Basin, it is difficult to deduce a populaton in the core area large enough to account for the growth evident in the Papaguería, the Santa Cruz Valley, the Roosevelt Basin, the Verde Valley, the Agua Fria Valley and the lower Gila Valley (Masse 1979: 178; Wilcox, McGuire and Sternberg 1981: 200; Wilcox and Sternberg 1981: 32). A more likely assumption is that local populations, not migrant Salt-Gila Hohokam, are responsible for the increases in site frequencies in these disparate areas. The development of local red-on-brown ceramics in the Tucson Basin and the persistence of unnamed Tucson Basin plain wares suggest that much of the growth in the Cañada del Oro phase was a result of local demographic developments.

While evidence for strictly nonsubsistence behavior for the early Colonial period in the Tucson Basin is limited, excavation data from the Hodges Site point to the

existence of some sort of ritualism in mortuary practices. This is inferred from standardized cremation burials during both the Snaketown and Cañada del Oro phases at that site, with all known burials located in a special crematory area (Kelly 1978: 125). Similar practices have been noted at the contemporary site of Snaketown in the Salt-Gila Basin (Haury 1976: 170). The lack of mixing with earlier burials suggests the use of grave markers or oral traditions which preserved some knowledge of their locations.

## The Rillito Phase (A.D. 700 to 900)

### Recorded Sites

The late Colonial period, termed the Rillito phase in the Tucson Basin and the Santa Cruz phase in the Salt-Gila Basin, is marked by the continuation of a number of trends in site frequency and distribution first noted in the early Colonial period. The most striking of these involves the proliferation of sites: site frequency for the project area increases from 15 to 69, a rise of 460 percent (Table 4.3A). Site frequencies for the general area increase 488 percent, from 25 to 122 (Table 4.3C). Class I sites with either trash mounds or architecture account for 25 of the 69 sites recorded in the project area. Eleven Class I sites are of such extent (30,000 square meters or more) that they were classified as "large village sites." It is admittedly impossible, without extensive excavation, to establish the extent of individual occupations at large multicomponent Class I sites, but the relative abundance of Rillito Red-on-brown at many large sites indicates extensive occupation during the period. Excavated sites in the project area containing architecture and dating to the Rillito phase, include AZ AA:12:18, AZ AA:16:26, AZ AA:12:57, and AZ BB:9:14 (Arizona State Museum site survey files).

Accompanying the increase in site frequency in the late Colonial are changes in the distribution of sites within the project area (Figure 4.4). The percentage of sites in the floodplain more than doubles—from 13 percent of the total in the early Colonial to 44 percent in the late Colonial (Table 4.3B). The increase in absolute terms is even more dramatic, rising from 2 to 30 sites in Zone 1. A significant proportion of Class II sites, 30 percent of the total, are found in bajada and mountain areas. Late Colonial loci include the earliest Hohokam site recorded in Avra Valley (other than AZ AA:16:70), the Werner Site (AZ AA:16:39). Thirty-eight percent of all large Class I sites containing late Colonial ceramics occur in the transitional zone, as do 55 percent of all Class I sites. Yet only 19 percent of all Class II sites are located in this area. This differential distribution of sites in the spatially restricted ecotone supports the model's assumption that transitional areas were preferred locales for habitation by the Hohokam; the low incidence of Class II sites in such areas indicates the ecotone was not as important in determining the location of sites occupied on an impermanent or limited basis.

## TABLE 4.3

**Rillito Phase Site Distributions and Frequencies**

### A. Site Frequency in the Project Area

| Site Type | Floodplain | Transition | Bajada | Mountain | Avra Valley | Total |
|---|---|---|---|---|---|---|
| Class I | 7 | 4 | 3 | 1 | 0 | 15 |
| Large Class I | 2 | 6 | 3 | 0 | 0 | 11 |
| Class II | 21 | 8 | 10 | 3 | 1 | 43 |
| Total | 30 | 18 | 16 | 4 | 1 | 69 |

### B. Site Distribution in the Project Area

| | | | | | | |
|---|---|---|---|---|---|---|
| Class I | 47% | 27% | 20% | 6% | 0 | 100% |
| Large Class I | 18% | 55% | 27% | 0 | 0 | 100% |
| Class II | 49% | 19% | 23% | 7% | 2% | 100% |
| Total Sites | 44% | 26% | 23% | 6% | 1% | 100% |

### C. Site Frequency in the General Area

| | | | | | | |
|---|---|---|---|---|---|---|
| Class I | 10 | 7 | 6 | 2 | 0 | 25 |
| Large Class I | 4 | 9 | 3 | 0 | 0 | 16 |
| Class II | 34 | 14 | 25 | 7 | 1 | 81 |
| Total Sites | 48 | 30 | 34 | 9 | 1 | 122 |

### D. Site Distribution in the General Area

| | | | | | | |
|---|---|---|---|---|---|---|
| Class I | 40% | 28% | 24% | 8% | 0 | 100% |
| Large Class I | 25% | 56% | 19% | 0 | 0 | 100% |
| Class II | 42% | 17% | 31% | 9% | 1% | 100% |
| Total Sites | 39% | 24% | 29% | 7% | 1% | 100% |

Changes in the topographic distribution of sites in the late Colonial are relevant to a debate central to models of Hohokam subsistence. While 73 percent of all Class I sites occur either in or adjacent to the floodplains of major streams, indicating a primary reliance on the resources of riverine areas, the distribution of 30 percent of all Class II sites in nonriverine environments implies that the resources of the bajada and mountains were also of major importance to the subsistence strategy of the Hohokam.

Rock alignments and stone features assumed to have agricultural functions have long been associated with Hohokam habitation sites in the Santa Cruz Valley (Frick 1954: 40; Hayden 1957: 115; Huntington 1914: 60) and elsewhere (Crown 1982). A typology of 10 agricultural features found in the Hohokam culture area has been compiled (Masse 1974). Nine of the ten types are found in association with Hohokam sites or ceramics within the project area or its immediate surroundings. These include:

1. boundary markers at AZ AA:16:6;
2. agricultural terraces at AZ AA:12:15, AZ AA:12:18, AZ AA:12:36, AZ AA:12:57, AZ AA:16:6, AZ AA:16:40, AZ BB:9:1, AZ BB:9:110, AZ BB:14:32, (Fritz 1973: 14);
3. a reservoir at AZ BB:10:6 (Masse 1974: 26);
4. water control features at AZ BB:9:97, AZ BB:13:139, and AZ BB:14:121;
5. check dams at AZ AA:12:108 (Rozen: 1979b: 59);
6. canals at AZ AA:12:15, AZ AA:12:57, AZ AA:12:90, AZ AA:12:92, AZ AA:12:118, AZ AA:12:120, AZ AA:12:144, and AZ BB:13:15;
7. a windbreak at AZ BB:14:73; 8. field gardens at AZ AA:12:15; AZ EE:1:17, and AZ EE:1:20; and 9 anomalous rock piles, thought to be related to dry farming, recorded at another 41 sites in the general area.

## Models

The frequency and diversity of agricultural features, often in association with Rillito and Rincon phase sites, has inspired models calling for an emphasis on dry farming by the Hohokam beginning in the Rillito phase (Doyel 1977b; Masse 1979: 174). The term "dry farming" has been used to denote a variety of agricultural practices. With true dry farming, crops are watered only by direct precipitation (Nabhan 1979: 246), and a minimum of 12 inches of precipitation per year is required. At present, annual precipitation in both the Tucson Basin and the Papaguería averages about 11 inches (Burkham 1970: 34). Environmental manipulation, however, can produce localized conditions conducive to agriculture. In southern Arizona, the clearing and piling of rocks, usually on bajada slopes, has been used to increase surface runoff, which is then channeled to areas where sufficient moisture accumulates, allowing the successful growing of crops. Such manipulative strategies have often been termed dry farming in order to distinguish them from floodwater and irrigation agriculture. Though somewhat inaccurate, the term dry farming will be used to refer to such systems. Cultigens associated with prehistoric dry farming systems in southern Arizona primarily consist of such drought-resistant forms as Onaveño maize and tepary beans (Masse 1978a: 174).

Some models have seen this emphasis on dry farming as a response to climatic conditions (Masse 1980b: 178), but paleoenvironmental data in the Southwest for the period A.D. 700 to 1200 are contradictory (Euler and others 1979: 1097; Masse 1979; Weaver 1972: 44). Other models have interpreted the increased emphasis placed by the Hohokam on dry farming as the response of a rapidly growing

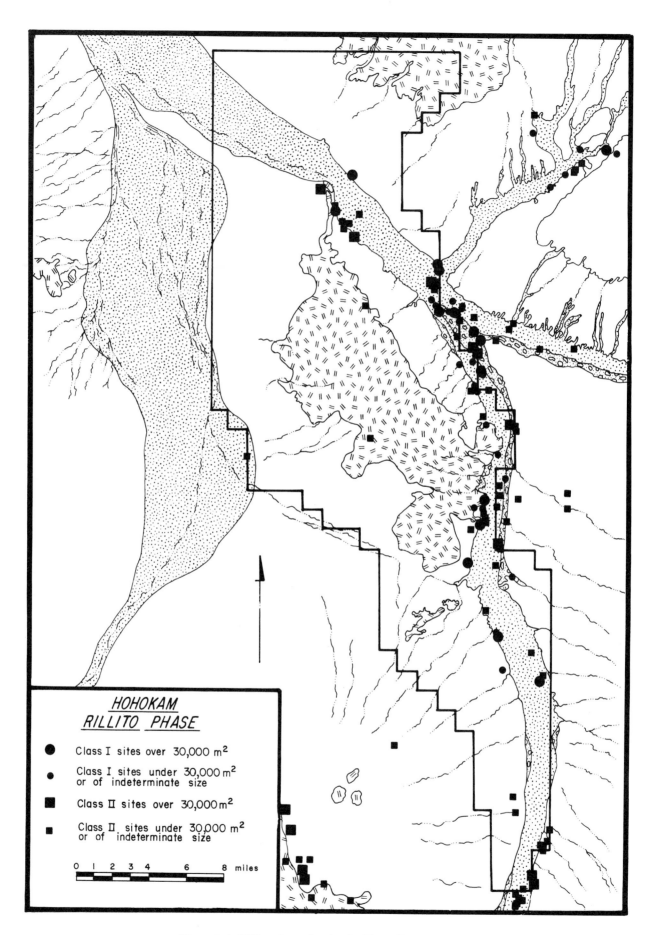

*Figure 4.4.* Rillito phase sites in the Phase B project area

population seeking to exploit all areas open to the practice of agriculture (Woosley 1980: 317).

A more plausible model associates the proliferation of dry farming systems with the spread of drought-resistant cultigens (primarily Onaveño maize and tepary beans) from Mesoamerica to the Southwest at about A.D. 700 (Masse 1980a; Miksicek 1979). For much of the Hohokam occupation, dry farming appears to be an integral part of the agricultural adaptation; to see dry farming as resulting from the failure of irrigation or floodwater agriculture is to denigrate its role as a major subsistence strategy of the Hohokam (Crown 1982).

This view of Hohokam agricultural development contrasts with models stressing a primary emphasis on irrigation agriculture by the Hohokam of the Tucson Basin (Grebinger 1971a, 1976; Grebinger and Adam 1978). Although some have assumed the impracticability of extensive irrigation in the flood plain of the Santa Cruz River (Doyel 1977b; McCarthy and Sires 1981: 15), historic and archaeological data contradict this. During the Historic period, irrigation systems operated in both the floodplains of the Santa Cruz (Betancourt 1978b: 89, Winter 1973: 73) and its upper terraces (Di Peso 1956: 42; Doyel 1977b: 4; Frick 1954: 32; Hastings and Turner 1965: 139). Several irrigation systems of modest size have also been found in prehistoric contexts in the Tucson Basin. Prehistoric canals and ditches have been recorded in the floodplain of the Santa Cruz at AZ AA:12:15, AZ AA:12:90, and AZ AA:12:92 (Fritz 1973: 15) and AZ BB:13:15 (Betancourt 1978b: 91) as well as in terrace areas at AZ AA:12:15, AZ AA:12:57, AZ AA:12:120, and AZ AA:12:144. Prehistoric irrigation systems in the Santa Cruz Valley have undoubtedly suffered severe impact from erosion and alluviation, urbanization, agricultural activities, land leveling, and gravel pit operations (Betancourt 1978a, 1978b; Rozen 1979a, 1979b). Of approximately 315 miles of prehistoric canals mapped in the Phoenix area from 1922 to 1929, only 5 miles had survived similar impact by 1965 (Midvale 1968). Given the smaller size of the irrigation systems of the Tucson Basin, the scattered portions of such systems presently known suggest that prehistoric irrigation agriculture in the area may have been quite extensive.

In summary, there is evidence for a diversity of prehistoric agricultural systems in the Tucson Basin. Floral data from the Hodges Site indicate that agriculture, probably in the form of floodwater farming, dates to the beginning of the Hohokam occupation (Kelly 1978). The association of extensive dry farming features with Rillito and Rincon phase habitation sites, points to the operation of dry farming systems as early as the late Colonial period. Irrigation canals and ditches associated with several large sites occupied in the Rillito, Rincon, Tanque Verde, and Tucson phases suggest the practice of irrigation agriculture may date from as early as the late Colonial, continuing until the end of the Classic period (Kelly 1978: 127).

Another development in the settlement pattern of the Rillito phase involves the distribution of sites in areas previously unrepresented in the archaeological record. During the late Colonial, sites increase south of Martinez Hill, primarily in distinct clusters. One group includes 12 Class II sites in, or near, the floodplain of the Santa Cruz near the present town of Continental. Many of these sites are associated with dry farming features (Frick 1954), and probably contain subsurface architecture. A second cluster of sites is located in the bajada northeast of the Sierrita Mountains, where eight sherd and lithic scatters have been recorded, one of which covers some 45,000 square meters. These loci, associated with exploitation of nonriverine resources, probably wild plants and animals or lithic sources, contain decorated ceramics from the Rillito and Rincon phases.

Some models have attempted to explain the increase in site frequency apparent in the Tucson Basin during the Colonial period as due to the movement of populations out of the Salt-Gila Valley (Masse 1979: 178). The proliferation of sites with exclusively local Tucson Basin ceramics, however, indicates that most of the growth during the Rillito phase should be associated with local demographic processes. Though the occurrence of Santa Cruz Red-on-buff at 31 sites in the area is a measure of the intensity of contacts between the Tucson and Salt-Gila basins, the presence of another 91 sites in the project area and its surroundings that have Rillito Red-on-brown as the only decorated type suggests that most of the system growth of the early Colonial was fueled by local populations, not immigration from outside the Basin.

The proliferation of sites in areas south of Martinez Hill may have resulted from two differing demographic processes: (1) the sites were established by Hohokam groups from the northern Tucson Basin through range-budding, the gradual occupation of empty niches (Grebinger 1971a), or (2) the sites were occupied by indigenous non-Hohokam populations who had adopted the material culture and subsistence practices of the Hohokam in the Tucson Basin. The striking similarity of ceramics from the newly occupied sites with those from the Hodges Site (Frick 1954: 53) points to a close relationship between the population of the southern Tucson Basin sites and existing Hohokam groups. Dissimilarities in the domestic architecture of sites south of Martinez Hill with the rest of the Tucson Basin implies, however, that much of the population of the newly occupied sites consisted of local groups outside of the Hohokam interaction sphere until the late Colonial (Greenleaf 1975a: 27). Most likely, a combination of both of these demographic processes is represented by the proliferation of Hohokam sites south of Martinez Hill.

It is with the Rillito phase that features often interpreted as representing integrative mechanisms—specifically, low, roughly parallel embankments of earth termed "ballcourts"—appear in the basin. Similarities between these features and Mesoamerican structures used in playing the historic game of *pok-ta-pok* have been considered superficial (Ferdon 1967), but the term has remained in vogue since its first use in the 1930s. Ballcourts are found in every region occupied by the Hohokam, other than the Papaguería (Masse 1980a; Haury and others 1975), including the Tucson Basin. The only ballcourt yet tested in the area, at AZ AA:12:18, was constructed in the Rillito phase and continued in use into the Sedentary period (Kelly 1978: 5). Other ballcourts have been recorded in the Tucson Basin at AZ AA:12:57, AZ AA:16:25, AZ BB:9:1, AZ BB:13:7, AZ BB:13:15, and recently at AZ BB:13:52 (Arizona State Museum site survey files). These are probably the remnants of a large number of ballcourts extant prior to the urban sprawl of Tucson: in 1914 one observer noted ballcourt-like features at many large village sites in the Tucson Basin (Huntington 1914: 47). Recent work outside the basin, however, suggests that many ballcourt features may have been reservoirs (Teague 1982: 4).

The role of ballcourts in the Hohokam system remains problematic, but their firm association with large villages, often in central locales, has led to their identification with redistributive systems, an association yet to be borne out by excavation data. Whatever the function of these semimonumental earthen structures, their existence and long-term use at sites in the Tucson Basin points to some sort of intersite system, perhaps related to regional socioeconomic integration. Another example of integrative behavioral systems during the Rillito phase in the project area is the continued use of special crematory areas at the Hodges and Punta de Agua sites (Greenleaf 1975a: 102; Kelly 1978: 125).

The Rillito phase in the project area was marked by an expanding population exploiting all available environments, especially those along major streams. The phase was also one with a growing emphasis on dry farming. Areas previously unoccupied by the Hohokam, such as the Santa Cruz Valley south of Martinez Hill, the bajada of the Sierrita Mountains, the Avra Valley (with the exception of the early Pioneer period site AZ AA:16:70), and the pediment of the Santa Catalina Mountains northwest of the project area were first exploited during the late Colonial. Probable integrative mechanisms, "ballcourts," appear, suggesting that the growth in site frequency was accompanied by an increase in social integration as well. Contact with areas outside the Tucson Basin was primarily with the Salt-Gila Basin; 21 percent of all late Colonial sites contain decorated ceramics from the Salt-Gila Basin. Isolated sherds of Trincheras Purple-on-red, Galiuro Red-on-brown, and Mogollon Red-on-brown have been noted at several sites in the Tucson Basin, indicating interregional contacts may have also been established with the Altar Valley of Sonora, the San Simon Valley, and the Mogollon culture area.

# The Sedentary Period (A.D. 900 to 1200)

## Recorded Sites

The Sedentary period, primarily the Rincon phase in the Tucson Basin and the Sacaton phase in the Salt-Gila Basin, is often viewed as the height of the Hohokam occupation. More sites are attributed to this period than any other in the Tucson Basin (Betancourt 1978b: 45; Wilcox 1979a, b), as well as in Avra Valley (Wilson 1980: 18, 100), and the Papaguería (Masse 1980a: 209). The Sedentary period has been considered the time of maximum integration of the Hohokam system (Doyel 1977a: 144, 147; Doyel 1980: 29; Haury 1976: 88), as well as a time when interregional contacts were at their greatest extent (Bowen 1972: 158; Doyel 1977a: 154, 159).

Data from the project area support the first of these assertions: 112 sites containing Sedentary period ceramics, primarily Rincon Red or Rincon Red-on-brown, have been recorded in the project area (Table 4.4A). Another 84 Rincon phase sites have been recorded in the immediate vicinity (Table 4.4C). No other prehistoric period is as well represented in the archaeological record of the project area. Site frequency for the project area increases 61 percent from Rillito phase levels; for the general area it increases 62 percent. Excavated sites with architecture in the Tucson Basin dating to the Rincon phase include: AZ AA:12:18; AZ AA:12:57; AZ BB:13:14; AZ BB:13:48; AZ BB:13:50; AZ BB:13:51; AZ BB:13:52; and possibly AZ BB:10:3.

The first dated Class III sites in the area are attributed to the Rincon phase. These are several isolated cremation burials at AZ BB:13:90 in the floodplains of the Santa Cruz, and at AZ BB:9:37, a cache of several Rincon Red-on-brown vessels in the Santa Catalina Mountains. Both sites are near village sites with Rincon phase components and offer additional evidence of ceremonial and mortuary traditions. Several other caches and shrines dating to the Sedentary period have been recorded in the Santa Cruz Valley (Bahti 1970; Stacey and Hayden 1975).

Occupational continuity is another hallmark of the Sedentary period: of the 17 large Class I sites occupied in the Rincon phase, 10, or 58 percent, were initially occupied in the Rillito phase; the same number would continue to be occupied in the Tanque Verde phase. This is in sharp contrast to the Salt-Gila Basin where very few sites span the Sedentary-Classic transition (Sires 1982). Stability in most occupations is attested to by the lack of change in existing site clusters along the Santa Cruz River—only one large Class I site dating to the Rillito phase (AZ AA:16:58) does not also contain Rincon phase ceramics. Population expansion during the Sedentary is evidenced by new site clusters along the Santa Cruz at Point of Mountain, Punta de Agua, and Martinez Hill, and by the proliferation of sites in existing site clusters at the confluences of Rillito Creek and the Cañada del Oro, in the Sierrita bajada, and near the town of Continental.

## TABLE 4.4

### Sedentary Period Site Distributions and Frequencies

#### A. Site Frequency in the Project Area

| Site Type | Floodplain | Transition | Bajada | Mountain | Avra Valley | Total |
|---|---|---|---|---|---|---|
| Class I | 12 | 11 | 5 | 1 | 0 | 29 |
| Large Class I | 3 | 7 | 3 | 0 | 0 | 13 |
| Class II | 21 | 16 | 21 | 10 | 1 | 69 |
| Class III | 1 | 0 | 0 | 0 | 0 | 1 |
| Total Sites | 37 | 34 | 29 | 11 | 1 | 112 |

#### B. Site Distribution in the Project Area

| | | | | | | |
|---|---|---|---|---|---|---|
| Class I | 41% | 38% | 17% | 4% | 0% | 100% |
| Large Class I | 23% | 54% | 23% | 0 | 0 | 100% |
| Class II | 30.5% | 23% | 30.5% | 14.5% | 1.5% | 100% |
| Class III | 100% | 0 | 0 | 0 | 0 | 100% |
| Total Sites | 33% | 30% | 26% | 10% | 1% | 100% |

#### C. Site Frequency in the General Area

| | | | | | | |
|---|---|---|---|---|---|---|
| Class I | 16 | 17 | 9 | 1 | 1 | 44 |
| Large Class I | 4 | 10 | 3 | 0 | 0 | 17 |
| Class II | 43 | 20 | 50 | 12 | 8 | 133 |
| Class III | 1 | 0 | 0 | 1 | 0 | 2 |
| Total Sites | 64 | 47 | 62 | 14 | 9 | 196 |

#### D. Site Distribution in the General Area

| | | | | | | |
|---|---|---|---|---|---|---|
| Class I | 36% | 39% | 21% | 2% | 2% | 100% |
| Large Class I | 23% | 59% | 18% | 0 | 0 | 100% |
| Class II | 32% | 15% | 38% | 9% | 6% | 100% |
| Class III | 50% | 0 | 0 | 50% | 0 | 100% |
| Total Sites | 33% | 24% | 32% | 7% | 4% | 100% |

Changes in the topographic distribution of sites are also evident during the Sedentary period (Figure 4.5). In the project area the percentage of sites located in the floodplain declines from 44 percent to 33 percent of the total (Table 4.4B). This is due to minimal growth in the numbers of Class II sites in the floodplain of the Santa Cruz River, in contrast to other zones. This is complemented by an increase in Class II sites in bajada and mountain

environments, which rise from 29 percent of the total in the late Colonial to 36 percent in the Sedentary. This can best be interpreted as evidence of an increasing use of nonriverine resources by the Hohokam, either by dry farming or the exploitation of wild resources.

In contrast, to these changes in the topographic distribution of Class II sites, is the relative stability in the location of Class I sites in the Rillito and Rincon phases. Seventy-three percent of all Class I sites in the earlier period are located in either the floodplain or terrace areas of major streams; 78 percent are located there in the Rincon phase. Forty-three percent of all Class I sites with Rincon phase ceramics are located in the transitional zone, an increase of 5 percent; 21 percent of all Rincon phase sites are found in bajada or mountain environments, a decline of 6 percent from the late Colonial period. Similar changes occur in the distribution of sites in the area surrounding the Phase B corridor (Table 4.4D). The stability in the distribution of Class I sites, however, indicates the riverine areas of Zone 1 remained the primary focus of the Sedentary population.

One development in the distribution of sites in the surrounding area that is not reflected in the site distribution within the project area, is a marked increase in the incidence of sites in Avra Valley. This results primarily from sample bias. Archaeological survey of Avra Valley has been limited and has taken place in the western portion rather than the eastern portion within the Phase B corridor. Thus, only one Rincon phase site has been recorded in that part of Avra Valley within the project area, while nine others are found in the valley outside of the project area, including a single component Rincon phase village (AZ AA:11:2).

The nine sites with Rincon phase ceramics in Avra Valley represent an increase of 800 percent over the site frequency for Avra Valley in the Rillito phase. Most of these sites are small sherd and lithic scatters dated to the late Rincon phase, a period of transition from the Sedentary to the Classic (Wilson 1981: 100). Most have been associated with seasonal agriculture similar to the *ak chin* farming of Historic Papago groups (Wilson 1980, 1981). Given sufficient moisture, *ak chin* or *de temporal* agriculture, the diverting of temporary surface flows from bajada canyon mouths to fields located as far as 5 miles away, has been shown to be as productive on an acre by acre basis as irrigation agriculture (Masse 1981: 203), allowing for the sedentary occupation of areas seemingly inhospitable to agricultural groups. The proliferation of sites in Avra Valley was probably the product of "range budding" (Grebinger 1971a: 182) as groups "normally resident outside of the area" (Wilson 1980: 100) entered the valley at the end of the Sedentary period.

The frequency of Class II sites relative to that of Class I sites reaches a peak in the Sedentary—61 percent of all sites dated to the Rincon phase are Class II sites, compared to 53

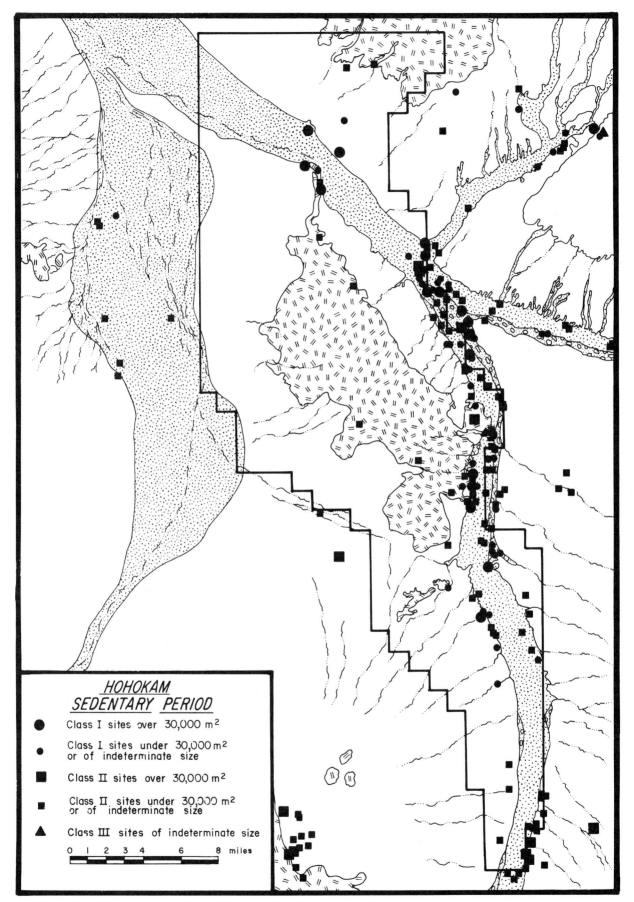

*Figure 4.5.* Sedentary period sites in the Phase B project area

HOHOKAM
SEDENTARY PERIOD

● Class I sites over 30,000 m²

• Class I sites under 30,000 m²
or of indeterminate size

■ Class II sites over 30,000 m²

▪ Class II sites under 30,000 m²
or of indeterminate size

▲ Class III sites of indeterminate size

0 1 2 3 4 6 8 miles

percent in the early Classic. Though this is no doubt due in part to the greater visibility of Classic period adobe-walled architecture relative to the wattle and daub structures of the Preclassic (McGuire and Schiffer 1982), it may also reflect an intensified exploitation of seasonal resources in the Sedentary period. The proliferation of sites in areas far removed from riverine zones has led to models calling for more moist environmental conditions during the Sedentary period (Masse 1980a: 205). The period from A.D. 950 to 1150, roughly corresponding to the Rincon phase (Haury 1976; Huckell 1980) has been termed "the time of greatest effective moisture in the last 2000 years on the Colorado Plateau" (Euler and others 1979: 1097). Data from the Salt-Gila Basin indicate the period from A.D. 920 to 1110 was considerably wetter than either preceding or subsequent periods (Miksicek 1982), resulting in the spread of desert grassland and desert riparian assemblages at the expense of more xeric vegetation communities. A significant increase in effective moisture would concur with the proliferation of Class I and Class II sites in Avra Valley and other nonriverine areas, where Rincon phase sites outnumber those sites of all other periods (Wilson 1980, 1981).

Evidence for integrative behavior increases during the Rincon phase in the Project area. In addition to the ballcourt features previously described, Class I sites containing Rincon phase ceramics have been firmly associated with defensive *trincheras* at the Tumamoc Hill Site (AZ AA: 16:6). While initial use of these trincheras may date to the Rillito phase (Hartmann and Hartmann 1979: 58), the first definite indications of their construction and use comes in the Sedentary period. Though it is the only defensive system in the Tucson Basin to be dated to before the Classic period, the existence of such a system, even as an isolated occurrence, poses great significance in the interpretation of Hohokam social organization. The construction and use of defensive features can best be taken as indications of intense resource competition on an intersite, or even interregional, level (Wilcox 1979a). Assumptions associating sociopolitical complexity with such features are, however, open to doubt, due to the use of even more massive *cerros de trincheras* by Historic Piman and Seri groups in Sonora and Arizona, groups that, as most ethnographic and archaeological data indicate, possessed minimal political organization (Bowen 1972: 172, 187; Di Peso 1953: 181; Doyel 1977a: 237).

## Models

One problem area in the archaeology of the Sedentary period in southern Arizona involves the late Rincon or Cortaro phase. Often neglected in archaeological syntheses of the area (Kelly 1978; Stacy and Hayden 1975), this period is marked by developments in the material culture that are often attributed to the subsequent Classic period.

These include: (1) the construction of multidwelling walled compounds; (2) inhumation burials found in association with Rincon phase occupations at the Punta de Agua sites (Greenleaf 1975), AZ BB:13:14 (Doyel 1979: 19), and AZ BB:13:4 (Hemmings 1969); (3) experimentation in polychrome ceramics (Rincon Polychrome); (4) production of a local red ware (Rincon Red); and, (5) the introduction of geometric motifs in ceramic decoration, a divergence from the traditional curvilinear motifs of the Hohokam (Greenleaf 1975a; Kelly 1978: 66; Zaslow and Dittert 1977: 197).

This gradual introduction of new traditions in architecture, ceramics and mortuary practices suggests that models calling for indigenous development behind the changes of the Classic (Doyel 1977a; Wasley and Doyel 1980) are more valid than those associating changes in material culture with population migration (Haury 1945; Hayden 1957). The late Rincon phase also seems to be the time when exploitation of nonriverine environments and the use of dry farming systems reached a peak (Masse 1979: 141, 162; Wilson 1980, 1981). External contacts in the Sedentary period resemble those of the late Colonial, as the number of sites with imported buff wares from the Salt-Gila Basin reaches an all time high with 40 sites, 20 percent of the total in the project area, containing Sacaton Red-on-buff, the principal decorated ware of the period in the Salt-Gila Basin. Other trade wares associated with Rincon phase sites include Encinas Red-on-brown from the San Simon Valley, San Francisco Red and Mogollon Red-on-brown from the Mogollon area, and Trincheras Purple-on-red and Nogales Polychrome from Sonora. These, however, are not commonly found in the Tucson Basin.

Settlement data point to the Sedentary as a period of stability with most sites occupied since the Rillito phase, and a comparable number continuing to be occupied into the early Classic. This contrasts with the general discontinuity in occupation of village sites during the Sedentary-Classic transition in much of southern Arizona, including the Papaguería (Masse 1980a), the San Pedro Valley (Masse 1980b), and the Salt-Gila Basin (Sires 1982). Site frequencies reached a height during the Rincon phase as 52 percent of all Hohokam sites in the area contain Rincon phase components. Over 55 percent of these are sites without surface habitation features, although subsurface architecture may be present at many of them. Many are in nonriverine environments and probably relate to the practice of two independent subsistence strategies by the Hohokam—dry farming and the gathering of wild plant foods. A number of prehistoric canals in the Basin are associated with large habitation sites with Rincon ceramics, suggesting the use of irrigation agriculture during the Sedentary period.

The stability in settlement and subsistence practices of the Hohokam from the Colonial to Sedentary periods is matched by continuity in the association of ballcourts with large village sites of both periods, implying continued use of these features. Continuity in mortuary practices, including avoidance of burials predating the Sedentary period, is, as earlier, apparent at a number of sites (Greenleaf 1975a: 101; Kelly 1978). Continuity in interregional contacts is evident, although such contacts were limited, except those with the Salt-Gila Basin. Trade with that area seems to reach a peak when 25 percent of all Sedentary period sites in the Tucson Basin contain Sacaton Red-on-buff.

The occupation of Avra Valley, an area termed "totally unsuited for agriculture" (Wilson 1980), can best be attributed to one or more possible causes.

1. Drought-resistant cultigens may have been introduced, enabling the practice of agriculture in areas formerly closed to it.
2. A temporary climatic change may have resulted in moister conditions in the area. The effects of increased moisture in Avra Valley would probably have been an expansion of desert grasslands and desert riparian communities at the expense of more xeric vegetation, primarily the creosote-bur sage community. This would result in more abundant potential food sources in Avra Valley, especially in the floodplain of Brawley Wash, as well as the temporary formation of water sources, such as *charcos* and springs, where none existed previously.
3. Some type of stress may have encouraged the settlement of formerly marginal areas by the Rincon phase population. Since the Rincon phase in the Tucson Basin has the highest site frequency of any prehistoric period, population stress may have been a factor in the occupation of Avra Valley.
4. Technological developments, such as the perfection of *ak chin* farming or tapping groundwater with wells, may have followed expansion of sedentary agriculturalists into areas previously closed to permanent occupation. *Ak chin* agriculture, typified by traditional Papago practices, has been associated with the spread of Sells phase sites in the Papaguería (Masse 1980a). Prehistoric wells have been recorded at two Hohokam villages in the Tucson Basin (AZ AA:12:57 and AA:16:80) as well as in Hohokam sites outside of the Tucson Basin (Crown 1982).

Several models have associated increased exploitation of nonriverine areas by the Hohokam in the Preclassic with the introduction of drought-resistant maize (Gasser 1976; Rosenthal and others 1978). The use of drought-resistant cultigens dates at least back to the early Colonial period (Miksicek 1979); hardy maize hybrids such as Harinoso de Ocho and Mais Blando first appear in the archaeological record of the Tucson Basin at about A.D. 700, the beginning of the Rillito phase. It seems improbable, therefore, that the introduction of drought-resistant cultigens was the primary factor in the occupation of the Avra Valley in the

Sedentary. Only one late Colonial period site has been recorded in the Avra Valley, despite the presence of Onaveño maize and tepary beans since the beginning of the period (Masse 1979). The principal occupation of the valley, in the late Sedentary, occurred some 400 years afterwards.

The second hypothesis, invoking environmental causation for the proliferation of sites during the Rincon phase in marginal areas, receives more support from both ethnohistoric and paleoenvironmental data. Major changes in the vegetation communities of Avra Valley have been documented during the Historic period. Much of the floodplain during the eighteenth century was apparently desert grassland, primarily Sacaton grass (*Sporobolus airioides*), with dense desert riparian growths along major washes, especially the braided channels of Brawley Wash (Wilson 1981). Thus, Avra Valley contained large amounts of a major food source of the Historic Papago (Masse 1980a: 338).

These conditions permitted the occupation of the valley, probably on a seasonal basis, by four small villages of Papago Indians prior to 1774 (Dobyns 1963: 177). The creosote-bur sage community that characterizes the valley at present apparently did not achieve dominance until after the widespread environmental changes of the late nineteenth century (Urban 1981: 10; Wilson 1980: 9). Models attempting paleoenvironmental reconstructions for southern Arizona have called for a period of increased moisture for much of the Sedentary (Masse 1979; Weaver 1972: 46). This is corroborated by dendrochronological data from the Colorado Plateau (Euler and others 1979: 1094). Such conditions probably would have resulted in less xeric plant communities similar to those of the seventeenth century.

The third possible factor leading to the occupation of Avra Valley during the Rincon phase, that of population stress, cannot be disregarded. Given the large numbers of Sedentary period sites throughout the Santa Cruz Valley and Papaguería (Betancourt 1978b; 102; Frick 1954: 39; Masse 1980b), and the intense inhabitation of most environmental niches along major streams, the opening of new areas of arable land due to an increase in effective moisture could well have encouraged the exploitation of such areas, especially with an increasing population in the Tucson Basin.

Equally probable is the perfection of agricultural techniques that allowed expansion by the Hohokam into marginal areas such as Avra Valley. The close association of alluvial fans with most Sedentary period sites in the valley suggests that most, if not all, of these sites were dependent on *ak chin* farming (Wilson 1981: 3). Coupled with an increase in effective moisture resulting in more readily available groundwater, development of this highly productive agricultural strategy may well have been the principal factor in the settlement of the Avra Valley, with or without the added impetus of population pressure. Whatever the cause, the expansion of sites into an area such as the Avra Valley indicates a flexible, broad-based adaptation by the Hohokam during the period, an adaptation marked by an extensive exploitation of wild resources and a diverse repertoire of dry farming techniques.

# The Classic Period
# (A.D. 1200 to 1400-1450)

The Classic period, unlike earlier Hohokam temporal units, has no one-to-one correlation between named decorated types and phases. This is due to the persistence of the principal decorated ware, Tanque Verde Red-on-brown, in both the Tanque Verde phase of the early Classic and the Tucson phase of the late Classic. In order to isolate early Classic assemblages from later components without excavation or chronometric dating, archaeologists have usually relied on the presence (or absence) of intrusive ceramics. This has most often resulted in all ceramic assemblages without late Classic imports such as Gila, Tonto, or Tucson Polychromes being dated to the early Classic. One line of reasoning used to support this has been the association of late polychromes with a migration of ethnic Saladoans into the Hohokam area (Haury 1945; Hayden 1957). More recent work has, however, associated the changes of the Classic period with the internal evolution of the Hohokam (Doyel 1977a; Wasley and Doyel 1980; Wilcox and Sternberg 1981). These archaeologists view the distribution of Saladoan polychromes as indicative of the spread of a pan-Southwest system of exchange, a system marked by the distribution of polychrome ceramics.

With this interpretation, the absence of late polychromes at a site with Tanque Verde Red-on-brown does not rule out its occupation in the late Classic, since the population of that site may not have participated in the polychrome system. This has rendered temporal identification of sites on the basis of ceramic assemblages suspect. In the Salt-Gila Basin, several large sites with few, if any, Saladoan polychromes have been dated to the late Classic (Hammack 1969; Wilcox and Shenk 1977).

The persistence of Tanque Verde Red-on-brown to the close of the Classic predicates use of the following temporal classifications: all sites without late Classic polychromes in their ceramic assemblages will be termed Classic period sites. Sites will be interpreted as definitely late Classic only if Saladoan polychromes are a part of their ceramic assemblages. Though sites without late Classic polychromes cannot be regarded as occupied only in the early Classic, it is probable that several large village sites without Saladoan polychromes were abandoned after the early Classic. According to Rich Lange of the Arizona State Museum, sites such as the Hodges Site (AZ AA:12:18), the Whiptail Site (AZ BB:10:3), the Hardy Site (AZ BB:9:14), and Los Morteros (AZ AA:12:57) have Tanque Verde phase occupations as their principal components (see also Kelly 1978: 10). These early Classic components contain numbers of nonlocal ceramics, including Casa Grande Red-on-buff, Pinto Polychrome, San Carlos Red, Sells Red, and Gila Red. Given the apparently high state of integration of these large village sites into regional exchange systems in earlier periods, the absence of late trade wares such as Gila Polychrome or San Carlos Red-on-brown indicates that their role may have changed after the early Classic due, most likely, to their decline in regional systems or abandonment. The establishment of large villages with typical late Classic material culture at AZ BB:9:33, adjacent to the Hardy Site; at AZ AA:12:90(?), adjacent to the Hodges Site; and at AZ AA:12:73, close to Los Morteros, contemporary with the apparent decline of the earlier villages, can be also interpreted as further evidence of population decline or disruption in the Classic.

## Recorded Sites

Although almost every site with Saladoan ceramics also contains Tanque Verde Red-on-brown (Betancourt 1978b: 40), the majority of sites with Tanque Verde Red-on-brown lack late polychromes: 152 of the 194 Classic period sites in the area (79 percent) contain Tanque Verde Red-on-brown without Saladoan polychromes, other than Pinto Polychrome. This type, restricted to the Globe-Miami region after A.D. 1250 (Breternitz 1966: 88), is probably limited to the early Classic in the Tucson Basin. Thirty-one Classic period ceramic assemblages contain Tanque Verde Red-on-brown with Saladoan polychromes; assemblages from six sites contain only polychromes; and four have Sells Red as the only non-plain ware.

Sites with only Tanque Verde Red-on-brown will be termed Classic, with the inference being that many were occupied only in the early Classic; all sites with late polychromes will be treated as late Classic in date, with the implication that other sites may have been occupied during the period as well. The frequency of Classic sites declines from that of the Sedentary: in the project area the number of sites drops from 112 to 99 (Table 4.5A); in the area as a whole, the number falls from 196 to 152, a decline of 22 percent (Table 4.5C). This decline is limited to Class II sites. The number of Class I sites in the project area rises from 42 with Rincon phase ceramics to 45 with Classic period pottery; the number of Class I sites over 30,000 square meters in area climbs from 13 in the Sedentary to 18 in the Classic, an increase of 38 percent. Class II sites decline from the Sedentary to the Classic, falling from 69 with Rincon phase ceramics in the project area, to 53 with Tanque Verde Red-on-brown, a decline of over 23 percent. The number of sites in bajada or mountain areas declines from 40 to 36, a reduction of 10 percent. A single Class III site (AZ BB:13:90) has been dated to the Tanque Verde phase. Consisting of several isolated cremation burials, this site, located in the floodplain of the Santa Cruz, contains vessels of both Rincon Red-on-brown and Tanque Verde Red-on-brown. Its use in both the Sedentary and Classic suggests continuity in mortuary traditions between the two periods.

### TABLE 4.5

**Classic Period Site Distributions and Frequencies.**

#### A. Site Frequency in the Project Area

| Site Type | Floodplain | Transition | Bajada | Mountain | Avra Valley | Total |
|---|---|---|---|---|---|---|
| Class I | 10 | 11 | 5 | 1 | 0 | 27 |
| Large Class I | 7 | 7 | 4 | 0 | 0 | 18 |
| Class II | 15 | 12 | 16 | 10 | 2 | 53 |
| Class III | 1 | 0 | 0 | 0 | 0 | 1 |
| Total Sites | 33 | 30 | 25 | 11 | 2 | 99 |

#### B. Site Distribution in the Project Area

| | | | | | | |
|---|---|---|---|---|---|---|
| Class I | 37% | 41% | 18% | 4% | 0 | 100% |
| Large Class I | 39% | 39% | 22% | 0 | 0 | 100% |
| Class II | 28% | 23% | 26% | 19% | 4% | 100% |
| Class III | 100% | 0 | 0 | 0 | 0 | 100% |
| Total Sites | 34% | 30% | 23% | 11% | 2% | 100% |

#### C. Site Frequency in the General Area

| | | | | | | |
|---|---|---|---|---|---|---|
| Class I | 14 | 18 | 11 | 2 | 1 | 46 |
| Large Class I | 8 | 9 | 4 | 0 | 0 | 21 |
| Class II | 24 | 16 | 27 | 12 | 5 | 84 |
| Class III | 1 | 0 | 0 | 0 | 0 | 1 |
| Total Sites | 47 | 43 | 42 | 14 | 6 | 152 |

#### D. Site Distribution in the General Area

| | | | | | | |
|---|---|---|---|---|---|---|
| Class I | 31% | 39% | 24% | 4% | 2% | 100% |
| Large Class I | 38% | 43% | 19% | 0 | 0 | 100% |
| Class II | 29% | 19% | 32% | 14% | 6% | 100% |
| Class III | 100% | 0 | 0 | 0 | 0 | 100% |
| Total Sites | 31% | 28% | 28% | 9% | 4% | 100% |

Changes in site frequency and distribution during the Classic have inspired models proposing a decrease in the importance of agriculture and a concomitant emphasis placed on the hunting and gathering of wild food sources (Gasser 1980: 75; Grebinger and Adam 1978: 242; Wilcox and Sternberg 1981: 13). The actual distribution of sites in

the project area tends, however, to contradict this. The decrease in Class II sites in all areas, especially nonriverine environments, indicates less emphasis on the resources of these areas than in the Rincon or Rillito phases. An increase in the importance of wild resources should be associated with an increase in the incidence of Class II sites, especially in areas with dense wild floral resources, such as the bajada. But in fact, the incidence of sites in bajada areas declines rather than increases (Table 4.5B). The number of Class II sites in all nonriverine environments for the surrounding area drops from 90 to 60, hardly an indication of more intense use of those areas.

The bajada of the Sierrita Mountains, extensively exploited in the Rillito and Rincon phases, contains fewer sites with Classic period ceramics; as the number of sites drops from 14 with Rincon phase ceramics to two with Tanque Verde Red-on-brown. This reduction suggests a lessening in the importance of nonriverine areas, hardly an indication of the intensification of the gathering of wild foodstuffs. Excavation and survey data from much of southern Arizona suggest that reliance on agriculture was increasing in the Classic, not declining (Gish 1979: 165; Haury 1976; Masse 1980a: 88; Withers 1973: 71).

The location of Class I sites with Classic period ceramics may indicate some systemic stress—such as population pressure—was beginning to affect the Hohokam. Most of these sites are situated in bajada areas adjacent to the floodplain; this has been associated with a need to allocate the maximum amount of arable land, a critical resource, for agriculture (Greenleaf 1975a: 15). The proximity of a number of Classic village sites to defensive *trincheras* at Tumamoc Hill, Black Mountain, and Martinez Hill (Fontana and others 1959) may also be a further indication of some type of stress, perhaps brought on by competition for scarce resources, most likely arable land and available water. Excavation data from a Tanque Verde phase site in the project area points to infant pathologies resulting from an exclusive reliance on agriculture in the Classic period (Doyel 1979: 25).

The distribution and frequency of large habitation sites with Classic period ceramics suggests the period was a time of population nucleation, as more sites of larger size were founded in several discrete clusters along the Santa Cruz River (Figure 4.6). The proliferation of sites in clusters near Point of Mountain, Martinez Hill, and what is now the area of the San Xavier del Bac Mission, suggests that the Hohokam continued to expand into new environmental niches open to agriculture. The decline in the number and density of sites at the confluences of Rillito Creek and the Cañada del Oro may indicate that the area's resources could no longer support the large sedentary populations that it had since the Rillito phase. Since the Hohokam adaptation, from its inception, appears to have been centered on agriculture, one interpretation is that the area's primary resources of arable land and available water were

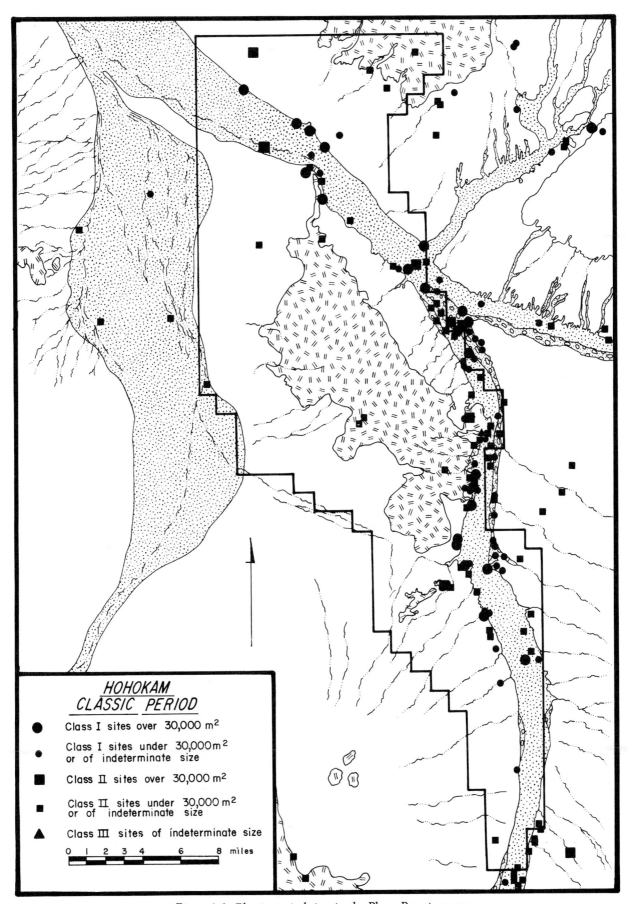

### HOHOKAM
### CLASSIC PERIOD

●   Class I sites over 30,000 m²

•  Class I sites under 30,000 m²
    or of indeterminate size

■   Class II sites over 30,000 m²

▪  Class II sites under 30,000 m²
    or of indeterminate size

▲   Class III sites of indeterminate size

0  1 2 3 4   6    8 miles

*Figure 4.6.* Classic period sites in the Phase B project area

[ 49 ]

declining in availability or productivity. This has been attributed to both environmental changes (Grebinger 1971a; Grebinger and Adam 1978: 128) and to maladaptive agricultural practices (Betancourt 1978a: 90).

## The Tanque Verde Phase
## (A.D. 1200 to 1300)

### Recorded Sites

The early Classic is marked by sweeping changes, not only in the Tucson Basin, but throughout the entire Southwest. Many of the changes of the early Classic were elaborations of trends first evident in the late Sedentary. These include: (1) continued divergence in the decorative motifs of decorated wares, both Tanque Verde Red-on-brown and Casa Grande Red-on-buff, from more traditional Hohokam designs (Zaslow and Dittert 1977); (2) an increase in the incidence of intentional smudging of vessel surfaces; (3) the proliferation of red wares—Sells Red in the project area and Gila and Salt Red in the Salt-Gila Basin; (4) the spread of multistructure domestic compounds; (5) a continued shift to inhumation as a common mortuary practice; and (6) an apparent realignment in interregional exchange systems. These changes should not, however, obscure the basic continuity between the Sedentary period, especially the late Sedentary Cortaro phase and the Tanque Verde phase. This includes stylistic continuities between Rincon Red-on-brown, late Rincon (Cortaro) Red-on-brown, and Tanque Verde Red-on-brown (Kelly 1978; Greenleaf 1975a). A majority of sites in the project area with Tanque Verde Red-on-brown also contain ceramics of the Sedentary period, pointing to occupational continuity between the two periods. Of the 45 Class I sites in the project area with Tanque Verde phase components, 30, or 67 percent, have Rincon phase components as well.

One significant development in the archaeology of the Tucson Basin in the Classic is a virtual absence of ceramics imported from the Salt-Gila Basin. In the Sedentary, 40 sites in the project area and its environs contain Sacaton Red-on-buff; only 2 sites include Casa Grande Red-on-buff in their ceramic assemblages. Gila Red and Salt Red, the most common decorated pottery types of the Gila Basin during the Classic, also are rarely encountered in Tucson Basin sites.

Contemporary with this decrease in ceramic imports from the Hohokam core area is a significant increase in the number of intrusive ceramics from other areas. Sites in the project area with trade wares dating to the Classic period include nine with San Carlos Red-on-brown and San Carlos Red from the Upper Gila area; eight with Pinto Polychrome from the Globe-Miami region; two with Tularosa Black-on-white and St. John's Polychrome from the White Mountain area; and one with Mimbres Black-on-white from southwestern New Mexico. Sells Red, a Classic type originating in the Papaguería, is also found at 40 sites in or near the project area. Its common occurrence in the Tucson Basin indicates close contact between the basin and the Papaguería. Sells Red has been associated with the migration of groups out of Sonora (Masse 1980a), an association recently challenged (McGuire and Schiffer 1982).

The proliferation of sites with intrusive ceramics from areas other than the Salt-Gila Basin, contemporary with a decline of 95 percent in the number of sites with ceramics from that area, suggest a significant realignment in the systems of regional exchange operative in the Tucson Basin in the early Classic. An expansion of the Tucson Basin sphere is also indicated by the spread of Tanque Verde Red-on-brown across the Papaguería, where the type may have originated (Masse 1980a: 281; Rosenthal and others 1978: 109), to the Gila Bend area, and eastward into the San Pedro Valley (Franklin 1978; Masse 1980a: 281; Rosenthal and others 1978: 109). Tanque Verde Red-on-brown is also more frequently encountered in the Salt-Gila Basin than Casa Grande Red-on-buff is in the Tucson Basin (Bradley 1980: 22), though its relative occurrence varies greatly from site to site.

### Models

These changes in the geographic distribution of Tucson Basin red-on-brown ceramics, contemporary with the retraction of Salt-Gila ceramic imports throughout southern Arizona, have been associated in several models with a collapse of the Hohokam regional system (Doyel 1977a; Masse 1980b; Wilcox 1979a). In the Papaguería, material culture assemblages with strong Hohokam affinities are replaced by Sells phase assemblages associated with non-Hohokam groups (Masse 1980a). Hohokam assemblages also disappear in the Gila Bend area, to be replaced by traditions similar to those of the lower Colorado Valley (Teague and Baldwin 1978). In the Agua Fria and Verde valleys, Hohokam systems are replaced by Sinaguan assemblages and in the Globe-Miami area and the lower San Pedro Valley by local Saladoan traditions (Masse 1980b). Groups from peripheral areas have been seen as retreating into the Salt-Gila core area, introducing new traditions in ceramics, architecture, and mortuary practices (Doyel 1977a; Masse 1980b: 221).

Models of the changes associated with the Sedentary-Classic transition invoke a number of causes: ethnic migrations (Haury 1945; Hayden 1970; Schroeder 1966); environmental deterioration, involving principally a drop in effective moisture (Masse 1980a: 310; Weaver 1972); or changes in interregional contacts. The latter often involves usurpation of a pan-Southwest shell distribution system formerly centered on the Salt-Gila

Basin, either by the Trincheras culture of Sonora (Bowen 1972: 164) or by the rise of Casas Grandes in Chihuahua (Di Peso 1974; McGuire 1980).

The role of migration in the changes of the early Classic has come under increasing criticism (Doyel 1977a; Wasley 1966; Wasley and Doyel 1980); more compelling data support other interpretations of the Sedentary-Classic transition. The decline of extensive Hohokam occupations along the principal trade routes (from the Salt-Gila Basin to the Gulf of California) in the Gila Bend area and the Papaguería, contemporary with the expansion of the Trincheras and Casas Grandes cultures, suggests that changes in regional economic relationships may have been a factor. Further study is necessary, however, before a clear understanding of marine shell procurement and distribution systems of the prehistoric Southwest emerges.

A more complete body of data supports the interpretation that the changes associated with the Sedentary-Classic transition may have been, in part at least, environmentally determined. If, as is often asserted, the rainfall regime for the Sonoran desert is analogous to that of the Colorado Plateau (Bryan 1941: 231; Euler and others 1979: 1097; Humphreys 1958: 39; Weaver 1972: 44), then the period from A.D. 1225 to 1300 was one of extreme aridity. Following the relatively moister period from A.D. 950 to 1150, this could have presented the Hohokam with significant environmental changes, changes that may have rendered many areas first occupied in the late Colonial and Sedentary periods less fit for the practice of agriculture.

The proliferation of defensive systems during the Classic in southern Arizona and northern Sonora supports the idea that the period was one of population stress. Some trinchera-like features in the Tucson Mountains have been associated with agriculture (Wallace in press; Downum and others 1980), but many rock walls, trincheras, and corrales in southern Arizona and northern Sonora are defensive systems, apparently occupied on an impermanent basis, most likely during times of conflict. Historic Pima groups have been recorded as using trincheras as refuges in times of war, during both internecine strife with other Pima and conflict with other groups, often Apache or Seri (Bowen 1972). One source, however, has challenged the use of trincheras by the Historic Pima (Johnson 1966: 28).

While the precise causes of conflict leading to the construction and long term use of defensive cerros de trincheras remain unknown, their occurrence in the Sedentary and Classic periods, when site frequencies reach an all time high across southern Arizona, may indicate that the burgeoning populations of these periods had exceeded the carrying capacity provided by their technological adaptation to the area, leading to competition for resources (Wilcox 1979b). If paleoenvironmental reconstructions calling for more arid conditions in the early Classic are correct, available resources, particularly the critical resources of arable land and water, were becoming more scarce. These resource shortages could have led to further intersite competition.

The location of major defensive trincheras at Tumamoc Hill, Martinez Hill, and Black Mountain, areas with readily available surface water in the seventeenth century (Betancourt 1978b: 46-49), may indicate such critical resources were a primary point of contention among that Classic period population.

Another model (Masse 1980a: 235) has linked the proliferation of defensive trincheras with ethnic migrations. This view associates the spread of Sells Red throughout the Papaguería and Santa Cruz Valley with a population originating in what is now Sonora, replacing or driving out Hohokam groups who retreated into the Salt-Gila Basin core area (Masse 1980a). This assumes a genetic relationship between Sells Red and cerros de trincheras; the existence of defensive trincheras at Tumamoc Hill in the Rillito and Rincon phases renders the validity of such an association suspect. At present, the processes behind the contemporary spread of Sells Red and trincheras systems during the Classic remain problematic.

The Classic period also produced marked change in the material culture of the Hohokam. Old ceramic traditions give way to new styles, some of which exhibit similarity with Mogollon traditions (Kelly 1978: 59; Greenleaf 1975a: 52, 109). Contemporary changes in mortuary practices suggest that the Hohokam were further influenced by non-local traditions from the northeast (Masse 1980b; Doyel 1972). The proliferation of red wares, however, though often attributed to external influences (Masse 1980a; Schroeder 1966), seems, instead, to be a local development in both the Salt-Gila and Tucson Basins (Doyel 1977a: 130; Greenleaf 1975a; Schroeder 1952: 323).

Settlement and subsistence data for the Classic period indicate that agriculture remained the principal means of subsistence, although fewer sites of the period are associated with dry farming features. Paleoenviromental data point to the Classic, particularly the early Classic, as a time of more xeric conditions in much of the Southwest. More arid conditions may have reduced the availability of resources critical to agricultural sedentism in many areas. Such conditions may have led to population stress and competition for resources, resulting in the proliferation of defensive systems in the Santa Cruz Valley, the lower Gila Valley, the Papaguería, and northern Mexico.

Changes in ceramics, mortuary practices, and interregional contacts in the Tucson Basin during the Classic indicate that the period was one of disruption and fragmentation of the Hohokam system as old traditions and patterns of exchange were abandoned or modified. The integrative and ideological systems of earlier periods also appear to be disrupted in the early Classic. This is manifested by a virtual cessation in the production of ceremonial palettes, censers, and figurines (Gladwin and others 1937: 125; Haury 1976), a decline in the production of red-on-buff ceramics (Doyel 1977a), and a decline in the incidence of cremation burials (Haury 1945: 205; Hayden 1957). The late Classic is also marked by the decline or abandonment of the majority of sites with ballcourts (Wilcox, McGuire and Sternberg 1981: 210). This growing acceptance of external traditions has been interpreted as "either a symptom or cause of the Hohokam...decline" (Wasley and Doyel 1980: 344).

Also evident is a change in the nature of contacts between the Salt-Gila Basin and other areas including the Tucson Basin. The Agua Fria and Verde valleys withdraw from the Hohokam sphere in the Classic, and are instead marked by local and Sinaguan traditions. Hohokam traditions also disappear in the Globe-Miami area and the San Pedro Valley, to be replaced by Saladoan expressions. Judging by the geographic distribution of ceramics, the lower Gila Valley and the Papaguería may have been reoriented towards the Tucson Basin, with a virtual cessation in contacts with the Salt-Gila Basin. What has yet to be determined is whether these shifts stem from environmental change, are migrations of Sells phase Hohokam, Sinaguan, or Salado groups, or whether a socioeconomic realignment resulted in the collapse of the traditional Hohokam system and the rise of peripheral systems in areas like the Tucson Basin (Wilcox 1979b), San Pedro Valley (Franklin and Masse 1976), and Roosevelt Basin (Doyel 1972).

## The Tucson Phase
## (A.D. 1300 to 1400–1450)

### Recorded Sites

The distribution and frequency of sites in the project area with Saladoan polychromes differs sharply from that of previous periods. The most striking change in the late Classic is a great reduction in site frequency. Ninety-nine sites have been recorded in the project area as containing only Tanque Verde Red-on-brown; only 29 contain late Classic polychromes (Table 4.6A). If most of the sites with only Tanque Verde Red-on-brown date to the early Classic, as may well be, then the late Classic is marked by a 70 percent decline in site frequency. The number of Class II sites (9) with Salado polychromes represents a decline of 83 percent from the number of Class II sites with exclusively Tanque Verde Red-on-brown ceramics (53). The decline in the number of large villages is much less precipitous; 18 Class I sites contain only Tanque Verde Red-on-brown ceramics, while seven have late Classic polychromes, a decline of 61 percent.

The distribution of definite late Classic period sites in the general project area differs from that of other Classic period sites (Figure 4.7). The incidence of Class II sites in bajada and montane environments increases from 46 percent in the Classic to 56 percent in the late Classic (Table 4.6B). No Tucson phase sites have been recorded in Avra Valley.

TABLE 4.6

**Tucson Phase Site Distributions and Frequencies.**

A. Site Frequency in the Project Area

| Phase | Floodplain | Transition | Bajada | Mountain | Avra Valley | Total |
|---|---|---|---|---|---|---|
| Class I | 4 | 5 | 3 | 1 | 0 | 13 |
| Large Class I | 3 | 4 | 0 | 0 | 0 | 7 |
| Class II | 1 | 2 | 3 | 3 | 0 | 9 |
| Total Sites | 8 | 11 | 6 | 4 | 0 | 29 |

B. Site Distribution in the Project Area

| | | | | | | |
|---|---|---|---|---|---|---|
| Class I | 31% | 38% | 23% | 8% | 0 | 100% |
| Large Class I | 43% | 57% | 0 | 0 | 0 | 100% |
| Class II | 11% | 22% | 33% | 33% | 0 | 100% |
| Total Sites | 27% | 38% | 21% | 14% | 0 | 100% |

C. Site Frequency in the General Area

| | | | | | | |
|---|---|---|---|---|---|---|
| Class I | 6 | 5 | 4 | 1 | 0 | 16 |
| Large Class I | 4 | 6 | 0 | 0 | 0 | 10 |
| Class II | 4 | 3 | 6 | 3 | 0 | 16 |
| Total Sites | 14 | 14 | 10 | 4 | 0 | 42 |

D. Site Distribution in the General Area

| | | | | | | |
|---|---|---|---|---|---|---|
| Class I | 38% | 31% | 25% | 6% | 0 | 100% |
| Large Class I | 40% | 60% | 0 | 0 | 0 | 100% |
| Class II | 25% | 19% | 37% | 19% | 0 | 100% |
| Total | 33% | 33% | 24% | 10% | 0 | 100% |

Late Classic sites are also absent in the Sierrita Mountains bajada. The seven sites south of Martinez Hill with Saladoan ceramics represent only one-quarter of the 28 sites in the area that have Tanque Verde Red-on-brown as the only decorated type.

### Models

Changes in site frequency and distribution can be interpreted two ways: if sites with late polychromes represent the majority of sites occupied in the late Classic then a precipitous drop in site frequency from the early Classic did occur. The drastic decline of Class II sites relative to that of Class I sites can be interpreted as an indication that the gathering and processing of wild resources was de-emphasized during the late Classic,

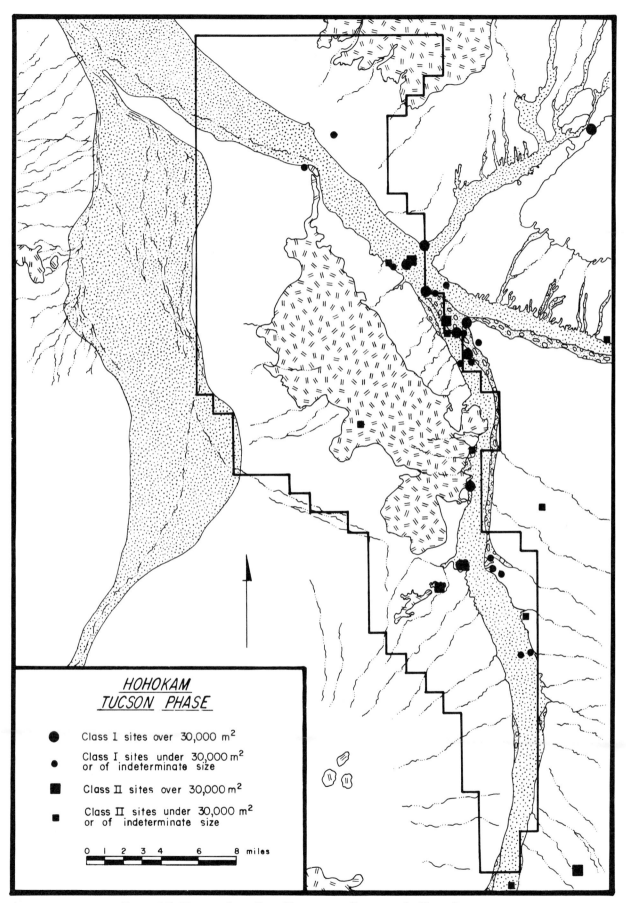

*Figure 4.7.* Tucson phase (late Classic period) sites in the Phase B project area

**HOHOKAM TUCSON PHASE**

● Class I sites over 30,000 m²

• Class I sites under 30,000 m²
or of indeterminate size

■ Class II sites over 30,000 m²

▪ Class II sites under 30,000 m²
or of indeterminate size

0 1 2 3 4 6 8 miles

possibly accompanied by a decline in the number of small farmsteads. The more gradual decline in the numbers of large villages has often been seen as a sign of population nucleation and aggregation in the late Classic (Grebinger 1971a; Stacy and Hayden 1975).

A differing interpretation allows for the occupation into the late Classic of those sites with only Tanque Verde Red-on-brown. Thus, the absence of late Classic polychromes at sites would be due to their lack of participation in the pan-Southwest Salado system. The predominance of large Class I sites with Salado ceramics relative to Class II sites would be due to the differing roles of the two site types in the polychrome system. Large village sites such as Martinez Hill or the Zanardelli Site would be much more likely to be well-integrated into the interregional exchange system represented by the distribution of exotic polychromes than would small Class II sites. These large sites, participating in a larger interaction sphere, would have preferential access to goods from other areas. Small sites occupied on an impermanent basis, integrated into a much more restricted interaction sphere, would have ceramic assemblages limited to purely local wares. This could account for the differential distribution of intrusive types like Gila Polychrome in large village sites.

Both of these models are open to criticism. The latter, viewing the presence of Saladoan polychromes at a site as due to its interaction in an interregional Saladoan system, can be faulted on three counts. (1) The ceramic assemblages of eight small Class II sites in the project area contain Saladoan polychromes, indicating that even limited activity sites were integrated into the Salado system. (2) Gila and Tucson polychromes are not necessarily intrusive at sites in the Tucson Basin. Local production of both wares has been proposed at Martinez Hill (Greenleaf 1975a: 75) and University Indian Ruin (Hayden 1957: 120; Doyel 1972: 23). If this is correct, then Salado polychromes could have entered the local redistributive system of the Tucson Basin as readily as Tanque Verde Red-on-brown, so that polychromes could occur as frequently in small Class II sites as in large village sites. (3) The apparent abandonment after the Tanque Verde phase of large village sites such as Romero Ruin, the Hodges and Hardy sites, and Los Morteros, sites that had been occupied since the Pioneer or early Colonial periods, suggests some sort of population disruption occurred in the Tucson Basin during the Classic. If many of the small Class II sites in the vicinity of the larger village sites were related to the occupation of those centers, as was the case in the lower San Pedro Valley (Masse 1980b), then the occupation of smaller sites may also have ceased with the abandonment of the larger sites. This would imply that occupation of many of the sites with only Tanque Verde Red-on-brown may have ceased after the early Classic. Thus the apparent decline in site frequency from the early

to late Classic is valid, and reflects actual demographic processes.

If this is correct, the decline in site frequency in the Tucson phase is not merely a function of an arbitrary archaeological criterion, the presence of polychromes, but reflects a real decline in site frequency for the period. The absence of sites yielding only Tanque Verde Red-on-brown, in association with non-Saladoan late Classic trade wares such as Jeddito Black-on-yellow, casts doubt on the existence of a significant late Classic population in the Tucson Basin producing only red-on-brown decorated wares outside of the polychrome system.

The alternative interpretation, that all sites occupied during the late Classic in the Tucson Basin did participate in the Salado system and thus will have late polychromes in their ceramic assemblages, can be faulted on the basis of examples from outside of the project area. Several large sites excavated in the Salt-Gila Basin have yielded little or no polychrome ceramics although they were occupied during the late Classic. These include Casa Grande and Las Colinas, where extensive late Classic occupations have been found with very few Salado polychromes (Schreiber and others 1981; Wilcox and Shenk 1977; Wilcox and Sternberg 1981). Both these sites were in close proximity to a number of roughly contemporary sites with abundant polychromes. The dearth of Saladoan ceramics at such sites is the best available evidence for the continued existence of a purely Hohokam system during the late Classic, a system apparently contemporaneous with, but distinct from, the more widespread Salado interaction sphere. Further data are necessary, however, before such a system can be postulated for the Tucson Basin.

Another change in the late Classic involves the proliferation of walled compounds. Often thought to be associated with a kin-based social organization (Doyel 1977a: 183; Di Peso 1956), some compounds appear to be at least partially defensive in function. Construction of massive encircling walls at Martinez Hill and at other sites outside the project area has been assumed to reflect a need for defense (Gabel 1931; Di Peso 1953, 1956, 1958). The continued use of defensive trincheras systems in the period indicates that conflict and resource competition was at least as prevalent in the late Classic as in earlier periods; the apparently violent destruction of Gila Pueblo in the Globe-Miami area (Shiner 1961: 11) offers physical evidence for conflict during the late Classic.

One development often cited as evidence for some type of stress during the late Classic is an increase in facilities associated with storage. Storage rooms have also been noted in Preclassic contexts (Haury 1976) but most are associated with Classic period sites. This apparent increase, however, may result from the greater visibility of Classic period architecture, allowing for firmer functional identification of architectural features (Sires 1982). Usually associated with compounds, the apparent proliferation of functionally distinct storage rooms in the late Classic has often been interpreted as representing a need for the stockpiling of surplus goods, most likely food (Doyel 1977a: 88; Wilcox and Sternberg 1981: 37). Excavation data have revealed a surprising array of goods in storage rooms, mostly domestic cultigens and wild plants (Doyel 1977a; Hayden 1957: 103). If a deteriorating environment, the result of either climatic shifts or the degradation and exhaustion of arable land from improper agricultural techniques, led to a decline in resources during the Classic, a possible response of a population to such stress might well be an increasing emphasis on storage.

Emphasis on the storage of resources has also been associated with intensification of redistributive systems, with surplus goods being apportioned among the population of a site, or even a group of sites. Such a redistributive system would probably require positions of authority and management for the allocation of resources. Such authority has often been proposed as the first step towards social ranking, differential status, and the formation of an elite subpopulation (Doyel 1977a: 182; Wilcox and Sternberg 1981). Although evidence for the existence of managerial elite groups is lacking in the Tucson Basin, data suggesting the presence of such groups are present in the Salt-Gila Basin (Upham and Rice 1980: 79; Wilcox and Sternberg 1981: 37). According to David A. Gregory of the Arizona State Museum, these include standardization in the orientation and dimensions of late Classic compounds and associated platform mounds (see also Haury 1945: 19).

## End of the Classic Period

Despite the late Classic populations' responses to the stresses cited above, the disruptions first evident in the early Classic became progressively greater. No data exist at present for any sedentary population in the Tucson Basin after A.D. 1400 to 1450. Virtually every site cluster in both the Classic and late Classic periods (see Figures 4.7, 4.8, and 4.9) disappears by the opening of the Historic period, which in the Tucson Basin begins with the first recorded entry of Europeans in 1692.

The apparent abandonment of the Tucson Basin was not an isolated occurrence. Other areas of the Southwest appear to have been abandoned by sedentary agriculturalists at about the same time, including the Salt-Gila Basin (Doyel 1977a; Wilcox, McGuire and Sternberg 1981: 183), the San Pedro Valley (Franklin 1978; Franklin and Masse 1976), the Globe-Miami area (Doyel 1972), and the Verde Valley (Fish and others 1980). Only in the Papaguería and upper San Pedro Valley is there a possible Postclassic occupation, although data remain contradictory (Di Peso 1953; Fontana and others 1962: 132; Goodyear 1977; Rosenthal and others 1978: 16).

The processes behind the apparent abandonment of much of the Southwest by sedentary populations during the Classic period remain problematic. In the Tucson Basin one site, Whiptail Ruin, was burned after the majority of homes had been stripped of all artifacts, implying a purposeful exodus (Grebinger and Adam 1978: 233). One site in the Gila Bend area, the Fortified Hill Site, has been associated with a migration of groups out of the Tucson Basin (Greenleaf 1975b: 275); however, Teague and Baldwin (1978) have questioned this interpretation. Data indicate abandonment of many sites was a gradual process, with the population apparently drifting away over a long period of time (Wright and Gerald 1950). Fires built in the ruins of the University Indian Ruin and the Zanardilli Site, the latter within the project area, may indicate the presence of a remnant population occupying those sites on a temporary basis (Hayden 1957: 95; Wright and Gerald 1950: 15). Reduced occupations during the late Classic have been proposed for the Casa Grande Ruin (Wilcox and Shenk 1977) and the Escalante Ruin (Doyel 1977a: 37, 96) in the Salt-Gila Basin.

Evidence for a violent end to the Hohokam occupation, although present elsewhere, it lacking in the Tucson Basin. One central objection to this interpretation is that the outcome of violent intersite conflict would leave the victorious group in possession of the "spoils." The apparent absence of any sedentary group in the area after the late Classic contradicts this view.

Other models of the end of the Classic involve the existence of a managerial elite (Wilcox and Sternberg 1981: 38). Classic period astronomical features have been recorded north of the Tucson Basin at the Zodiac Site (AZ AA:5:27) (Hewitt and Stephen 1981: 64), and at Casa Grande (Wilcox and Sternberg 1981: 25), with alignments apparently keyed to the scheduling of agricultural activities. This suggests that the Hohokam depended on astronomical observations, at least in part, for the scheduling of agricultural tasks, principally spring planting and fall harvesting. Historic Papago are recorded as tying their summer planting to the dawn rise of the Pleides (Underhill 1939: 125). The disruption in mortuary practices (Doyel 1977a: 25, 136) and other integrative systems evident in the Classic may have spread to these astronomical scheduling systems as well, with the elite group associated with such systems finding their preferential socioeconomic positions jeopardized. A similar collapse has been proposed for Classic Mayan elite groups (Culbert 1973). Persistence of a village economy after the abandonment of large ceremonial centers such as Tikal has been interpreted as resulting from a peasant revolt overthrowing the managerial priestly elite. A similar situation, on a much more modest scale, has been proposed for the Hohokam Classic period (Doyel 1977a: 229; Wilcox and Sternberg 1981: 40).

The fate of the late Classic populations remains problematic, with possible explanations offered by several

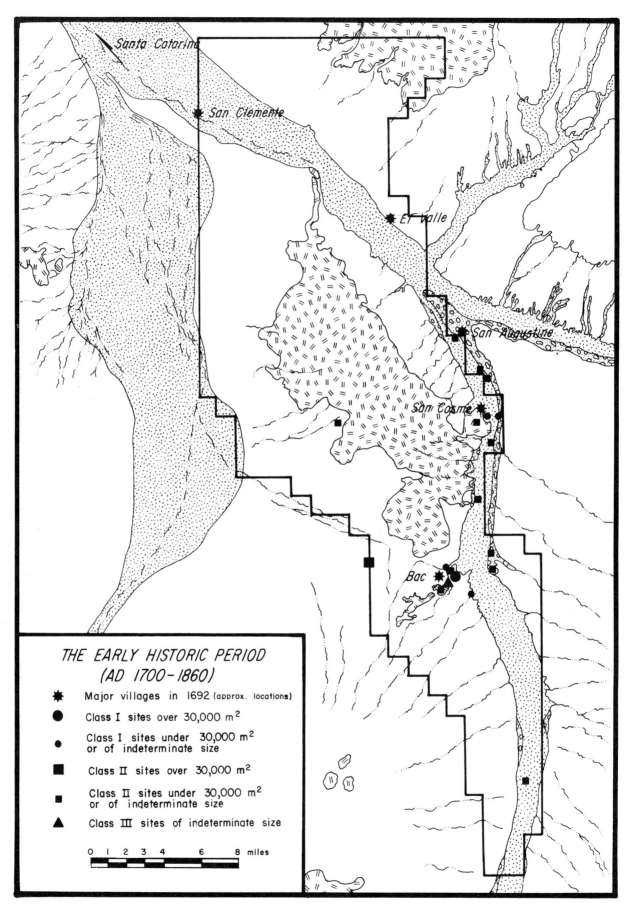

THE EARLY HISTORIC PERIOD
(AD 1700-1860)

⭐ Major villages in 1692 (approx. locations)

● Class I sites over 30,000 m²

• Class I sites under 30,000 m²
  or of indeterminate size

■ Class II sites over 30,000 m²

▪ Class II sites under 30,000 m²
  or of indeterminate size

▲ Class III sites of indeterminate size

0 1 2 3 4   6   8 miles

*Figure 4.8.* Early Historic period sites in the Phase B project area

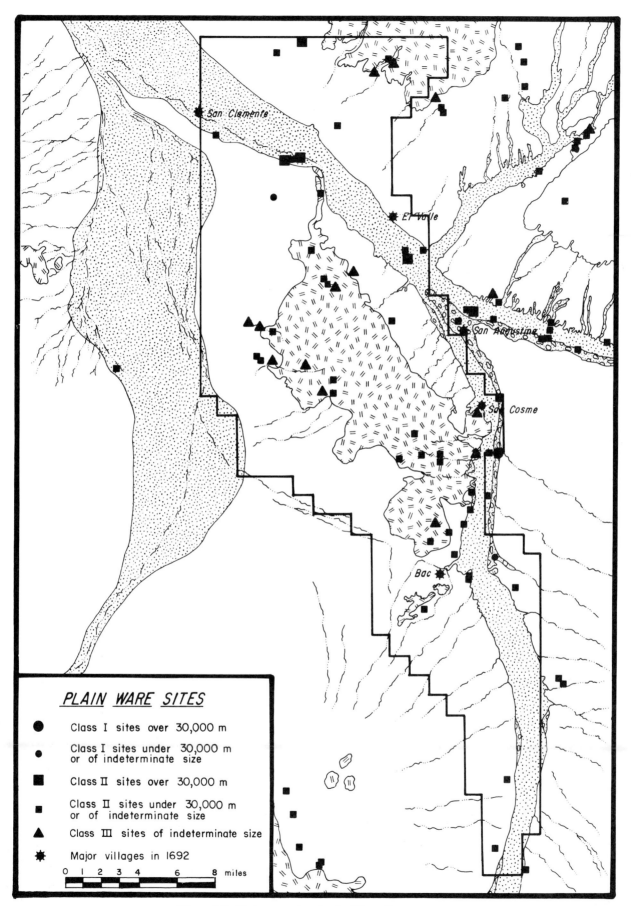

PLAIN WARE SITES

● Class I sites over 30,000 m

• Class I sites under 30,000 m or of indeterminate size

■ Class II sites over 30,000 m

▪ Class II sites under 30,000 m or of indeterminate size

▲ Class III sites of indeterminate size

✳ Major villages in 1692

0 1 2 3 4 6 8 miles

*Figure 4.9.* Plain ware sites in the Phase B project area

models. The continued deterioration of the environment, due either to climatic changes or degradation of resources central to agriculture (arable land), may have rendered any type of agriculture impossible, leading to the end of sedentary life as well, as the remnant Postclassic population adopted a seasonally transhumant settlement pattern. The absence of permanent habitation sites associated with this Postclassic occupation has led to assumptions that areas were not abandoned but rather occupied solely by nonsedentary populations. This "reorganization model" has several proponents (Grebinger and Adam 1978: 238; Doyel 1972; 1977a: 196).

A second hypothesis is that with the collapse of the elite in the late Classic the final integrative means left to the Hohokam was the production of decorated ceramics. If this system was also abandoned, as were the ballcourt, platform mound, and polychrome systems, then the material culture of the Postclassic population would consist of nondistinctive plain ware that, along with much of the architecture and lithics from the period, cannot be isolated from previous Hohokam components. In short, the area was not abandoned after the late Classic; the failure to recognize the undistinguished material culture of the Postclassic population has, however, led to an illusion of abandonment. An analogous situation has been proposed for the Postclassic in Sonora (Bowen 1972: 176).

A less likely interpretation associates the abandonment of the late Classic with the spread of epidemic diseases introduced by the Spanish in the sixteenth century. This "epidemic model" can be found in Di Peso (1958), Weaver (1972: 49), and Ezell (1963: 65). Until chronometric data establishing the persistence of the Hohokam into the sixteenth century are forthcoming, the model remains questionable.

A fourth model calls for the assimilation of the Hohokam by Piman groups entering the area from the south. Producing only plain ware, the Piman presence would, like that of the nonelites, escape archaeological detection, leading to an apparent abandonment despite the presence of sedentary agriculturalists (Bowen 1972: 188; Masse 1980a).

A similar hypothesis, termed the "continuum model," involves direct ethnic affiliation of several Historic Piman groups, the Sobaipuri, Pima, and Papago, with the Hohokam (Di Peso 1953, 1956; Haury 1976; Rosenthal and others 1978). The changes after the end of the Classic are seen as due to the decline or reorganization of the Hohokam, and do not involve significant population movements.

The third model has already been dismissed as lacking chronometric or stratigraphic evidence establishing the persistence of the Hohokam into the sixteenth century. The first model, invoking environmental determinism in the cessation of the occupation of the area by sedentary agriculturalists, is not corroborated by available paleoenvironmental data. Dendrochronological data from the Colorado Plateau establish the existence of a lengthy period of increased aridity on the plateau during the early Classic; much of the late Classic, however, appears to be associated with a period of less xeric conditions from A.D. 1400 to 1500 (Euler and others 1979: 1094). Data from the Salt-Gila Basin further indicate that the late Classic was a time of considerably more moist conditions than the present, especially the period from A.D. 1280 to 1340 (Miksicek 1982: 13). Why the Hohokam would abandon sedentary agriculture during a more moist period seems inexplicable. Most paleoenvironmental models for the Sonoran Desert agree that the period from A.D. 1300 to 1450 was not one particularly unfavorable to agricultural pursuits (Robinson 1978: 62; Schoenwetter 1970; Weaver 1972: 46; Wilcox, Sternberg and McGuire 1981: 202); in short, paleoenvironmental data for southern Arizona indicate that the late Classic was a time when agriculture was no more difficult than in previous periods.

For consideration of the other models of the end of the Hohokam occupation of the project area, examination of the early Historic period in the Tucson Basin is in order.

# Post-Hohokam Ceramic Periods

## The Protohistoric Period
### (A.D. 1400 – 1450 to 1690)

The Protohistoric period, lasting from the end of the Tucson phase to the entry of the Spanish into the area, is poorly known. Very few sites from this period have been identified in southern Arizona. A number of sherd and lithic scatters with Protohistoric brown ware have been recorded in the Slate Mountains to the northwest of the project area (Goodyear 1977). Four sites dating to the period have been excavated in southern Arizona: Santa Cruz de Gaybanipitea and Quiburi in the San Pedro Valley (Di Peso 1953), and, in the upper Santa Cruz Valley, the Paloparado Ruin (Di Peso 1956) and the England Ranch Site (Doyel 1977b). Of these, all but the England Ranch Site have European goods, associating them more with the Historic period.

One site, AZ AA:12:131, thought to possibly date to the Protohistoric, has been recorded in the project area. Located in the bajada of the east slope of the Tucson Mountains, this site consists of a small sherd and lithic scatter with Kechipawan Polychrome and Whetstone Plain. The former, a White Mountain Red Ware from the Zuni region (Huckell and Huckell 1981) has been dated from A.D. 1375 to 1475–1500. Whetstone Plain has often been identified with the Protohistoric Sobaipuri; however, its temporal parameters are poorly known (Masse 1981; Wilcox and Masse 1981b). Bruce Huckell of the Arizona State Museum has supplied information that new radiocarbon dates indicate that the site was occupied in the late seventeenth century.

## Phase I of the Historic Period (A.D. 1700 to 1860)

### Recorded Sites

Since the period immediately after the end of the Hohokam Classic is not well represented in the project area, sites with ceramics dating to the early Historic period will be compared to Hohokam sites, since this period precedes the integration of Native American groups into the industrialized Anglo economy. As defined (Fontana and others 1962: 104), this earliest period in the Papago ceramic chronology is marked principally by Papago Plain Ware and Papago Red-on-brown. Only sites with exclusively Papago Plain and Papago Red-on-brown are considered to date exclusively from this period. Sites with the ubiquitous Papago Red are dated to Period 2 of the Historic period since red ware was not produced until after 1870 (Betancourt 1978b: 94); these will not be discussed, though many may contain Period 1 components as well. Pima ceramics are very poorly known prior to 1850 (Fontana and others 1962: 118). Production of ceramics among the Gila Pima may even postdate initial contact by the Spanish (Fontana and others 1962: 5). A poorly known type, perhaps related to Whetstone Plain, termed Pima Plain Ware, has been identified in the Tucson Basin (Arizona State Museum site survey files). Sites whose assemblages include this type will also be considered as early Historic sites. From initial contact in 1692 until 1762, the Piman Sobaipuri occupied the Tucson Basin and are the population associated with Pima Plain. After 1774 the less sedentary Papago occupied the Basin, especially the area around Mission San Xavier del Bac (Dobyns 1963).

All sites with early Papago and Pima ceramics were classified by the same typology used for sites with Hohokam ceramics. Site distribution was plotted in the same manner (Figure 4.8). Comparison of the frequency and distribution of sites dating to the early Historic with those from the Hohokam Classic yields some provocative results. The frequency of early Historic sites in the project area is lower than all Hohokam phases later than the early Colonial: only 17 early Historic sites are recorded in the project area, a decline of 41 percent from late Classic frequencies (Table 4.7A). Only two other sites with early Historic ceramics have been recorded in the general area (Table 4.7C). Thirteen of the sites in the general area lack habitation features, and only one is identified as a large village site.

One Class III site (AZ AA:16:13), dates to the early Historic period. A cemetery with cist inhumation burials, this site contains Papago ceramics dated to before 1850 (Arizona State Museum site survey files). It continued to be used until the mid-twentieth century. The high incidence of Class II sites compared to Class I sites, and the concentration of the former on the alluvial floodplain, would suggest that agriculture was not a principal means of subsistence, although it was practiced in early Historic times. The distribution of habitation sites with early Pima and Papago ceramics supports this inference of subsistence practices—only 25 percent of all village sites are located in the floodplain; 50 percent are located in the adjacent transitional ecotone (Table 4.7B). Eight of the 13 early Historic Class II sites are to be found in nonriverine environments. This can be interpreted as reflecting an adaptation centered less on agriculture than that of the Hohokam, with greater emphasis on the hunting and gathering of wild resources.

---

TABLE 4.7

**Early Historic Period Site Distributions and Frequencies.**

A. Site Frequency in the Project Area

| Site Type | Floodplain | Transition | Bajada | Mountain | Avra Valley | Total |
|---|---|---|---|---|---|---|
| Class I | 1 | 2 | 1 | 0 | 0 | 4 |
| Large Class I | 0 | 0 | 1 | 0 | 0 | 1 |
| Class II | 4 | 2 | 1 | 2 | 2 | 11 |
| Class III | 0 | 0 | 1 | 0 | 0 | 1 |
| Total Sites | 5 | 4 | 4 | 2 | 2 | 17 |

B. Site Distribution in the Project Area

| | | | | | | |
|---|---|---|---|---|---|---|
| Class I | 25% | 50% | 25% | 0 | 0 | 100% |
| Large Class I | 0 | 0 | 100% | 0 | 0 | 100% |
| Class II | 37% | 18% | 9% | 18% | 18% | 100% |
| Class III | 0 | 0 | 100% | 0 | 0 | 100% |
| Total Sites | 30% | 23.5% | 23.5% | 11.5% | 11.5% | 100% |

C. Site Frequency in the General Area

| | | | | | | |
|---|---|---|---|---|---|---|
| Class I | 1 | 2 | 1 | 0 | 0 | 4 |
| Large Class I | 0 | 0 | 1 | 0 | 0 | 1 |
| Class II | 5 | 3 | 1 | 2 | 2 | 13 |
| Class III | 0 | 0 | 1 | 0 | 0 | 1 |
| Total Sites | 6 | 5 | 4 | 2 | 2 | 19 |

D. Site Distribution in the General Area

| | | | | | | |
|---|---|---|---|---|---|---|
| Class I | 25% | 50% | 25% | 0 | 0 | 100% |
| Large Class I | 0 | 0 0 | 100% | 0 | 0 | 100% |
| Class II | 39% | 23% | 8% | 15% | 15% | 100% |
| Class III | 0 | 0 | 100% | 0 | 0 | 100% |
| Total Sites | 32% | 26% | 21% | 10.5% | 10.5% | 100% |

Archaeological evidence for interregional contacts during the period is primarily limited to the influx of European goods associated with the colonization of the area by Hispanic and Anglo groups. One complete vessel of an unidentified Hopi Polychrome has been recorded in the project area at AZ BB:13:94. Found with a flexed (non-Christian) Pima burial, it has been dated to approximately A.D. 1700 and is associated with the Pima occupation of the village of Bac (Ayres 1970b). Together with marine shell found with the same burial, this vessel provides the major archaeological evidence for contact between the Native American groups of the Tucson Basin and non-European populations of other areas during the period.

Sharply differing views of the possible relationships between the prehistoric Hohokam and Historic Pima groups can be found in the literature. Some propose a genetic relationship between the two, with a direct cultural continuum. Haury (1945, 1976) and Rosenthal and others (1978: 109) cite similarities in material culture, subsistence practices, and site structure. Others dispute this association, pointing to basic differences in ceramic techniques (Fontana and others 1962: 132; Masse 1980a: 224) as well as in subsistence practices (McGuire and Schiffer 1982). Significant differences have also been noted in the two groups' domestic cultigens (Bohrer, Cutler and Sauer 1969) and in the working of shell and lithics (Doyel 1977b: 118ff).

Alternative models call for the absorption of the Hohokam after the Classic period by Piman groups migrating out of Sonora (Wilcox and Masse 1981a: 38), an event perhaps triggered by the depredations of the Spanish in northwestern Mesoamerica in the early sixteenth century (Wilcox and Masse 1981a: 47). Another proposes that the Papago are descended from remnant populations of the Trincheras and Hohokam cultures driven westward by Pimas emanating from the Rio San Miguel Valley of Sonora (Bowen 1972: 182ff).

Another model associates the Papago, especially the Kohatk of the northeastern Papaguería, with the non-Hohokam Sells phase population (Goodyear 1977: 208). This association has, however, been challenged (Masse 1980a: 251). At present much more research is necessary before the origin of the Historic Native American groups of southern Arizona can be established, including their relationship, if any, to the prehistoric Hohokam.

## Historical Data

The early Historic period is the first for which data from other sources can be used to supplement archaeological information. Historic data, primarily records kept by Spanish colonial officials, are often contradictory to inferences from archaeological sources. Archaeological data indicate that the population in the project area during the period was confined to five villages—three in the area of the San Xavier del Bac Mission and two at the foot of Sentinel Peak. Historic data, however, mention the existence of at least 10 more villages in or near the project area (Smith and others 1966).

The village of San Agustín de Oiaur, termed the "area of greatest Sobaipiri population" (Betancourt 1978b: 60), has not been archeologically identified. Due to changes in the course of the Santa Cruz River, the site of this village may be either east or west of the present channel. The locations of the villages of Santa Catarina de Cuitubaga, San Clemente, and El Valle are also unknown, although the latter two were apparently within the project area. Four small rancherias north of Bac and south of San Agustin, noted by the Spanish in 1690, are missing from the archaeological record. Also unrecorded at present are four small villages in Avra Valley occupied by the Papago prior to 1774 (Dobyns 1963: 177). Other evidence indicates the archaeological record is not in agreement with the historical record. The material culture of early Historic Pima apparently consisted only of plain ware, if that, and nondistinctive forms in architecture that are so poorly known that they cannot be separated from earlier Hohokam loci. Bruce Huckell of the Arizona State Museum notes, however, that the Historic Pima flaked stone is distinctive and Historic Pima projectile points are separable from Hohokam points. Thus, Pima remains may be present in the area, but archaeological criteria for their recognition are difficult to define, with the possible exception of projectile points.

Much of the material culture of the Pima was apparently perishable; what little of it that survives in archaeological contexts cannot be readily recognized. The high proportion of wooden tools among Pima and Papago groups is well documented (Goodyear 1977: 225; Rosenthal and others 1978: 218; Withers 1973: 70). If most of the tool assemblage used by Pima and Papago groups was of wood, then numbers of Class II sites associated with resource exploitation would be missing from today's archaeological record. If pottery was not manufactured by the Gila Pima until the 1700s, the seventeenth century Pima of the Tucson Basin may also have been essentially aceramic, with baskets as their principal containers. This would account for the survival of little Pima material culture into the present. (Fontana and others 1962). If early Pima architecture was as insubstantial and informal as the accounts of the first Europeans indicate (Smith and others 1966) the archaeological remains of an entire village might be all but impossible to interpret.

One line of inference used in support of the first hypothesis has been that, since the ceramic repertoire of early Historic Pima consisted mostly of plain wares, many ceramic assemblages without decorated types may date from the period. While this possibility cannot be dismissed, the distribution of sites with only plain ware ceramics in the project area does not approximate the location of the Pima villages in the seventeenth century (Figure 4.9; Table 4.8). One Class I site with exclusively plain ware ceramics, AZ BB:13:69, may be one of the historic villages mentioned by Kino and Manje, but no other sites with Pima ceramics recorded in the area agree with seventeenth century descriptions.

### TABLE 4.8

**Unclassified Ceramic Site Distributions and Frequencies**

A. Site Frequency in the Project Area

| Site Type | Floodplain | Transition | Bajada | Mountain | Avra Valley | Total |
|---|---|---|---|---|---|---|
| Class I | 0 | 2 | 0 | 0 | 1 | 3 |
| Class II | 6 | 11 | 11 | 12 | 5 | 45 |
| Class III | 0 | 0 | 5 | 6 | 3 | 14 |
| Total Sites | 6 | 13 | 16 | 18 | 9 | 62 |

B. Site Distribution in the Project Area

| | | | | | | |
|---|---|---|---|---|---|---|
| Class I | 0 | 67% | 0 | 0 | 33% | 100% |
| Class II | 14% | 24% | 24% | 27% | 11% | 100% |
| Class III | 0 | 0 | 36% | 43% | 21% | 100% |
| Total Sites | 9% | 21% | 26% | 29% | 15% | 100% |

C. Site Frequency in the General Area

| | | | | | | |
|---|---|---|---|---|---|---|
| Class I | 0 | 2 | 0 | 0 | 1 | 3 |
| Class II | 13 | 20 | 32 | 14 | 6 | 85 |
| Class III | 0 | 2 | 5 | 7 | 3 | 17 |
| Total Sites | 13 | 24 | 37 | 21 | 10 | 105 |

D. Site Distribution in the General Area

| | | | | | | |
|---|---|---|---|---|---|---|
| Class I | 0 | 67% | 0 | 0 | 33% | 100% |
| Class II | 15% | 24% | 38% | 16% | 7% | 100% |
| Class III | 0 | 12% | 29% | 41% | 18% | 100% |
| Total Sites | 12% | 23% | 35% | 20% | 10% | 100% |

Other areas of disagreement exist between the archaeological and historic records. The distribution of most sites with early Historic ceramics in bajada areas can be interpreted as signifying relatively little emphasis on agriculture. A similar inference can be derived from the absence of agricultural tools or irrigation canals at early

Historic sites. Yet, according to the Spanish, extensive fields of maize, beans, and cotton around Bac and San Agustín de Oiaur were under irrigation by the Pima upon first contact. The villages north of Bac were also described as primarily agricultural, pointing to serious discrepancies between archaeological interpretations and historical data.

The archaeological record would also indicate a general lack of contact with areas outside of the Tucson Basin during the period. Historic evidence, however, shows that the Pima and Sobaipuri held trade fairs with Moquinos (Hopis) and Cibolans (Zuni) as late as the eighteenth century (Di Peso 1953; Ayres 1970b). References by the Spanish to the raising of red macaws by the inhabitants of Bac in 1692 (Wilson 1981: 63) suggest possible contact with Mesoamerica, although archaeological evidence fails to indicate such contacts for the period.

Probably the most significant discrepancy between available archaeological and historic data involves population size. The limited number of early Historic sites and the small size of most of them would suggest that the population of the project area at the time of contact was not very substantial. The small site clusters at Bac and San Cosme apparently represent the centers of the area's population (Figure 4.8).

These assumptions are belied by historical data. These indicate a population in 1696 of 830 at Bac in 176 houses, while another 758 Pimas occupied 177 houses at San Agustin. This village, not Bac, has been considered the apparent center of population at the time of contact (Betancourt 1978b: 60; Smith and others 1966: 73). At present, the only evidence of that population is a sherd scatter at AZ AA:12:90, which may be related to the occupation of San Agustín de Oiaur. The population of El Valle in 1696 was estimated at 100 in 20 houses (Smith and others 1966: 44). A 1699 census revealed 100 people residing in both Santa Catarina and San Clemente, 800 at San Agustin, and 900 at San Xavier (Dobyns 1963: 179). The total population of Pima between Bac and San Agustin in the seventeenth century has been estimated at 2580, a population barely represented in the archaeological record.

The following discrepancies between the archaeological record and historic data emerge.

1. Population size during the period was much larger than site frequency and site size would indicate.
2. Many, if not most, of the villages occupied in the seventeenth century have not been recorded or recognized.
3. Many artifacts recorded by the Spanish at time of contact are not found in archaeological contexts, including agricultural tools, macaws and irrigation canals.
4. Interregional contacts known to have existed with the Hopi, Zuni, and Mesoamerican areas are either underrepresented or altogether absent in the archaeological record.

The relevance of these discrepancies between the archaeological and historical data may be significant for interpretations of the Hohokam. If Hohokam material culture consisted of perishable materials as did those of Historic groups, many Hohokam sites in the project area have not been recorded, due either to poor preservation or failures in their recognition by existing archaeological criteria. If prehistoric material culture is as unrepresentative of levels of social complexity as is early Historic data, the Hohokam probably evidenced more complex and various interrelated subsystems than is often assumed.

If the low-level presence of nonlocal trade wares on most Hohokam sites is similar to Historic conditions, then the Tucson Basin Hohokam were far more integrated into regional and interregional exchange systems than previously thought. Historic documentation of interregional trade with Mesoamerican, Zuni, and Hopi areas by Tucson Basin Piman groups is in sharp contrast to available archaeological data, limited to one vessel each from the Hopi and Zuni areas and a few marine shells. Given the relative abundance of nonlocal ceramics at many Hohokam sites, the volume and intensity of prehistoric interregional contacts must have been considerably greater than in the Historic period.

Three major implications are suggested by these discrepancies: (1) archaeological data from unexcavated sites cannot be used as a means of reconstructing past adaptations without serious reservations: (2) much of the material culture of precontact populations was perishable—the part preserved in the archaeological record is only a small fraction of the original; and (3) a majority of sites occupied in any particular period will not be recorded, due to poor preservation of artifacts, site attrition, or lack of survey. This suggests that archaeological data, especially from unexcavated sites, should be used only with the utmost caution in reconstructing past adaptations of both prehistoric and historic populations.

# Chapter 5

# HISTORIC PERIOD CULTURAL RESOURCES

## James E. Ayres and Lyle M. Stone

During January and February, 1982, Archaeological Research Services, Inc. (ARS) completed a class 2 "Field Sampling Inventory" of historic cultural resources for Phase B of the Tucson Aqueduct, a feature of the Central Arizona Project. This study was authorized by the Arizona State Museum, University of Arizona, as a part of its comprehensive evaluation of cultural resources for the Central Arizona Project Tucson Aqueduct.

The Tucson Aqueduct Phase B study area is relatively large, in that it extends from the southwestern corner of the Tortolita Mountains on the north to the community of Green Valley on the south. This area includes approximately 392 square miles, is 42 miles long (north-south) and between 2 and 15 miles wide.

The objective of this study has been to develop and evaluate data pertaining to historic cultural resources within the study area at a class 2 (sampling inventory) level, such that an objective appraisal of the type, frequency, and distribution of historic sites within the area could be made. This information would then be applied to the comparison of specific project features (for example, alternative aqueduct alignments) from the perspective of historic cultural resources.

In performing this study it has been necessary to define an approach commensurate with these objectives, which would consider the unique nature of the available historic site data base (historical documentary sources), and which could be accomplished within reasonable funding and time constraints. This approach involved three study phases:

Phase I (Historical Site Documentation) focused on development of an inventory of pre-1936 historic cultural resources within the study area. These historic site inventory data could then be applied to estimating the occurrence of historic sites within specific project features assuming that these sites, or their archaeological equivalents, are present at this time. Due to post-1930s land use activities (such as mining, housing and commercial development, highway construction, and agriculture), as well as to natural processes such as erosion and flooding, this predictive approach would have produced biased results since many of the Phase I inventory sites would have been destroyed or otherwise adversely affected. In order to consider the effects of such environmental or land-use actions in determining which inventory sites would likely be present at this time, it was necessary to gain a perspective on the quantity and location of inventory sites that have been lost.

In order to address this information need in Phase II (Field Sampling Survey), a sample of inventory sites was field checked to produce information on the basis of which the first level inventory could be refined.

Sample surveys of randomly selected land areas were not performed within specific environmental zones or regions in order to predict site density for that zone. This approach is commonly used when little is known about the cultural history of an area. Rather, the project survey was site-specific and directed to historic sites previously referenced. In this manner we had hoped to maximize results produced by a limited amount of field time by field checking the locations of historically documented sites rather than surveying randomly selected land areas that would have less relevance to the project's objectives. The purpose of this survey and analysis has therefore been to determine if a historically documented site is present or absent through a sample field check, to determine what percentage of inventory sites are in fact present, and to then apply this percentage figure to inventory sites located at project features as a basis for estimating the number of sites expected to be present within that feature or alignment.

Phase III (Data Analysis) involved an evaluation of inventory and field sampling survey data as a basis for estimating the number of historic sites expected to be present in relation to alternate project features. This process is discussed later in the report.

# The Study Area

Geographically, the study area is within the Middle Santa Cruz River Basin (Westfall 1979). Specifically, it extends from the south end of the Tortolita Mountains and the Marana area on the north to the vicinity of Green Valley on the south. It includes all of the Tucson Mountains, a small segment of Avra Valley, and most of the Santa Cruz River between the northern and southern limits (Figure 1.1). The space within these confines is unevenly occupied; the extremes range from the densely populated urban area of greater Tucson's west side, which lies on the east side of the Tucson Mountains, to the sparse settlement characterizing eastern Avra Valley and the western slope of the Tucson Mountains. Agricultural activity predominates beyond the limits of greater Tucson. A thorough discussion of the pertinent aspects of the environment within the study location is presented elsewhere (Westfall 1979; McCarthy and Sires 1981).

The study location includes three major aqueduct corridors, two on the west side of the Tucson Mountains, and one on the east side, and several shorter segments and related water control features (see Figure 6.1, page 80).

Sources used to compile the brief historical overview of the study area are secondary in nature. These are believed acceptable due to their high quality and because the overview section is not central to the purpose of the report.

# *Culture History*

Historical developments in the Tucson area can be characterized as being slow and relatively stable rather than dramatic in nature. Even major political events, such as the end of Spanish rule in 1821 or the Gadsden Purchase in 1854, appear to have been treated with a large degree of equanimity by local residents.

The historic period is defined as beginning with the arrival of Padre Eusebio Francisco Kino in 1692 and extends into the 1930s. Although the National Register of Historic Places generally has a 50-year age requirement for eligible sites, an arbitrary three-year extension beyond this figure was deemed necessary to take into account an expected time lapse between planning and the actual mitigation process. Therefore, for the purpose of this study, 1935 was considered the end date for the historic period. It is also possible that some sites within the study area dating later than 1935 may be eligible for the National Register.

The historic era can be divided into three periods based on the source of political control: the Spanish period, 1692-1821; the Mexican period, 1821-1843; and the American period, 1854 to the present (1935 for the purposes of this study).

## Spanish Period

In 1682, a Jesuit missionary, Padre Kino, made the first of several trips down the Santa Cruz River from his headquarters in Sonora to what is now the Tucson area. During the course of his missionary endeavors he established *visitas* at what were probably existing Indian settlements along the river downstream from San Xavier del Bac. Those at San Cosme del Tucson and San Agustín de Oiaur are best known; however, their exact locations are uncertain. Both settlements are now covered by the City of Tucson.

In 1700 Kino began construction of the first church at San Xavier. The exact location of this building is not known, and in fact it may never have been completed (Wagoner 1975: 86). Kino died in Sonora in 1711 and was buried in the town of Magdalena. Seventy-two years later the Franciscans started construction of the present church at San Xavier.

The city of Tucson began in 1776 with the construction of a presidio whose complement of troops was transferred from Tubac because of a restructuring of a line of presidios on the northern Spanish frontier. The presidio was completed in 1783 (Wagoner 1975: 145).

At the site of San Cosme, whose name had been changed to San Agustin, a large, two-storied adobe building was erected sometime between 1797 and 1810. Early photographs lead one to believe that the site was in ruin by the 1870s, and it may have been abandoned as early as the 1840s (Hard and Doelle 1978: 10). A detailed account of the various excavations conducted at this site is reported in Hard and Doelle (1978: 14-22). No surface remains of this building, or of the site generally, exist, although subsurface features may be present along the western edge of the site. The site has been destroyed by landfill operations.

During the 129-year Spanish period, sites and transportation routes were situated near the Santa Cruz River, a source of water for humans and livestock and the location of small irrigation systems and fields. All known sites of this period, both in and out of the study area, are located within 0.75 mile of the river channel.

## Mexican Period

With the Mexican Revolution and subsequent independence in 1821, and the concomitant removal of troops from the Spanish presidio in Tucson, increased Apache Indian depredations restricted the movement and settlement of people away from the population centers.

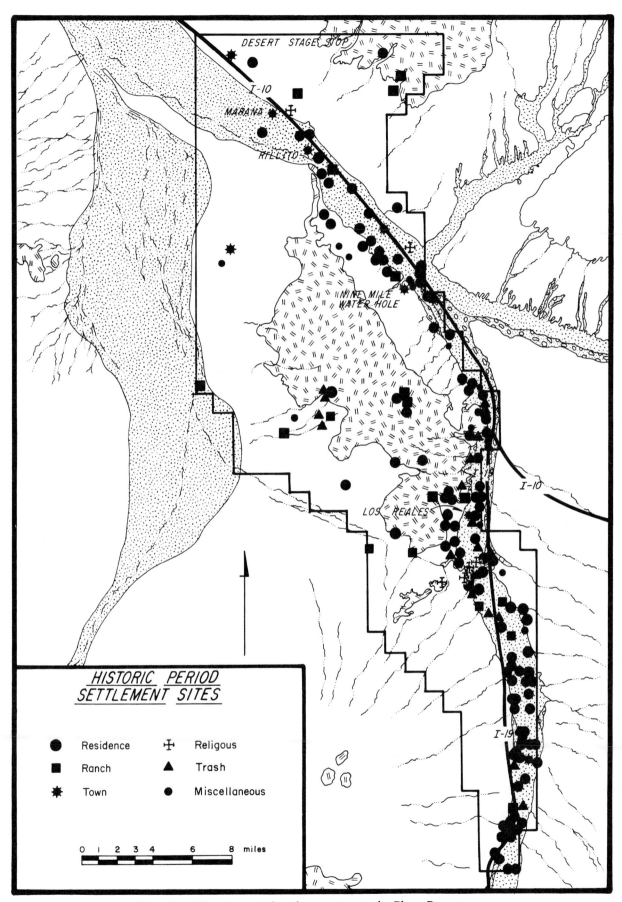

## HISTORIC PERIOD SETTLEMENT SITES

| | | | |
|---|---|---|---|
| ● | Residence | ✚ | Religous |
| ■ | Ranch | ▲ | Trash |
| ✴ | Town | ● | Miscellaneous |

0 1 2 3 4 6 8 miles

*Figure 5.1.* Historic period settlement sites in the Phase B project area

[ 65 ]

Most sites previously occupied by the Spanish continued to be held during the Mexican period. With the secularization of the missions in 1828, several sites were abandoned and, with the exception of San Xavier del Bac, probably never reoccupied (Hard and Doelle 1978: 10).

The severely limited documentation available for the 33-year-long Mexican period suggests that while some attempts were made to establish ranches along the Santa Cruz River south of San Xavier, most were short lived. This was generally a period of retrenchment with the major population foci at the Tucson presidio and San Xavier.

No sites established during this period have been identified within the study area.

## American Period

The American period begins with the ratification of the Gadsden Purchase Treaty in 1854 when the Tucson area became part of the United States.

The number of individuals living in Tucson at this time is unclear because the available information is not based on sound census data. Wagoner (1975: 286) cites Bartlett's report that Tucson had a population of about 300 individuals plus about 300 Mexican military personnel in 1852. Getty (1951: 2) quotes Poston that there were between 300 and 400 Mexicans and about 30 Americans in Tucson in 1856. The first formal U.S. census, that of 1860, indicates that 650 people were living in Tucson (Wagoner 1975: 392), but that figure appears not to be particularly accurate.

Two years after Tucson became part of the United States, the Mexican Army still maintained its garrison there. The Mexican troops left in the spring of 1856 and were replaced by the U.S. Army (Wagoner 1975: 395).

Despite a continuing problem with Apaches, in the 1850s individuals slowly began to establish small ranches, farms, and other businesses along the Santa Cruz River in the vicinity of Tucson. The Punta de Agua Ranch was established south of San Xavier by Fritz Contzen in 1855. The ranch appears to have been abandoned in 1877 because of the creation of the San Xavier Indian Reservation which included the ranch (McGuire 1979: 5). The site was partially excavated in 1965 by the Arizona State Museum (McGuire 1979). In 1856 the Silver Lake Dam was constructed near Tucson as a flood control structure to keep water from fields and irrigation systems downstream. Water from the pond was used in 1857 to power the first flour mill in Tucson (Betancourt 1978b: 81). Shortly thereafter, in 1858, the Butterfield Overland Mail Stage line was founded. In addition to a stop in Tucson, a station was constructed at Point of Mountain near the present-day community of Rillito. The line was terminated in 1861 (Wagoner 1975: 351-359). Another stage station, Desert or Desert Well, is reported north of Marana but little

is known about it (Gregonis and Huckell 1980: 27). In addition to the establishment of these sites, a number of undocumented sites in existence or created during the 1850s and 1860s are likely to have been present. As with the Mexican period, the documentary record for the early American period is poor.

Creation of the Territory of Arizona in 1863 provided further impetus for development. By 1870, Tucson's population had reached 3,224 including the U.S. Army contingent stationed at Fort Lowell. According to the census, this figure represented 907 families or almost 2.5 times more than were recorded six years earlier during the special 1864 census (U.S. Senate 1965).

The 1870s saw increasing population, increasing development of agriculture, and a corresponding decrease in the occurrence of Apache activities in the Tucson area. During this time the community of Sahuarita was established and Maish and Driscoll, among others, began ranching south of San Xavier. The San Xavier Indian Reservation was created around San Xavier del Bac for the Papago Indians in 1874 (McGuire 1979: 10).

The most significant event in Tucson in the nineteenth century was the construction of the Southern Pacific Railroad which arrived in Tucson in the spring of 1880. Along with improving Tucson's connections with the outside world, sidings were built at what is now Marana and at Rillito which had been in existence from about 1870 (Granger 1975: 278).

The 1880s began a period of unprecedented settlement and development along the Santa Cruz River and in the Tucson Mountains. The 1880s and 1890s saw the spread of farming and ranching along the Santa Cruz both north and south of Tucson and into Avra Valley to the west; extensive exploitation of mineral resources, such as copper, gold, lead, and silver, throughout the Tucson Mountains; and establishment of the community of Los Reales in 1888 north of San Xavier. This period also saw the end of the Apache problems.

At the turn of the century, farming and ranching continued to be predominant activities along the Santa Cruz River excluding, of course, Tucson and other communities, and much of the San Xavier Indian Reservation.

In 1910 C. W. Post began subdividing land near Marana. He established a small community known as Postvale and advertised family farms. Both settlements had post offices in the early 1920s, but eventually they were combined under the name Marana. The farms were bought out in the 1930s by Cortaro Farms (Granger 1975: 271-272). Cortaro, near the Santa Cruz River, also related to Cortaro Farms, had its own post office by 1920, and in Avra Valley the community of Avra had a post office for the year 1932 (Granger 1975: 264, 259). Around many of these communities, where urban expansion has not occurred, agriculture remains an important enterprise to the present.

During the period of time between 1900 and the end of the study period, 1935, mining activity in the Tucson Mountains declined to a sporadic endeavor, flourishing when prices were good and ceasing when they were not; mostly they were not.

Along with a gradually increasing population spreading over the valley, primarily along the east slope of the Tucson Mountains, the small farms and ranches have been overrun by urban expansion or incorporated into larger, commercial farms.

During the first 81 years of the American period in the Tucson area, dramatic changes in settlement arrangements occurred. In the early years the pre-Anglo patterns persisted, but gradually expansion and in-filling from the Spanish and Mexican core areas of Tucson and San Xavier took place. The expansion process, which is still in operation today, led to increasing use of the Santa Cruz River drainages by ranchers and farmers near the core areas, and to the construction of flour mills, and dams and other water control devices. Establishment of additional commercial enterprises in the immediate Tucson vicinity followed. In the late nineteenth century a local mining boom occurred, resulting in the creation of hundreds of small sites in the Tucson Mountains. Later, the bulk of these sites were incorporated into Saguaro National Monument (West) and Pima County's Tucson Mountain Park. The thousands of acres included in these parks have been effectively excluded from further development and settlement as has the San Xavier Indian Reservation.

Major transportation routes, both north and south along the Santa Cruz River, were defined and improved gradually, others were extended onto and around the Tucson Mountains.

Little settlement took place in Avra Valley, in the area north of the Tucson Mountains, or in the southern Tortolita Mountains until well after 1900. These began for the most part as ranches and farms and many, incorporated into commercial agricultural enterprises in the 1920s, were short lived. By this time the last of the small towns had been founded.

The 1930s saw the end of many small farms and ranches whose land and water were gradually subsumed within urban and suburban developments. The 1930s also mark a period of considerable home construction on the east side of the Tucson Mountains. The trend was accelerated after World War II.

## Previous Investigation of Historic Sites

The search for historic sites in the greater Tucson area has been carried out over many years but systematic surveys are relatively recent. The first large scale attempt to record Tucson's historic sites was that of the Historic Sites Committee organized by Ray Brandes of the Arizona

Historical Society. The committee, conducting its work from approximately 1960 to 1963, used a documentary rather than a field search technique; hence, specific site locations were often not known or recorded.

In 1978, a narrow area on both sides of the Santa Cruz River from Ruthrauff Road south to Los Reales Road was surveyed as part of the study for the proposed Santa Cruz River Park. Twenty-four historic sites, many of which were previously unreported, were recorded by the survey (Betancourt 1978b, also see 1978a).

A number of smaller surveys have also recorded historic sites within the Tucson area. In 1980 a study was conducted for the Corps of Engineers within the Tucson area (Gregonis and Huckell 1980), a survey was made of the Midvale Farms property (Stephen 1980; Stephen and Hewitt 1980a) and sites were added to the record in 1981 as a result of the Pima County land exchange survey (Hartmann 1981).

All five of the surveys cited above recorded specific sites located within the Central Arizona Project Tucson Aqueduct Phase B cultural resource study area.

Excavations of historic sites within the study area have concentrated primarily on sites of the Spanish period; however, a few sites dating to the nineteenth century have been partially excavated.

At San Agustin, five separate limited excavation projects were conducted between 1949 and 1967. Although the data have never been published, maps, field notes, artifacts, and human skeletal remains are housed in the Arizona State Museum. Hard and Doelle describe in detail the existing information in their report on San Agustin (1978: 14-23).

San Xavier also has experienced numerous excavation efforts beginning in 1958 (Robinson 1963). Later, during the period from 1962 to 1973, Bernard Fontana, with the assistance of University of Arizona students, conducted several small excavations. His efforts are reported by Cheek (1974). In 1970 an historic burial with a Hopi ceramic bowl was excavated by Ayres (1970b) in the village of Bac south of the mission.

Another important Spanish period site is the Tucson presidio. Although it is located outside the project study area on the east, this site is nevertheless central to much that occurred within the study area during the Spanish and Mexican periods. A small excavation was conducted by Emil Haury in 1954 (Chambers 1954) to locate one of the presidio walls. More extensive excavations within the presidio were conducted by James Ayres in the late 1960s as part of the Tucson Urban Renewal project (Ayres 1970c). One of these excavations is the subject of a Ph.D. dissertation currently in preparation by Mark Barnes of the National Park Service.

Nineteenth century sites have been excavated as parts of three projects. The Punta de Agua Ranch, dating to 1855, was excavated during a highway salvage project in 1965

(McGuire 1979). In 1979 Bruce Huckell of the Arizona State Museum excavated the remains of a three-room house in the old community of Los Reales. The sites of the Elias and Angulo ranches dating at least to the early 1870s were partially excavated in 1981 and 1982 by David Stephen and James Hewitt of Pima Community College. In addition, Stephen and Hewitt have excavated a lime kiln and what they believe to be an early smelter. Formal reports on the latter two projects have not yet been written.

## Study Methods

As indicated in the introduction, this study was completed within a three phase framework. Each of these phases is discussed in detail below.

### *Phase I. Historical Site Documentation*

The initial step in the data collection process required the location and evaluation of the major documentary resources available for the study area. From these, the initial site inventory was compiled. For the purposes of this study, the term "documentation" includes all sources, published or otherwise, which provided information on historic site locations.

One federal agency and four state entities were visited to search for appropriate documentary sources that would provide information on sites, buildings, and structures predating 1936 in the study area. Included in the category "appropriate documentary sources" are archaeology and geology reports, general and site-specific histories, and a wide variety of maps. In some instances where documentation could not be located for known, occupied buildings, brief telephone interviews were conducted with knowledgeable individuals to determine the age of the property.

In Phoenix, the files of the Bureau of Land Management (BLM) were searched to obtain the General Land Office (GLO) cadastral survey maps (35 sheets) of the study area. These maps, dating from various years between 1871 and 1945, illustrate buildings, structures, roads, fields, mines, canals, and other cultural features. The GLO maps are an invaluable and generally accurate resource of use to the historical archaeologist for determining potential site locations.

Also available at the Bureau of Land Management office are records pertaining to historic mining activities. (Only one district, the Amole Mining District, which covers most of the Tucson Mountains, exists in the study area). The mining district maps, organized by township and range, are first consulted to obtain the location and number designation of claims. There are four maps for each township. When the claim number is acquired, the Mineral

Survey Plat Books are consulted. These provide documentation as to claim size and location, name of the claimant, improvements, and date of filing.

The acquisition of land from the federal government by individuals was achieved, for our purposes, through one of four ways. When the legal requirements for these were met, a patent was issued indicating transfer of ownership to the individual concerned. For the homesteader, a homestead entry (HE), which was intended to be used for farming, or a stock raising homestead entry (SRHE) were available under the provisions of the Homestead Act of 1862, the Desert Land Act of 1877, the Enlarged Homestead Act of 1909, and the Stock Raising Homestead Act of 1916 (Stein 1981). The 1862 law allowed a homestead entry to be no more than 160 acres; subsequently, under some circumstances, this figure was increased to 320 acres and then to 480 acres. The 1916 Act allowed 640 acres if they were to be used for grazing purposes. Homesteading requirements could be avoided by cash purchase of land, a process known as cash entry (CE). A mining claim also could be patented as a mineral entry (ME). Approximately 200 homesteads (HE and SRHE) were patented in the study area.

In addition to the Bureau of Land Management records, those of the State Historic Preservation Office were utilized to locate sites placed on the National Register of Historic Places, to identify National Historic Landmarks, and to obtain historical information about specific sites.

In Tempe, the historical resources available in the Arizona Room, the Arizona Historical Foundation, and the Map Room at the Hayden Library, Arizona State University, were evaluated. Maps that were consulted are listed below.

The greatest number of documentary sources were located at the University of Arizona and at the Arizona Heritage Center (AHC) of the Arizona Historical Society, Tucson. The Arizona Heritage Center made available a number of maps including Roskruge's very useful 1893 map of Pima County. The Arizona State Museum and the Main Library at the University of Arizona were successfully consulted for numerous historic site locations. At the State Museum, site survey files and maps, both pre-1936 USGS maps and pre-1900 maps of the San Xavier Indian Reservation, were extremely helpful in providing site locations. The Map Room of the Main Library provided a number of useful maps, and Special Collections was a source of information specifically from rare Arizona mining journals and Geology Department master's theses, both covering mining in the Tucson Mountains.

The maps used to locate and assign occupation dates to sites are dated. Often, however, the field work from which the map was compiled was carried out a year or more before the map was prepared in its final form. The field work date reflects the actual date the building or structure was seen and recorded. In Appendix B, where a listing of sites and the dates of their occupation is presented, it is important to note that wherever possible, the dates used reflect the date of the field work rather than the date the map was prepared.

More than 70 maps were consulted during the course of the project; however, only those that provided usable site occupation dates are mentioned in this report.

## Phase II: Field Sampling Survey

Upon completion of the initial inventory which was constructed from documentary and other sources, a field evaluation of a number of sites was required. The initial inventory consisted of 229 sites, 140 of unknown status and 89 known to be present. The field evaluation was necessary primarily to provide data with which site occurrence within the proposed alternative aqueduct routes could be projected. In addition, information relative to site condition, site function, time occupied, and factors contributing to site destruction or deterioration was to be collected.

Preceding the actual field checking process, it was necessary to define an approach that would assure that sites to be surveyed were representative of study area sites in general. A number of possibilities were considered for dividing the study area into meaningful zones for the purpose of selecting the number of sites to be field checked. An environmental approach based on vegetation zones such as that presented by Westfall (1979) was considered inappropriate for historic resources because historic site locations are usually sensitive to environmental variables in a manner too general to be of use for this study. Dividing the area on the basis of the USGS quadrangle maps was also rejected. Ultimately the study area was divided into three major zones or subdivisions based on physiographic considerations. The boundaries of these subdivisions are not absolute although they closely approximate the actual mountain, bajada, and riverine zones within the study area. Zone 1 consists of the Tucson Mountains and outliers with a small segment of the Tortolita Mountains; 2a is the area that is primarily bajada extending along the east side of the Santa Cruz River through the entire study area south and west of the Tortolita Mountains; 2b is the bajada between the Santa Cruz River and the Tucson Mountains; 2c is the bajada to the west and south of the Tucson Mountains on the west side of the Santa Cruz River. This unit extends through the entire study area. The riverine zone is designated as Zone 3. It also extends through the entire study area.

Once the study area subdivisions were defined, the number and types of sites to be field evaluated had to be determined. A number of factors was considered in establishing the sites to be field checked. Time and culture were not thought to be appropriate variables on the basis of

which to select inventory sites because reliable information pertaining to cultural affiliation and period of occupation for many of the sites was not available from the documentary survey. On the other hand, site function was more easily determined from the names of sites listed in the documentary sources (for example, Gould Mine, Silverbell Road, St. Mary's Hospital, cemetery, lime kiln). Based on these considerations, site function and spatial representativeness were selected as the appropriate criteria. To the extent present in the study area, sites associated with nine functional categories in each of the five zones and subzones were field checked. The nine functional categories are: Residential (R), Mining (M), Town (TOW), Ranch-Farm (RAN), Trash deposition (T), Water control (W), Transportation (TRA), Religion (REL), and Miscellaneous (MIS). These are discussed below in detail. Because of the small potential sample size that resulted from this procedure, no attempt was made to randomize the sites to be field evaluated.

The field sample survey or field check of representative inventory sites was conducted from 22 February to 3 March 1982. Recording of information at the sites visited, beyond verification of site presence or absence, probable date of occupation, and probable function, was kept at a minimum. It was considered unnecessary to relocate 89 sites, buildings, and structures recently recorded by Arizona State Museum archaeological surveys or buildings and structures known to exist (for example, San Xavier del Bac, mines and related structures, The Manning House) (Betancourt 1978a, 1978b; Hartmann 1981; Gregonis and Huckell 1980). The exclusion of these 89 sites left a remainder of 140 sites of which 58 (41 percent), covering most of the major functions known to be represented within the three physiographic zones, were evaluated.

## Phase III: Data Analysis

Data analysis involved an evaluation of both historical documentary (inventory) and site survey data within a predictive framework. In developing a procedure for estimating the frequency of historic inventory sites that would actually be present within a specific project feature location, several assumptions were made:

1. The historic inventory sites that were field checked, while not a probabilistic sample due to the small sample size, are broadly representative of study area cultural activity (and sites) in general, in that the sample included sites that were spatially distributed throughout the study area, and that were representative of all study area functional categories that had been defined during the documentary research phase.

2. Given this representativeness, then, the percentage of inventory sites that are *actually* present in either the study area or a specific physiographic zone is expected to be

approximately the same as the percentage of sites present in the area or zone as demonstrated by the results of the field sampling survey. For example, if 100 sites are identified in a specific zone on the basis of documentary research, and 15 sites were actually found by a survey of 30 site locations, a total of 50 sites (15 of 30; or 50 percent of the inventory number, 50 of 100) would be expected to be present in that zone. This same percentage (of inventory sites that were present in the zone) could then be applied to estimating the number of sites in any given project feature location by applying the percentage to the number of inventory sites in a project feature in that zone.

These percentages for each zone are computed in Study Results below and are applied to the description and comparison of project features.

# Study Results

At the conclusion of the field survey, 245 sites had been entered on the inventory (Appendix B). This final inventory includes the 229 sites on initial survey (89 present or assumed present and 140 from which those sites to be field checked were selected) and 16 previously unrecorded sites located during the field survey.

As a basis for evaluating the historic resources located through documentary and field resarch, it was first necessary to categorize these sites into meaningful, workable units. All 245 sites were assigned to one of nine categories based on actual or, in a few cases, presumed, function. The categories and general comments on the sites found in each are presented below.

## *Functional Categories*

### Residential (R)

Sites listed as residential include all buildings shown on historic maps that are identified as homes, have a family name attached, or are unidentified buildings. In several cases, especially in rural areas, the location of a building on a map may indicate a ranch or farm but because it was not identified as such it was recorded simply as residential. This procedure is based on the assumption that a ranch or farm would have a residence associated with it.

Seven sites classified as residential actually contain more than one pre-1936 house each. The total number of houses included in the seven sites probably exceeds 200. In addition, the 1905 (reprinted 1916) USGS Tucson quadrangle map (HM-6) shows approximately 80 houses in the immediate vicinity of Tucson. None of these were included on the inventory because map scale and radical changes in street patterns would make locating them exceedingly difficult.

A total of 112 sites is identified as residential on the final inventory; in addition, a minimum of 280 pre-1936 buildings not on the inventory may exist within the study area. Twenty-eight of the 112 inventory sites were field checked. Eight residences (J-18, 32-34, 39; CM-23, 38, and 41) were located as a result of field investigation. One building, the Manning House (T-22), is on the National Register of Historic Places.

### Mining (M)

Included under this heading are sites such as shafts, adits, dumps, camps, smelters, lime kilns, prospects, and claims related to mining. For the most part these sites occur in the Tucson Mountains and its outliers. Forty mining sites were identified; nine of these were checked during the field survey. National Park Service employees in the Saguaro National Monument (West) reported that they were aware of approximately 100 mining-related sites in the Monument. These sites were not added to the inventory as most are undocumented. One site, M-17, was discovered during the field evaluation process.

For the purposes of this study all mining sites in the Tucson Mountains were assumed to be present. None of these sites is currently on the National Register of Historic Places.

### Town (TOW)

This category includes eight former and existing unincorporated communities which, with the exception of Avra, are located along the Santa Cruz River, most in Zone 3, some in Zone 2. Sahuarita, Rillito, Marana, Cortaro, and Avra are all viable entities; only Desert, Los Reales, and the site of Laguna have been abandoned. Very little is known about Desert except that it was an early stage station. The community of Laguna had a population of at least 71 individuals in 1870 according to census records (U.S. Senate 1965: 156). Some confusion exists as to the exact location of Laguna, also known as the "Nine Mile Water Hole." Both the generally reliable GLO cadastral survey map of 1871 and the 1893 Roskruge map show the site in T13S, R13E, Sec. 18. No cultural remains were located in the area indicated by the maps during the field survey. The Arizona State Museum site files place the site in T13S, R13E, Sec. 7. The site of the community of Los Reales has for the most part been leveled. However, a cemetery and a few buildings, which may or may not date from the original occupation, are present. (Los Reales was inadvertently omitted from subsequent calculations in this chapter.)

None of these sites are on the National Register of Historic Places.

## Ranch or Farm (RAN)

Twenty-one sites identified as ranches or farms are listed on the final inventory; six of these were field checked. Bureau of Land Management records list 199 Homestead and Stock Raising entries as having been patented within the study area. Most of these would be expected to have, or to have had, buildings and structures associated with them. These 199 homesteads may include some of the sites listed here or under the residential category. Because of the large number of possibilities, no work was done with the homesteads and the total was not included on the inventory. One site, BM-9, was discovered during the course of the field evaluation.

None of these sites are on the National Register of Historic Places.

## Trash Deposition (T)

Included in this category are 20 sites consisting primarily of trash scatters; 17 sites are recorded in the Arizona State Museum site survey files and were assumed present, one site was known to be present from another source, and two sites (SXM-18 and TSW-30) were discovered during the course of the field evaluation.

None of these sites are on the National Register of Historic Places.

## Water Control (W)

Nine sites including five canals, a dam, two City of Tucson pumping plants, and a reservoir, are related to water control and use. Only one of these sites was field checked.

None of these sites are on the National Register of Historic Places.

## Transportation (TRA)

The transportation category contains six roads, one railroad depot, and three railroad lines. There were dozens of formal and informal roads and trails in the study area historically; however, only the major roads to mines and to communities outside of the study area are listed on the inventory. Most important roads followed the Santa Cruz River, but three important east-west roads crossing the Tucson Mountains provided connections to the mines in the Tucson Mountains, to the Avra Valley, and beyond. These are the Silverbell, Gates Pass, and Starr Pass roads. Railroads traverse the study area north and south, primarily following the Santa Cruz River.

None of these sites are on the National Register of Historic Places.

## Religion (REL)

Seven sites, including San Xavier del Bac, San Agustin mission, two isolated burials, and three cemeteries reflect a religious function. None of these sites was field checked.

San Xavier del Bac is a National Historic Landmark.

## Miscellaneous (MIS)

A number of functions have been assembled into this general category. The functions involved are commercial, recreational, science, health, education, quasi-military, and unknown. Six of the 18 sites were field evaluated. Included are schools, a swimming pool, businesses, the Desert Laboratory, a Civilian Conservation Corps (CCC) camp, a series of earth and rock ridges, guest ranches, hospitals, a golf course, and a tuberculosis sanatorium.

The Carnegie Institution Desert Laboratory on Tumamoc Hill and several acres surrounding it is a National Historic Landmark.

## *Physiographic Zones*

Three major physiographic zones were defined for this project: the Tucson Mountains, Zone 1; an area that is primarily bajada on the east side of Santa Cruz River, Zone 2a; the bajada between the Tucson Mountains and the river, Zone 2b; the bajada on the west and south sides of the mountains on the west side of the river, Zone 2c; and the area adjacent to the Santa Cruz River, Zone 3.

Historic sites were found in all zones in the study area (Figures 5.1 and 5.2); however, only Zones 2c and 3 contained sites representing all nine functional categories. Zone 1 had no towns, water-related sites, or trash scatters; Zone 2a contained no mining remains or sites with a religious function, and Zone 2b had no towns or water-related sites. Only residential, ranch or farm, transportation, and miscellaneous functions occurred in all zones.

One hundred forty sites on the initial inventory were available for field evaluation (Table 5.1); 58 were actually visited and of these, 33 were located: six in Zone 1; five in Zone 2a; nine in Zone 2b; eight in Zone 2c; and five in Zone 3.

As might be expected, Zone 1 contains 75 percent (30) of the mining related sites on the final inventory. With those reported for Saguaro National Monument (West), and those probably in Pima County's Tucson Mountain

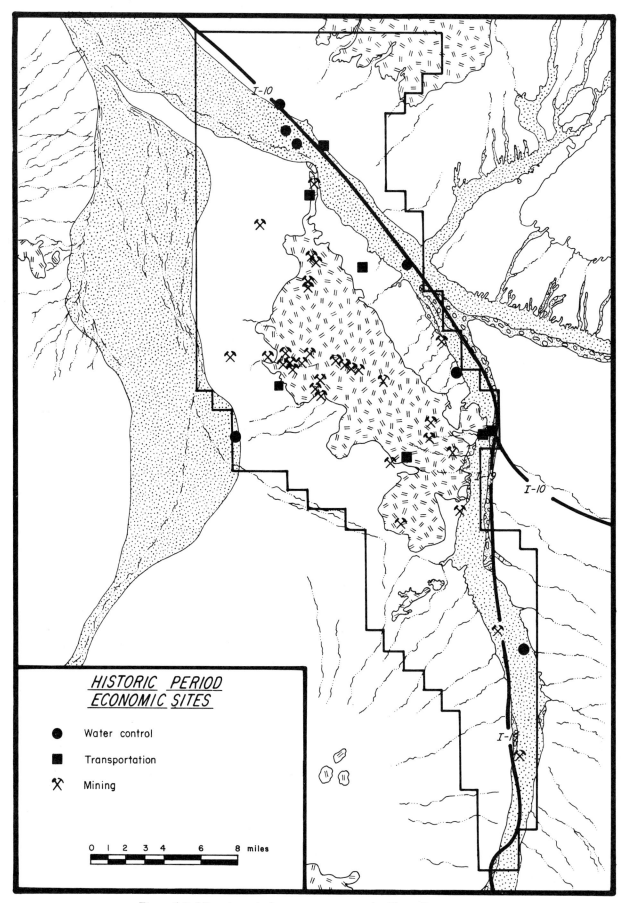

*Figure 5.2.* Historic period economic sites in the Phase B project area

TABLE 5.1

**Sites Available to Field Check and Sites Field Checked**

| Known sites Recorded sites | R | M | TOW | RAN | T | W | TRA | REL | MIS | Total |
|---|---|---|---|---|---|---|---|---|---|---|
| **Zone 1** | | | | | | | | | | |
| Sites available* | 1 | 5 | 0 | 1 | 0 | 0 | 1 | 0 | 0 | 8 |
| Sites field checked | 0 | 5 | 0 | 0 | 0 | 0 | 1 | 0 | 0 | 6 |
| **Zone 2a** | | | | | | | | | | |
| Sites available* | 15 | 0 | 2 | 3 | 0 | 1 | 1 | 0 | 1 | 23 |
| Sites field checked | 9 | 0 | 1 | 1 | 0 | 1 | 1 | 0 | 1 | 14 |
| **Zone 2b** | | | | | | | | | | |
| Sites available* | 5 | 2 | 0 | 1 | 0 | 0 | 0 | 0 | 4 | 12 |
| Sites field checked | 3 | 2 | 0 | 1 | 0 | 0 | 0 | 0 | 4 | 10 |
| **Zone 2c** | | | | | | | | | | |
| Sites available* | 10 | 2 | 1 | 8 | 0 | 1 | 0 | 1 | 2 | 25 |
| Sites field checked | 3 | 2 | 1 | 4 | 0 | 0 | 0 | 0 | 1 | 11 |
| **Zone 3** | | | | | | | | | | |
| Sites available* | 58 | 1 | 2 | 2 | 1 | 5 | 2 | 0 | 1 | 72 |
| Sites field checked | 13 | 0 | 2 | 0 | 1 | 1 | 1 | 1 | 1 | 20 |
| **Total** | | | | | | | | | | |
| Sites available* | 89 | 10 | 5 | 15 | 1 | 7 | 4 | 1 | 8 | 140 |
| Sites field checked | 28 | 9 | 4 | 6 | 1 | 1 | 3 | 1 | 7 | 160 |

*Sites available to field check, based on initial inventory

Park and elsewhere in the Tucson Mountains, possibly more than 300 mining sites are located in Zone 1. All are expected to be present. Zone 3 contains 58 percent (65) of the residential sites, nearly 78 percent (7) of the water-related sites, and 62 percent (5) of the towns. The percentage of residential sites would be higher in Zone 3 if the number of houses in subdivisions were treated separately. Nearly 50 percent (10) of the ranches and farms occur within Zone 2c. This percentage will probably not change if the 199 homesteads are added to the inventory. Also, over half (4) of the religious sites are found in Zone 2c. Zone 2b accounts for over half (10) of the miscellaneous sites. The remaining sites are more or less evenly distributed. Zone 2b has the fewest number of sites (29) and Zone 3 has the most (96) which is twice as many as the next largest total, Zone 2c with 48 sites (Figures 5.1 and 5.2).

From the perspective of population, the tables clearly indicate that Zone 3 was the most heavily occupied zone in the study area. This appears to have been the case throughout the historic period. Zone 1, with the fewest functional categories represented, would appear to have been the least heavily occupied. Beyond these observations, few meaningful generalizations can be made given the small numbers involved (Figures 5.1 and 5.2).

Twenty-five of the 58 field-evaluated sites were not located and were presumed destroyed. Thirteen sites were found destroyed in Zone 3, eight in Zone 2a, three in Zone 2c, one in Zone 2b, and none in Zone 1. Subsurface remains may be present in some cases, but without being able to pinpoint site locations the presence of subsurface remains is moot. Over 70 percent (18) of the sites were destroyed by agriculture, one each was destroyed by a gravel pit, a shopping center, and flooding (?) and four from unknown causes. Ten of the agriculturally destroyed sites are in Zone 3, five in Zone 2a, and three in Zone 2c.

In the Sahuarita area, agriculture is responsible for all 12 of the destroyed sites noted. These sites account for nearly half (48 percent) of the total number of sites destroyed in the entire study area.

## Corridor Evaluation

With the completion of the final inventory and plotting of sites on USGS quadrangle maps, an overlay of project features (for example, proposed alternative canal alignments) was placed on the maps to determine which sites would be affected in a 1-mile-wide corridor. To estimate the number of sites actually expected to be present within the project features, it was first necessary to determine the number of sites on the initial inventory that could be expected to be present within each physiographic zone. This number was based on the field checking process; when the number of sites on the initial inventory had been established and the field checks completed, the relationship between the number of sites field checked in each zone and the number actually located in each zone was expressed as a percentage. These percentages are: 100 percent for Zone 1, 38.5 percent for Zone 2a, 90 percent for Zone 2b, 73 percent for Zone 2c, and 28 percent for Zone 3. This means, for example, that all of the sites searched for in Zone 1 and only 28 percent of those in Zone 3 were located. These percentages were treated as being representative of the total number of sites expected to be present within each zone. That is, if 28 percent of those sites selected for field checking were present, 28 percent of all the inventoried sites whose status was *unknown* in that zone would be present as well.

This same reasoning was applied to the project features in the study area. The applicable percentage for each zone was applied to the number of sites located by zone in the appropriate project feature.

Corridors 1 and 2 are listed together since, except for a short distance, they are in the same location. No sites were located in the approximately 3-mile-long segment where the two diverge. The 1-mile-wide alignment of Corridors 1 and 2 would affect the 17 sites listed in Table 5.2.

73, and 28 respectively, to the sites in Zones 1, 2c, and 3, results in eight sites that are expected to be present.

In addition to the eight sites expected as a result of the field evaluation, three sites known to be present (P) were excluded from the field checking process. Therefore, a total of eleven sites is expected to be impacted by either Corridor 1 or 2.

Seventy-nine sites are present within the 1-mile-wide B-5 alignment (Table 5.3).

### TABLE 5.2

**Sites within Corridors B-1 and B-2**

| Inventory No. | Zone | Status | Type |
|---|---|---|---|
| M-3 | 3 | U | Irrigation Canal |
| M-5 | 3 | U | Irrigation Canal |
| M-9 | 3 | SP | Road |
| M-16 | 3 | P | Southern Pacific Railroad |
| A-15 | 2c | SP | CCC Camp |
| BM-3 | 2c | U | Temanalberes Ranch |
| CM-11 | 2c | SP | F. Canes and Lime Kiln |
| CM-12 | 2c | U | House |
| CM-40 | 1 | SP | Lime Quarry |
| SXM-12 | 1 | P | Cemetery |
| S-5 | 3 | SD | House |
| S-8 | 2c | SD | Baga Ranch |
| S-9 | 2c | SP | Houses (2) |
| S-13 | 2c | SD | Democrat Mill Site |
| S-20 | 3 | SD | S.E. Brown House |
| S-24 | 2c | P | Twin Buttes Railroad |

P= present　　　　　SP= field checked and present
U=unknown　　　　SD= field checked, but destroyed

Three sites were checked in Zone 1, five in Zone 2c, and one in Zone 3. Applying the appropriate percentages, 100,

### TABLE 5.3

**Sites within Corridor B-5**

| Inventory No. | Zone | Status | Type |
|---|---|---|---|
| J-2 | 3 | SD | Canas House |
| J-6 | 3 | SD | Talmadge-Rodriquez House |
| J-7 | 3 | U | De Bascano House |
| J-8 | 3 | U | Pumping Plant |
| J-9 | 2b | SP | Ranch House |
| J-10 | 3 | SD | House |
| J-11 | 3 | SD | Nine Mile Water Hole |
| J-12 | 3 | U | Allison Canal |
| J-17 | 2b | SP | Concrete Foundation |
| J-18 | 2b | SP | Adobe Ruin |
| J-19 | 2b | P | Trash Scatter |
| J-22 | 3 | U | Martinez House |
| J-23 | 3 | U | Cuevas House |
| J-25 | 2b | SP | Lime Kiln |
| J-26 | 3 | P | Laguna |
| J-27 | 2b | P | Building |
| J-28 | 3 | P | Isolated Burial |
| J-31 | 2b | SP | Lime Kiln |
| J-32 | 2b | SP | House |
| J-39 | 2b | SP | House |
| J-42 | 2a | P | Badger Hole Ranch |
| M-9 | 3 | SP | Road to Silverbell Mines |
| M-16 | 3 | P | Southern Pacific Railroad |
| CM-7 | 3 | P | Upper Reales (7 Houses) |
| CM-13 | 3 | U | House |
| CM-14 | 3 | SP | J.M. Elias House |
| CM-15 | 1 | P | Sunshine Mine Claims |
| CM-17 | 1 | P | Copper Queen Claim |
| CM-19 | 3 | SP | Angulo House |
| CM-20 | 3 | U | Hughes House |
| CM-21 | 3 | U | Herrera House |
| CM-22 | 3 | U | Burrel House |
| CM-24 | 2b | SD | Mission Pool |
| CM-26 | 2b | U | Leon House |
| CM-31 | 1 | P | Desert Laboratory |
| CM-42 | 3 | P | Midvale Farms |
| T-1 | 3 | U | Ortega House |
| T-2 | 3 | U | Castro House |
| T-3 | 3 | U | House |
| T-12 | 3 | U | T. Elias House |
| T-13 | 3 | U | School |

TABLE 5.3 (continued)

**Sites within Corridor B-5**

| Inventory No. | Zone | Status | Type |
|---|---|---|---|
| T-14 | 3 | U | Etchell House |
| T-18 | 3 | P | Trash Scatter |
| TSW-3 | 3 | U | House |
| TSW-9 | 3 | P | Trash Scatter |
| TSW-11 | 3 | U | Frederico House |
| TSW-12 | 2a | SD | Sayze House |
| TSW-13 | 2a | SD | Arctic Ice Co. |
| TSW-14 | 2a | SD | Shortridge House |
| TSW-15 | 3 | U | M.C. Shortridge House |
| TSW-18 | 3 | P | King House |
| TSW-21 | 3 | U | Lopez House |
| TSW-22 | 3 | U | Merrill House |
| TSW-28 | 2a | P | Trash Scatter |
| TSW-34 | 3 | U | Houses (27) |
| TSW-35 | 3 | U | Houses (4) |
| S-1 | 2a | SD | Hartt House |
| S-2 | 2c | U | Houses (2) |
| S-3 | 2a | SP | Sahuarita |
| S-4 | 2c | SD | House |
| S-6 | 3 | U | Durazo or Alfredo Ranch |
| S-7 | 3 | SD | Houses (2) |
| S-8 | 2c | SD | Baga Ranch |
| S-9 | 2c | SP | Houses (2) |
| S-12 | 2a | SD | House and Pump House |
| S-13 | 2c | SD | Democrat Mill Site |
| S-15 | 3 | U | Doyle House |
| S-16 | 3 | U | Buchman House |
| S-17 | 2a | SD | Hartt House |
| S-18 | 3 | SD | J. K. Brown House |
| S-19 | 3 | U | G. Morales House |
| S-20 | 3 | SD | S. E. Brown House |
| S-21 | 3 | SD | Moreno House |
| S-24 | 2c | P | Twin Buttes Railroad |
| S-25 | 2a | P | Tucson and Nogales Railroad |
| S-26 | 2a | U | House |
| S-27 | 3 | U | House |
| S-28 | 3 | U | House |
| S-29 | 3 | U | House |

P= present     SP= field checked and present
U= unknown     SD=field checked but destroyed

Of the 62 sites available for field checking, seven were checked in Zone 2a, eight in Zone 2b, three in Zone 2c, and 11 in Zone 3. Applying the appropriate percentages, 38.5, 90, 73, and 28 respectively to the inventory sites in the zones, results in a total of 26 sites expected to be present. Of the 26 sites, three are in Zone 2a, eight are in Zone 2b, four are in Zone 2c, and 11 are in Zone 3.

In addition to the 15 sites expected as a result of the field evaluation, 17 sites known to be present were excluded from the field checking process. Therefore, a total of 43 sites is expected to be present in the 1-mile-wide Corridor B-5.

In addition to the major corridor alternatives, the B-2 alternate (Table 5.4), the Indian Delivery and Feeder and Avra Valley Feeder corridors (Table 5.5), and the two reservoir sites (Table 5.6) contained historic cultural resources. Predictions on the number of sites expected within these Phase B project features were not made because of the small sample, which in some cases was only one site. Tables 5.4, 5.5, 5.6, show that most of the sites inventoried for these corridors are present.

TABLE 5.4

**Sites in Alternative Corridors**

| Route B-2 Alternative Number | Zone | Status | Type |
|---|---|---|---|
| A-4 | 1 | P | Shaft |
| A-14 | 1 | P | Lime Kilns (2) and Quarry |
| A-17 | 2c | SP | Avra |

P= present     SP= field checked and present
U= unknown     SD= field checked but destroyed

TABLE 5.5

**Sites in Delivery and Feeder Corridors**

| A. Routes B-1 and B-2 — Indian Delivery Line Number | Zone | Status | Type |
|---|---|---|---|
| A-1 | 1 | P | Shaft and Tunnel |

| B. Routes B-1 and B-1 — CM Number | Zone | Status | Type |
|---|---|---|---|
| CM-28 | 1 | P | Building |

| C. Route B-5 — Indian Delivery Line Number | Zone | Status | Type |
|---|---|---|---|
| CM-23 | 2c | NSP | House |

| D. Route B-5 — CM Number | Zone | Status | Type |
|---|---|---|---|
| CM-15 | 1 | P | Sunshine Mine Claim |

| E. Avra Valley Feeder Number | Zone | Status | Type |
|---|---|---|---|
| M-15 | 3 | U | Residence |

TABLE 5.6

**Sites in Reservoir Flood Pool**

*A. Twin Hill Reservoir*

| Number | Zone | Status | Type |
|--------|------|--------|------|
| CM-10 | 1 | P | Goat Ranch |
| CM-17 | 1 | P | Copper Queen Claim |
| CM-38 | 1 | NSP Riddell | House |
| CM-39 | 1 | P | House |

*B. Cat Mountain Reservoir*

| Number | Zone | Status | Type |
|--------|------|--------|------|
| CM-16 | 1 | P | Old Pueblo Copper Company Claim |
| CM-28 | 1 | P | Building |
| CM-29 | 1 | P | Starr Pass Road |
| CM-30 | 1 | P | Well and Enclosure |

| | |
|---|---|
| P= present | SP= field checked and present |
| U= unknown | SD= field checked but unknown |
| N= found on survey | |

## Conclusions and Recommendations

During January and February 1982, Archaeological Research Services, Inc., completed a Class II field sampling inventory of historic sites in a study area established for the Phase B, class 2 cultural resource study of the Central Arizona Project Tucson Aqueduct.

The study began with the creation of an initial inventory of 229 sites, 140 of which were of unknown status and 89 of which were assumed to be present. These sites, dating from the Spanish period to the mid-1930s, were identified from a variety of sources, including historic maps, published sources, interviews, and site survey files. Subsequently, these sites were classified into nine functional categories, and the study area was divided into three major physiographic zones (mountains, bajada, and riverine), to better enable the investigators to evaluate the historic sites, to provide spatial control, and to assist in the definition of a procedure for estimating frequency of historic sites expected to be present at the locations of specific Tucson Aqueduct features.

A field check or evaluation of 58 of the 140 sites whose status was unknown followed. This sample was constructed on a judgmental basis taking into account site function and geographic location. More formal sampling procedures would not have produced meaningful results because of the small numbers of sites involved. Table 5.1 presents the relevant figures. The field check provided information on 16 new sites bringing the total inventory number to 245. Twenty-five of the sites field checked could not be located. These sites appear to have been destroyed primarily because of agricultural activities.

With the completion of the field evaluation of sites, a procedure for estimating the expected frequency of sites within the route of a specific project corridor or feature was constructed. The approach is based on data acquired from the field check of sites. Basically, the procedure assumes that the percentage of sites found to be present as a result of the field evaluation in a zone would provide an estimate of the number of sites expected to be present in a corridor or other project feature in that zone. The procedure for establishing site number estimates seems sound, but the small number of sites obviates the usefulness of the system especially for Corridors 1 and 2. When dealing with project features where the number of sites affected is small, a thorough literature and documentary search combined with a complete field check of the sites located by the search would provide an adequate base from which to determine project impact on historic resources.

Of the 17 sites located in the 1-mile-wide B-1 and B-2 corridors, eight sites are expected to be present given the results of the field evaluation process and the predictive approach, and three sites were previously known to exist. Therefore, 11 sites are expected to be present in Corridors B-1 and B-2. The same results applied to Corridor B-5 indicate that of the 79 inventory sites within the corridor, 26 are likely to be present. Seventeen sites were previously known. Corridor B-5, therefore, is expected to contain 43 historic sites.

On the basis of the expected numbers of sites, it is suggested that Corridors B-1 or B-2 would have the least effect on historic resources. Corridor B-5 is less attractive because a greater number of historic sites could be potentially affected. The number of sites in a corridor that would be directly impacted by the aqueduct depends on the final route and right-of-way width. The more sites a corridor is expected to have, the greater the chances that a larger number of them will be affected by construction.

When a specific corridor is selected, and prior to an intensive archaeological survey of the route chosen, the appropriate homestead files at the Bureau of Land Management should be thoroughly studied for potential site data. Most of the homestead entries and stock raising homestead entries are expected to have had buildings and structures. In addition, records relating to cash entries and mining entries should be studied along with the homesteads filed on but not proven up. All would be expected to have associated cultural remains. Armed with this information and existing site data, field survey will be more efficient and effective.

**Note:**

Prior to publication of this report, several sections of the Phase B canal-pipeline alternatives were modified or deleted by Bureau of Reclamation planners. These changes are reflected on the appropriate maps for the report and in the discussions of prehistoric site type locations, expected site densities, and known site locations. The preceding discussion of historic cultural resources in the Phase B area was not completely modified to reflect these realignments, however, because the principal author of the chapter was out of the country while revisions were made. Minor revisions were made when they did not affect the original data or interpretations (such as including historic site data for the Avra Valley Feeder Line, which was added to the original Phase B alternatives). The major change involved the lower one-third of the B-5 Alternative and would have involved deleting certain sites from Table 5.3, which, while not a difficult problem, would have changed other related site number estimates, modified other B-5 corridor estimates, and required review of data with which only the primary author was familiar. Instead, historic sites located within 1 mile of the realigned portions of the B-5 Alternate are listed below (Table 5.7). Sites listed in Table 5.3 that are no longer within the B-5 corridor include all but two "TSW" and all "S" site designations.

TABLE 5.7

**Historic Sites Within One Mile of Realigned B-5 Alternate**

| Inventory No. | Zone | Status | Type |
|---|---|---|---|
| SXM-4 | 2c | SP | Lime Kiln |
| SXM-6 | 2c | P | San Xavier del Bac |
| SXM-7 | 3 | U | Berger (3 buildings) |
| SXM-8 | 3 | U | Brush House |
| SXM-9 | 3 | U | House |
| SXM-10 | 3 | U | Bedoya House |
| SXM-11 | 2c | U | Leopold Carrillo's Stock Ranch |
| SXM-14 | 2c | P | Trash Scatter |
| SXM-15 | 2c | P | Building |
| SXM-16 | 2c | P | Trash Scatter |
| SXM-18 | 2c | NSP | Trash Scatter |
| TSW-5 | 2c | P | Puntada de Agua Ranch |
| TSW-6 | 2c | U | Raglans Ranch |
| TSW-7 | 2c | U | "Ruins" |
| TSW-9 | 3 | P | Trash Scatter |
| TSW-10 | 3 | U | House |
| TSW-11 | 3 | U | Frederico House |
| TSW-27 | 3 | SP | Trash Scatter |
| TSW-30 | 2c | NSP | Trash Scatter |

P= present          SP= field checked and present
U=unknown          SD=field checked but destroyed

# Chapter 6

# PHASE B PROPOSED CANAL/PIPELINE EVALUATIONS

## James Mayberry and Jon S. Czaplicki

Discussion and evaluation of the various proposed canal/pipeline alternatives is based on Bureau of Reclamation maps No. 344-330-3501 and 3501A. The routes discussed below are the result of on-going engineering and planning studies by the Bureau and represent modifications of earlier alignments. Since Phase B planning continues at the time of this writing, additional modifications may be made before final selection of a preferred Phase B alignment.

Phase B of the Tucson Aqueduct consists of three possible canal pipeline routes (B-1, B2, B-5), two possible reservoir sites (Cat Mountain and Twin Hills), three reservoir feeder lines (B-1 and B-2 CM and TH; B-5 CM; B-5 TH), three Indian Distribution Lines (B-1, B-2, B-5), two sump sites (Bopp Road and Marana), and an Avra Valley feeder line. There are also several minor alternative alignments for routes B-1 and B-2 (Figure 6.1). Since these routes were tentative at the time this study was done, cultural resources within one-half mile on either side of the alignments were also identified. Assessment of known cultural resources in an area adjacent to the proposed alignments will provide Bureau planners with data on cultural resource sensitivity, should portions of an alignment change. It will also provide archaeologists with a more complete picture of site distribution along the Phase B alternatives.

The Phase B alignment begins at the pumping plant at the Marana Sump and heads south. After a short distance, routes B-1 and B-2 turn west and then south down the east side of Avra Valley before turning southeast at the southern end of the Tucson Mountains to cross the San Xavier Indian Reservation, and terminate at the southern border of the reservation. Route B-5 stays on the east side of the Tucson Mountains and roughly parallels the Santa Cruz River. It also terminates at the same location as the B-1 and B-2 routes (Figure 6.1).

Two alternative reservoir sites are located at the southern end of the Tucson Mountains. The Twin Hills and Cat Mountain reservoirs would each have a capacity of from 10,000 to 60,000 acre-feet of water, and have feeder lines leading to them from the three major canal alternatives.

Two sump sites are also under consideration. The Bopp Road sump site, approximately one square mile in area, is located in Avra Valley west of the junction of routes B-1 and B-2 with the B-5 Indian Delivery Line. The Marana sump site also covers approximately one square mile and is located at the beginning of the Phase B system, east of the community of Marana.

The topographic landforms comprising the Phase B project area have been assessed for their known and expected cultural resource sensitivity (for example, low, moderate, or high sensitivity). These are relative ratings and indicate the possibility that an area may contain certain kinds of cultural resources. The floodplain of the Santa Cruz River is expected to be highly sensitive for all site types. The lower bajadas of the Tucson, Tortolita, and Sierrita mountains are expected to be moderately to highly sensitive for Hohokam Class II sites, and low to moderately sensitive for Archaic period sites, Hohokam Class I and III sites, and Historic period sites. Mountain areas of concern within the project area, limited to the Cat Mountain and Twin Hills reservoir sites, are expected to be of low to moderate sensitivity for Historic period sites, moderately sensitive for Archaic and Hohokam Class II sites, highly sensitive for Class III sites, and low in sensitivity for Hohokam Class I sites. Much of the proposed canal/pipeline alignments are located in the transition area between floodplain and bajada. This zone is generally expected to be highly

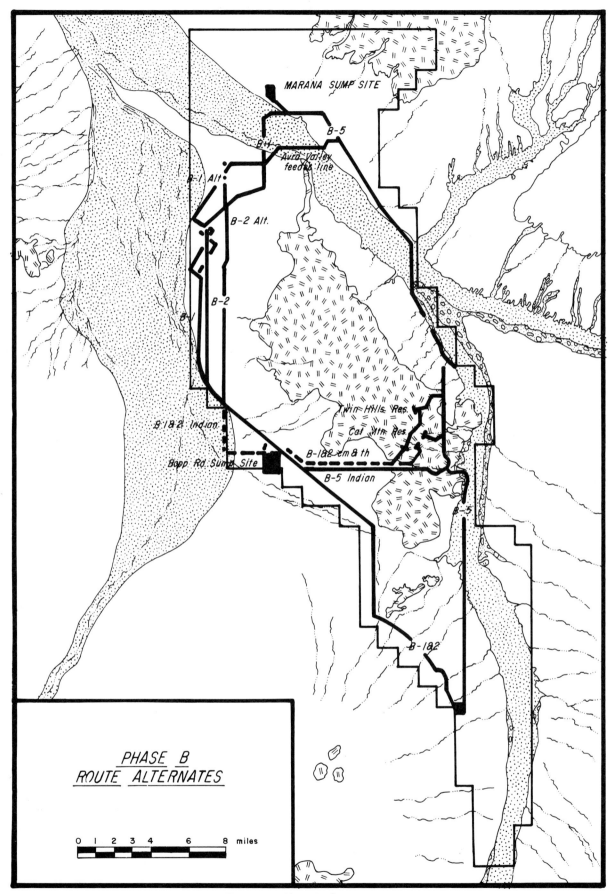

*Figure 6.1.* Phase B alternatives

sensitive for Hohokam Class I sites, moderately sensitive for Archaic and Hohokam Class II sites, and of low sensitivity for Hohokam Class III sites. Areas of known and expected cultural resource sensitivity are discussed below for individual route alignments.

# Route B-1

Route B-1 has a potentially moderate to high sensitivity for all site types for its first 2 miles, until it leaves the Santa Cruz River floodplain and enters Avra Valley. Although few sites are presently recorded for this part of Avra Valley, Route B-1 is expected to have a moderate sensitivity for Archaic period and Hohokam Class II sites. Of particular concern are buried Archaic sites in the Brawley Wash floodplain and shallowly buried sites—both Archaic and Hohokam—along the lower bajada-floodplain transition zone. The route appears to be confined to this transition zone and only crosses floodplain areas for short distances. Nonetheless, the possibility of buried and surface sites adjacent to drainage arroyos in the transition zone is good.

The portion of the B-1 route that crosses the bajada of the Sierrita Mountains has a potentially low to moderate sensitivity for Hohokam Class II and Class III, and Archaic period sites. Historic cultural resource sensitivity for this route is considered to be low.

# Route B-2

This alignment is identical to B-1 except for several miles at the northern end of Avra Valley where an alternate alignment exists. Consequently, cultural resource sensitivity for Route B-2 is essentially the same as that described for Route B-1. The B-2 Alternate Alignment, located to the east of the B-2 route, is expected to have a moderate sensitivity for Archaic period and Hohokam Class II and III sites.

# Route B-5

This route begins in the lower bajada of the Tortolita Mountains, in an area of expected high sensitivity for Hohokam sites, and low to moderate sensitivity for Archaic and Historic period sites. After turning south it is generally limited to areas of expected high sensitivity for Hohokam Class II sites, until it enters Section 26, T12S, R12E. From this point until it reaches Ironwood Drive, Route B-5 is in an area of expected high sensitivity for all site types. A number of Archaic, Hohokam, and Historic period sites are recorded along this portion of the alignment.

From Ironwood Drive to Ajo Way, Route B-5 crosses an area expected to be of moderate to high sensitivity for

Hohokam Class II sites. After re-entering the floodplain of the Santa Cruz at Ajo Way, the route is once again in an area considered to be highly sensitive for all site types. The alignment crosses the Santa Cruz River Park Archaeological District which is eligible for nomination to the National Register. Upon entering the San Xavier Indian Reservation at Los Reales Road, the route enters an area of moderate to high cultural resource sensitivity for Hohokam and Historic Native American sites. A number of such sites are recorded in the area of San Xavier Mission. The Indian village of Bac (AZ AA:16:6), reported by Father Kino and other Spanish explorers, is thought to be located in the vicinity of the Mission, which lies about one-quarter mile west of the B-5 route.

# Indian Delivery Lines

Indian Delivery Line Route B-1 and B-2 crosses an area of expected low to moderate sensitivity for Archaic period sites, particularly in the floodplain area of Brawley Wash where buried sites may occur. Hohokam Class I sites may also be present in this area. The area appears to have a low sensitivity for Historic period sites.

The B-5 Indian Line, until it enters Avra Valley, is in an area of moderate sensitivity for Hohokam Class II and Class III sites, and low sensitivity for Hohokam Class I sites and Archaic period sites. Once in the Avra Valley it crosses an area of expected low to moderate sensitivity for Archaic and Hohokam period sites, and of low sensitivity for Historic period sites. Where the alignment crosses washes emanating from the Tucson Mountains, buried and surface Archaic period sites may be present.

# Feeder Lines, Reservoir Areas, and Sump Areas

The B-1 and B-2 TH and CM feeder alignment parallels a portion of the B-5 Indian Delivery Line and has the same sensitivity ratings as this line. The B-1 and B-2 feeder lines into the reservoir areas and the Cat Mountain and Twin Hills reservoir sites, are located in areas of low to moderate sensitivity for Archaic, Hohokam Class II and Class III, and Historic period sites.

The Bopp Road Sump Site is in an area of low to moderate sensitivity for Archaic and possibly Hohokam period sites, but of low sensitivity for Historic period sites. The Marana Sump Site is in an area of moderate to high sensitivity for Class I and Class II Hohokam site types. As planned, its construction will directly impact at least one recorded Hohokam Class II site. The Avra Valley feeder line crosses an area of moderate sensitivity for Hohokam and possibly Archaic sites where it crosses the Santa Cruz floodplain.

Where it crosses lower bajada areas, cultural resource sensitivity for Hohokam and possibly Historic period sites is expected to be low to moderate.

# Conclusions

Recorded archaeological sites within the individual corridors are listed in Table 6.1, and the number of sites for each corridor can be found in Table 6.2. On the basis of known and expected sites, Routes B-1 and B-2 are preferable to B-5, as fewer sites of all periods are recorded along these routes. While much of the B-5 corridor crosses areas of known high cultural resource sensitivity, including a small portion of the proposed Santa Cruz River Park Archaeological District, the B-1 and B-2 corridors cross areas of primarily low to moderate sensitivity for Archaic period, Hohokam Class II and III sites, and Historic period sites, and low sensitivity for Hohokam Class I sites. As Figure 1.2 shows, the area traversed by the B-5 alignment has undergone considerably more cultural resource survey than that covered by the B-1 and B-2 alignments, possibly accounting for the greater number of recorded sites in and adjacent to the B-5 alignment.

TABLE 6.1

**Prehistoric and Historic Sites Within Phase B Corridors**

*Routes B-1 and B-2*
| | |
|---|---|
| Direct Impacts: | prehistoric:none |
| | historic: none |
| Adjacent Sites: | prehistoric: AZ AA:12:125, 128; |
| | AZ AA:16:85 |
| | historic: M-3, 5, 12; A-15, 17; BM-3; |
| | CM-11, 12, 40 |

*Route B-2 Alternate*
| | |
|---|---|
| Direct Impacts: | prehistoric: AZ AA:12:70 |
| | historic: A-4, A-17 |
| Adjacent Sites: | prehistoric: AZ AA:12:63, 71, 133 |
| | historic: A-14 (AZ AA:12:101), 15 |

*Avra Valley Feeder Line*
| | |
|---|---|
| Direct Impacts: | prehistoric: possibly AZ AA:12:73 |
| | and 87 |
| | historic: none |
| Adjacent Sites: | prehistoric: AZ AA:12:57, 58, 88, 125, |
| | 158, 160, 161 |
| | historic: M-11, 15 (AZ AA:12:54) |

*Route B-1 and B-2 Indian Distribution Line*
| | |
|---|---|
| Direct Impacts: | prehistoric: AZ AA:16:39 |
| | historic: BM-1 |
| Adjacent Sites: | prehistoric: none |
| | historic: none |

TABLE 6.1 (continued)

**Prehistoric and Historic Sites Within Phase B Corridors**

*Route B-1 Alternate*
| | |
|---|---|
| Direct Impacts: | prehistoric: none |
| | historic: none |
| Adjacent Sites: | prehistoric: none |
| | historic: none |

*Routes B-1 and B-2 and TH Feeder Lines*
| | |
|---|---|
| Direct Impacts: | prehistoric: possibly AZ AA:16:81 |
| | historic: none |
| Adjacent Sites: | prehistoric: AZ AA:16:78 |
| | historic: Cm-28 (AZ AA:16:79) |

*Route B-5*
| | |
|---|---|
| Direct Impacts: | prehistoric: AZ AA:12:38, 42,93, 96, |
| | 102, 105, 206; AZ AA:16:15, 19, |
| | 25, 45, 46, 48, 54, 60, 67, 86; AZ |
| | BB:13:48, 75, 126, 148 |
| | historic: J-12, 18, 19, 25 (AZ |
| | AA:12:106), 26 (AZ AA:12:55), |
| | 31, (AZ AA:12:150), 32; CM-22; |
| | SXM-4, 7, 8, 9 |
| Adjacent Sites: | prehistoric: AZ AA:12:1, 2, 9, 10, 11, |
| | 36, 46, 56, 59, 86, 92, 95, 97, 100, |
| | 104, 107, 108, 111, 113, 118, 159, |
| | 162, 163, 164, 165, 166, 193; AZ |
| | AA:16:3, 4, 14, 18, 21, 33, 49, 53, |
| | 68; AZ BB:13:14, 16, 18, 41, 42, 43, |
| | 44, 45, 50, 51 |
| | historic: M-8; J-6, 8, 11, 16 (AZ |
| | AA:12:90), 17 (AZ AA:12:93), 21, |
| | 22, 23, 28 (AZ AA:12:98), 42, (AZ |
| | AA:12:40); CM-8, 13, 14 (AZ |
| | AA:16:61), 19, 20, 21, 24, 31 (AZ |
| | AA:16:51), 42; SXM-6 (AZ |
| | AA:16:6, 7, 8, 9, 10, 35), 10, 11, |
| | 14, 15 (AZ AA:16:69), 16 (AZ |
| | AA:16:55), 18; TSW-5, 6, 7, 9 (AZ |
| | BB:13:19), 11, 27 (AZ BB:13:14), 30 |

*Route B-5 Indian Distribution Line*
| | |
|---|---|
| Direct Impacts: | prehistoric: none; |
| | historic: none |
| Adjacent Sites: | prehistoric: AZ AA:16:76 |
| | historic: CM-23 |

*Route B-5 CM Feeder Line*
| | |
|---|---|
| Direct Impacts: | prehistoric: none |
| | historic: none |
| Adjacent Sites: | prehistoric: none |
| | historic: CM-15 |

*Route B-5 TH Feeder Line*
No impacts

TABLE 6.1 (continued)

**Prehistoric and Historic Sites Within Phase B Corridors**

*Cat Mountain Reservoir*
Direct Impacts:
    prehistoric: AZ AA:16:2, 82
    historic: CM-28 (AZ AA:16:79), 29
      (AZ AA:16:83), 30 (AZ AA:16:80)
Adjacent Sites:
    prehistoric: none
    historic: CM-16

*Twin Hills Reservoir*
Direct Impacts:
    prehistoric: AZ AA:16:16
    historic: CM-17, 39
Adjacent Sites:
    prehistoric: none
    historic: CM-10, 38

*Bopp Road Sump Site*
No known impacts

*Marana Sump Site and Feeder to Routes B-1, B-2, B-5*
Direct Impacts:
    prehistoric: AZ AA:12:354, 355, 357,
      358, 368
    historic: M-2, M-4
Adjacent Sites:
    prehistoric: AZ AA:12:208, 209, 211,
      212
    historic: M-16

TABLE 6.2

**Numbers of Recorded Sites in Phase B Corridors**

| Route | Direct Impacts | | Adjacent Sites | | |
|---|---|---|---|---|---|
| | ASM# | ARS# | ASM# | ARS# | Total |
| B-1 and B-2 | 0 | 0 | 3 | 9 | 12 |
| B-2 Alternate | 1 | 2 | 4 | 1 | 8 |
| B-1 & B-2, Indian Line | 1 | 1 | 0 | 0 | 2 |
| B-1 Alternate | 0 | 0 | 0 | 0 | 0 |
| B-1 & B-2 CM-TH Feeder Lines | 1 | 0 | 2* | 0 | 3 |
| B-5 | 24* | 9 | 66* | 23 | 122 |
| B-5 Indian Line | 0 | 0 | 1 | 1 | 2 |
| B-5 CM Feeder Line | 0 | 0 | 0 | 1 | 1 |
| B-5 TH Feeder Line | 0 | 0 | 0 | 0 | 0 |
| Cat Mountain Reservoir | 7* | 0 | 0 | 1 | 8 |
| Twin Hills Reservoir | 1 | 2 | 0 | 2 | 5 |
| Bopp Road Sump Site | 0 | 0 | 0 | 0 | 0 |
| Marana Sump Site | 5 | 2 | 4 | 1 | 12 |
| Avra Valley Feeder Line | 2 | 0 | 10 | 1 | 13 |

*Indicates that one or more sites identified by ARS were previously recorded by ASM and are assigned to the ASM site number category.
ASM= Arizona State Museum
ARS= Archaeological Research Services, Inc.

The B-1 and B-2 TH and CM feeder line and the B-5 Indian Delivery Line parallel each other and are basically identical in their expected cultural resource sensitivity.

The B-1 Alternate is preferable to the B-2 Alternate. Both are in areas of expected low to moderate sensitivity for Archaic period sites, but the B-2 Alternate impacts several known Hohokam and Historic period sites.

The two alternate reservoir sites affect areas of expected low to moderate sensitivity for Historic period sites, and moderate sensitivity for Archaic and Hohokam Class II and III sites. The Twin Hills reservoir site impacts fewer recorded sites and is therefore preferable to Cat Mountain.

Of the various alternative feeder lines, the B-5 TH and B-1 and B-2 CM routes are better choices than the B-5 CM route. All four affect similarly sensitive areas; however, the B-5 CM route may impact at least one previously recorded site. The Avra Valley feeder line affects an area of moderate sensitivity for Hohokam sites.

The Bopp Road Sump Site appears preferable to the Marana Sump Site which is in an area expected to be of moderate to high cultural resource sensitivity.

The projected impact of the B-5 alternative on known cultural resources in the proposed Santa Cruz River Park Archaeological District appears minimal. The alternative runs along the western edge of the proposed district for about 3.5 miles in T13S, R13E, Sections 20, 28, 29, and 33, and appears to directly impact only four sites: AZ AA:12:93, 96, 105 and 106. AZ AA:12:96 is recorded as a large, probably buried, Archaic (Cochise) site, whie AA:12:93 is a small pit house village, AA:12:105 a small Hohokam sherd and lithic scatter, and AA:12:106 a single historic lime kiln.

In T14S R13E, Section 34 and T15S R13E, Section 3, the alignment again intersects the proposed archaeological district impacting five sites: AZ AA:16:45 (sherd and lithic scatter), AA:16:46 (large pit house village, partially disturbed), AA:16:48 (small sherd and lithic scatter), AA:16:54 (sherd and lithic scatter associated with bedrock mortars), and possibly AA:16:60, a disturbed sherd and lithic scatter.

Previous surveys along portions of the Santa Cruz River (Betancourt 1978b; Rozen 1979a) indicate that many of the recorded sites in the floodplain have been disturbed to varying degrees by urbanization and agricultural and industrial development. Therefore, while the B-5 route does not directly impact numerous sites, mitigation efforts on some of these may not be as extensive as might first appear because of their disturbed condition. Nonetheless, this route remains the least preferable alternative.

# Chapter 7

# FUTURE RESEARCH IN THE PHASE B AREA

### Jon S. Czaplicki, James D. Mayberry, and James E. Ayres

One of the main goals of this report was an assessment of the various Phase B canal and reservoir alternatives in terms of their potential impacts to known and expected cultural resources.

Since a large body of survey data for the area is available, research focused on using these data to develop as complete a picture of the prehistory and history of the project area as possible. The various canal alternatives were then viewed in light of their potential impacts on the known and expected cultural resource base and each alternative judged accordingly.

The previous chapters have discussed the paleoenvironment and the Paleo-Indian, Archaic, Hohokam, Protohistoric, and Historic occupations of the Phase B area and adjacent regions. Settlement patterning and site function inferences for the Archaic and Hohokam occupation of the project area, and in fact for the Tucson Basin, are often based soley on survey data. These data are not always reliable as indicators of site function and can lead to misinterpretation and distortion. Once excavation is completed and data analyzed, site interpretations may be considerably different from preliminary assessments based on survey data. To rely on survey data alone in assessing subsistence and settlement strategies and generating models can distort the researchers' view with what Simmons (1981: 14) calls a "survey mask." "Sometimes the discrepancies between survey and excavation data are so severe that to use only the former in model building and reconstructing settlement and subsistence systems, for which site function is critical, is to ensure spurious results" (Simmons 1981: 14).

Realizing that interpretations of settlement patterns, subsistence, site types, cultural interactions, and formulation of models based almost entirely on survey data are not without some serious problems, this chapter will discuss various research topics that may be addressed during future Phase B cultural resource investigations. These research topics or orientations deal with some of the more important questions and problems concerning prehistoric and historic occupation of the project area. In addition, the following discussion will alleviate some of the acknowledged shortcomings of interpretation and modeling based almost exclusively on survey data.

While some of the interpretations and models discussed in the previous chapters will undoubtedly be modified as new information becomes available, the canal route rankings are based primarily on known site location and can be considered reliable.

## Paleoenvironmental Research

### Jon S. Czaplicki

An accurate view of the paleoenvironment is critical to a better understanding of prehistoric development; however, as noted in Chapter 2, the paleoenvironment of the study area is not well known. Climate was certainly a limiting factor in the occupation of semiarid southern Arizona and was reflected in the environment, hydrology, and geomorphology of the area. Although not completely reconstructed, the paleoclimate of the Santa Cruz River Valley may be inferred from studies in other southwestern river valleys. Paleoclimatic reconstruction of Avra Valley is comparatively unknown, and needs to be better defined and interpreted, especially as it compared to the Santa Cruz Valley.

It appears that Avra Valley had little, if any, surface water after the early Holocene. Prior to this it may have been a grass covered valley, with some surface water. Ground water has apparently been deep, compared to the shallow water table of the Santa Cruz River; but whether this has always been the case is not known. A cienega deposit, exposed in a tributary of Brawley Wash, contains fossilized camel and horse remains and indicates that marsh conditions existed in at least one part of the valley. Similar evidence for a considerably wetter climate is not uncommon in floodplain arroyos of the Santa Cruz and other southwestern rivers. McCarthy (1982: 39) points out that "...the plant community associated with the desert washes may have little in common with the prehistoric environment of these areas." Riparian communities are sensitive to climatic changes, and the present location and extent of these communities should not be extrapolated into prehistoric time. Their appearance in the prehistoric past undoubtedly changed over time, and was different, perhaps significantly so, than that of today.

Paleoenvironmental reconstruction is dependent on interdisciplinary study, including geologic, geomorphologic, hydrologic, pollen, radiometric dating, faunal, and archaeological information. Some of the most important paleoenvironmental data for the late Pleistocene and early Holocene are available either directly or indirectly from archaeological investigations. The association of man and animals at a site usually signifies the presence of ancient surface water that can provide paleohydrologic data. Conditions may have been favorable for the preservation of molluscs, plant remains, and pollen, which can provide data on the local paleoenvironment (Haynes 1965: 61).

Of primary importance to any paleoenvironmental study is a detailed stratigraphic description. Stratigraphy is the framework to which all other data are referenced, and should be completed and identified before pollen, radiocarbon, or other analyses begin, to avoid unnecessary sampling. Samples can then be selected to provide the most meaningful data (Haynes 1965: 61-62). In the San Pedro Valley, the most useful sequences of late Quaternary sediments have been exposed at archaeological sites where the geology has been studied in order to obtain detailed stratigraphic controls for paleoenvironmental studies and for establishing a radiocarbon-calibrated chronology (Haynes 1968: 79). Similar work needs to be undertaken in the Phase B area. C. Vance Haynes has been monitoring several buried sites in Brickyard Arroyo in the Santa Cruz floodplain, and has begun stratigraphic mapping at these sites. More work is needed in the Santa Cruz floodplain and Brawley Wash floodplain, but it should be done after consulting with Haynes to determine what has been completed and what remains to be done.

Pollen samples must be taken with the full understanding of stratigraphic relationships. The best opportunity for obtaining a pure pollen assemblage is from sediments representing semipermanent or intermittent ponding along a stream channel, such as cienega deposits (Haynes 1965: 62). Investigations by University of Arizona palynologists

of recently exposed buried deposits in the Santa Cruz River may provide the kinds of data needed for paleoenvironmental reconstructions.

Disconformities and gaps in the sedimentary record can lead to errors in interpretation and confusion in radiocarbon dates. To avoid these problems it is necessary to obtain adequate exposures of sediments. Because of the soft nature and limited thickness of late Pleistocene and Holocene sediments, it is often practical to make exposures at critical places by stratigraphic trenching or by uncovering stream banks (Haynes 1965: 64). The areas where the preferred Phase B canal crosses floodplain deposits, or stream or tributary arroyos, should be carefully examined. Backhoe trenching, core drilling, or bank profiling should be considered if the area appears likely to provide good stratigraphic data.

Radiocarbon dating is best used for correlation over any distance, and it is the best aid available for correlation of stratigraphic units, provided its limitations are understood (Haynes 1965: 64). Radiocarbon dating used in conjunction with stratigraphic investigations has shown that alluvial deposits of numerous tributary streams can be correlated over wide areas on the basis of soils, fauna, and archaeology (see Haynes 1966). Alluvial deposits appear to represent a similar and synchronous sequence of deposit, soil formation, and erosion throughout the Southwest (Haynes 1966: 18-19).

Haynes (1966) has defined stratigraphic levels for an alluvial chronology for the greater Southwest, and has identified cultural and faunal material associated with these depositional strata. Stratigraphic studies in critical Phase B areas (for example, where the canal corridor crosses the Santa Cruz River or a major tributary drainage with alluvial deposits) should determine if comparable depositional units are present. Such information could be ascertained during the testing phase of a class 3 survey, thereby identifying areas where buried cultural or faunal remains may be encountered. Identification of indurated red and yellow sand layers, like those found in Brickyard Arroyo and elsewhere in the Santa Cruz River floodplain, containing Archaic period cultural remains, would be an example of this kind of investigation. Backhoe trenching or core drilling, or both, could be used to determine the depositional history of a particular area and acquire data for a stratigraphic chronology.

How well the paleoenvironment can be reconstructed will depend on the location of the preferred Phase B canal alignment and the opportunities this alignment provides for obtaining the kinds of data necessary for these reconstructions. Where it crosses alluvial deposits, stratigraphic studies should be made and should include pollen, faunal, and radiometric studies when possible. Archaeological sites that will be directly impacted by canal construction need to be evaluated in terms of the kinds of data they can provide for stratigraphic studies and paleoenvironmental reconstructions. Stratigraphic, pollen, faunal, radiocarbon, hydrologic, and geomorphologic data potential all need to be evaluated during testing phases and when evaluating sites for excavation.

Should either the B-1 or B-2 route be selected as the preferred Phase B alternative, the opportunity to obtain significant paleoenvironmental data is considerably less than if Route B-5 were to be selected. As they are now defined, Routes B-1 and B-2 cross only small margins of the Brawley Wash floodplain. Consequently, the likelihood of obtaining the kinds of samples needed to provide paleoenvironmental data will most likely be minimal at best. The one possible exception may be pollen samples that could be obtained from drill core samples or trench profiles in certain floodplain, tributary wash, or other alluvial deposits along these routes.

The B-5 route offers a considerably better opportunity for acquiring paleoenvironmental data. This route crosses the Santa Cruz floodplain in several areas, providing an opportunity to sample floodplain stratigraphy and obtain pollen and other samples at different areas along the floodplain.

No matter which canal route is finally selected for construction, it should be accurately plotted on topographic maps and, if possible, on aerial photographs, and assessed in terms of its potential for providing paleoenvironmental data prior to the class 3 intensive survey. Areas where the alignment crosses alluvial deposits or other deposits likely to provide paleoenvironmental data should be identified and examined during the survey. Consultation at this time with specialists in alluvial stratigraphy, pollen and macrofloral analysis, paleohydrology, and geomorphology would help in identifying these particular areas. If these areas appear promising after being examined during the survey, they should be included in the testing program. Testing will enable archaeologists to determine if stratigraphy, pollen, hydrologic and other kinds of pertinent data are present at these sites, and whether more intensive studies are possible or even justified during the final data recovery phase. Continued consultation with specialists during analysis of the survey data will save time and money and insure that testing will focus on those sites most likely to yield paleoenvironmental data.

## Paleo-Indian and Archaic Research

### Jon S. Czaplicki

Except for two fragmentary and two complete Clovis points, virtually no other reliable evidence of Paleo-Indian occupation in the Phase B area exists. Other isolated Clovis points are known from surrounding areas,

and Clovis occupation has been documented for the San Pedro Valley; however, it remains to be definitely identified in the Santa Cruz and Avra valleys. As mentioned in Chapter 3, the lack of Paleo-Indian data is most likely due to sites of that period being deeply buried in the Santa Cruz floodplain. Whether this is the case for Avra Valley is not known.

Future Phase B archaeological investigations may report new surface finds of Paleo-Indian material that would provide additional indirect evidence for a Paleo-Indian presence in the area. There is no apparent reason why Clovis hunters and their families should not have occupied the Phase B area. Stratigraphic studies may identify the depositional units discussed by Haynes (1966) and known to contain Paleo-Indian material elsewhere in the Southwest. Even if evidence for a Clovis presence is not found, identification of these units would be important, alerting archaeologists to their presence and to the potential for finding Clovis or other Paleo-Indian material.

The presence of a cienega deposit and associated Pleistocene fauna indicates that swampy areas were present in Avra Valley, at one time and evidence for them can be found within several meters or less of the surface. Other arroyos in this area may show evidence of cienega deposits and possibly Paleo-Indian material associated with the deposits. It is important that survey crews examine all arroyos carefully for such evidence, and identify those that may provide stratigraphic data. Alluvial deposits in the Santa Cruz floodplain are very deep, and depositional units that may contain Paleo-Indian material may be buried considerably deeper than excavation for canal construction would reach. Similar deposits in Avra Valley may not be as deeply buried.

Archaic sites and numerous isolated projectile points in the Phase B area indicate occupation by Archaic people, and additional sites may be discovered during the class 3 survey. Buried sites in Avra Valley, but particularly in the stratigraphic studies identifying depositional units known to contain Archaic period material will enable archaeologists to identify areas in the canal corridor that may contain buried sites. The stratigraphic studies discussed previously for paleoenvironmental reconstruction can be used for documenting buried Paleo-Indian and Archaic site presence and potential.

Huckell (1982c) has defined two major problem domains for Archaic studies on the ANAMAX-Rosemont Mitigation Project: (1) subsistence-settlement strategy and (2) cultural-temporal affinities. These problem domains should be considered for future Phase B investigations; they will tie in directly to Huckell's study of Archaic occupation in the mountainous ANAMAX-Rosemont area of the Santa Rita Mountains southeast of the Phase B area, and the two studies together will provide much new data on the Archaic occupation of the Tucson Basin. Huckell (1982c: 8) sees the ANAMAX-Rosemont Archaic sites as an incomplete record of the subsistence-settlement system. They represent resource procurement and processing locales that were part of a seasonal round in an assumed, defined territorial range. The Phase B project area contains base and camp sites in addition to resource procurement sites and can provide settlement data that will complement Huckell's study.

In order to define the subsistence strategy of his sites, Huckell is looking at the paleoenvironment and using pollen, macrofossil, and faunal studies to aid in reconstruction. These studies will also attempt to identify the specific resources used by the Archaic families. Similar studies at Phase B sites can add to the paleoenvironmental record and provide information on riverine and bajada subsistence strategies.

The ANAMAX-Rosemont project will address cultural-temporal affinities, trying to relate Archaic groups in the ANAMAX area to those elsewhere in the Southwest (Huckell 1982c: 16). This needs to be done for the Phase B area, as pointed out in Chapter 3. The project area contains both Cochise and poorly-defined Amargosa cultural remains, and the relationship, if any, between them is not clear (see Bruce Huckell 1979: 19-20; 1980: 226; Westfall 1979: 35). Pinto Basin-style projectile points have been found in considerable quantities in the Avra Valley, suggesting some kind of relationship to Archaic groups typical of southern California and western Arizona. Certain Archaic sites in the preferred canal corridor may provide the data needed to better define this relationship. As Huckell points out (1982c: 16), perhaps it may be possible to do no more than define and describe these Archaic cultural entities, but it needs to be done in order to integrate the Archaic occupation of the area into a larger cultural framework. Lithic studies should be geared toward technological attributes and, as much as possible, toward functional analyses. These studies will be the primary basis for defining specific cultural relationships and are needed to interpret those sites that do not contain diagnostic projectile points, but are considered to be Archaic (see Rozen 1981).

Simmons (1981: 13) points out that a critical problem with aceramic site studies is the identification of their gross cultural affiliation. "Many researchers have *a priori* assumed that most aceramic sites relate to preceramic horizons; that is, Archaic, or more rarely, Paleo-Indian. This may be the case in most instances, but it is a tenuous assumption to make without supporting evidence." Simmons (1981: 14) goes on to say that an emphasis on lithic debitage may "ultimately provide researchers with greater precision in dealing with fundamental problems regarding aceramic sites. What is clear even now is that projectile points alone may not be as culturally diagnostic as initially thought." Aceramic lithic scatters are present in the project area, and their cultural affiliation is often noted as "unknown" or is assumed to be Archaic.

An important aspect of Archaic studies is better chronological control, without which support for ideas about cultural affinities or documentation of cultural or paleoenvironmental changes through time will be difficult (Huckell 1982c: 16). Radiocarbon dating should be an important goal of future Phase B investigations, and every effort should be made to identify sites (preferably stratified sites) having a potential for supplying datable organic material. These sites should be carefully assessed during the testing program.

Among other problems peculiar to the Phase B area is the question of a late Archaic-early Hohokam continuum (Gregonis and Huckell 1980: 13). The archaeological record for the Tucson Basin indicates an apparent gap between the late Archaic and the earliest Hohokam occupation. "It is improbable that a region as rich in natural resources as the Tucson Basin was completely uninhabited for this 300-year period. Recognizing that current knowledge of the late Archaic and early Hohokam periods is quite limited, it is possible that this gap is more apparent than real" (Gregonis and Huckell 1980: 13). New, as yet unpublished survey data from the Arizona State Museum's Tucson Basin Survey indicate that Pioneer period Hohokam sites are present in the floodplain-lower bajada transition zone along the Santa Cruz River in the northern part of the Phase B area. Several Archaic sites are recorded in the floodplain in this area, and future investigations may provide an opportunity to study the relationship between the Archaic and Pioneer period Hohokam occupations in the project area. Sites that may shed more light on this problem are most likely to be located in or immediately adjacent to the Santa Cruz floodplain, where late Archaic groups may have been experimenting with agriculture (see Hemmings and others 1968; Whalen 1973). The river would have been the only place where adequate water and the proper soil were available for such experimentation. Early Hohokam farmers would also have settled here for these same reasons. The Pantano Site on the east side of the basin yielded maize pollen and dated to the first centuries of the Christian era. Late Archaic groups were present in the basin, and the discovery of Pioneer period Hohokam sites may provide the data needed to answer the question of a late Archaic-Hohokam continuum, and may also provide data on late Archaic agricultural development and sedentism.

Paleo-Indian and Archaic studies in the Phase B area face potential limitations similar to those for paleoenvironmental studies. With either the B-1 or B-2 route the opportunities to study some of the problems discussed above will be limited, if for no other reason than the smaller number of known and expected Archaic sites along either route. Major floodplain areas where buried sites may exist are not crossed by either alignment as currently defined. Only one Archaic site—AZ AA:16:39—is directly impacted (by the B-1 and B-2 Indian Distribution Line), although the possibility for other Archaic campsites being located within either canal corridor is good, especially in areas adjacent to tributary drainages crossed by the canal. AZ AA:16:39 is important because it appears to have a Chiricahua or San Pedro stage Cochise component overlain by a Hohokam component, and may provide data on middle and late Archaic occupation of the Avra Valley, in addition to new information on Archaic lithic technology and possibly Archaic-Hohokam relationships.

The B-5 canal route may offer a somewhat better chance for Archaic studies because more such sites are known in and adjacent to the floodplain. No known Archaic sites are impacted by the current B-5 route, however.

The final Phase B canal route has not been selected, however, and may, in fact, be significantly modified from either of the three alternatives currently under consideration. Until the actual route is selected and its exact alignment determined, discussion about specific research problems that might be addressed by future studies will be somewhat limited. The construction corridor can vary in width from several hundred to a thousand or more feet. Once it and other related construction areas such as detention basins have been defined, areas likely to or known to contain unrecorded sites should be identified and earmarked for careful examination during the class 3 survey. Likewise, areas where buried Archaic sites may be present need to be identified. These areas may include washes, tributary drainages, and floodplain areas.

The class 3 intensive survey will locate and identify cultural resources in the preferred corridor. To avoid problems concerning inadequate site survey data, class 3 survey efforts should focus on accurate and detailed site mapping, systematic surface artifact collections, and an intensive testing program. The testing program is critical for assessing site significance and developing data recovery recommendations. Testing will enable archaeologists to define specific research problems that can be addressed at sites recommended for excavation.

Sites selected for testing need to be evaluated in terms of their potential for providing various kinds of data needed to address the questions discussed earlier in this section. Of particular importance is the problem of a late Archaic-early Hohokam continuum in the Tucson Basin. In the northern portion of the Phase B area several Pioneer period sites have been recorded and others have recently been identified by the Arizona State Museum Tucson Basin Survey along the lower bajada bordering the Santa Cruz floodplain. These sites may contain evidence of early Pioneer period occupation (Vahki, Estrella, and Sweetwater phases) and may also show a relationship to late Archaic groups that lived nearby in the floodplain. Although it does not appear that the current B-5 route will directly affect these sites, other Pioneer period sites may be located along the northern part of the route. Should Pioneer period sites be found during the class 3 survey, testing should focus on identifying

stratigraphic cultural sequences and obtaining definite evidence for early Pioneer period occupation. Even if no direct evidence for a late Archaic-early Hohokam relationship is found, identification of Vahki or other early Pioneer period components would be significant for interpretations of Hohokam develoment in the Tucson Basin and possibly for Hohokam origins in southern Arizona.

One late Pioneer period site (AZ AA:12:93), located south of the confluence of the Santa Cruz and Rillito Creek, appears to be directly impacted by the B-5 route, while still further south, another late Pioneer period site (AZ AA:16:49) is in the vicinity of the B-5 route. Both of these sites may contain early Pioneer period components that may provide evidence indicating a relationship to late Archaic groups.

Testing should also include pollen and flotation analyses at Archaic and early Pioneer period sites. Identification of economic pollen, especially early domesticates like maize (*Zea*), will indicate that additional studies may provide important data on agricultural development in the late Archaic and early Hohokam periods.

The B-5 route may provide similar opportunities to investigate middle and late Archaic occupations in the Middle Santa Cruz River Valley. A large Cochise period campsite or possibly a base camp (AZ AA:12:86), is within one-half mile of the current B-5 alignment. This site has been intensively surface collected and mapped, including the point proveniencing of collected surface artifacts. The collection, although in private hands, may be accessible for study. This site offers great potential for yielding new data on the middle and late Archaic of the Tucson Basin, and other similar sites may be located along the B-5 alignment.

Buried Archaic sites are scattered along the Santa Cruz floodplain and appear to concentrate at the southern end of the Phase B area in tributary channels downcutting into the alluvium. The class 3 survey should pay particular attention to identifying and investigating areas that are actively downcutting, which could yield either cultural evidence for Archaic occupations or stratigraphic evidence suggesting their possible presence.

West of the southern portion of the B-5 route, the B-1 and B-2 routes cut across the lower bajada of the Sierrita Mountains before terminating north of Green Valley. No Archaic sites are known in this area; however, they may be present. At least one large Archaic campsite has been reported by Henry Wallace of the Arizona State Museum in the lower bajada of the Santa Rita Mountains east of the floodplain. Archaic sites along this portion of the B-1 and B-2 routes are likely to occur adjacent to drainages cutting across the bajada, and may provide new data on settlement patterning and nonriverine subsistence practices.

Of the two proposed reservoir locations, the Cat Mountain site will directly impact two late Archaic sites (AZ AA:16:2 and 82). These are apparently campsites and are important because they are situated away from major riverine resources, and at least one of the sites may be a long-term base camp. While other Archaic sites may exist in the Cat Mountain Reservoir area, these two sites may contribute data on late Archaic settlement patterns and subsistence activities in a mountainous, nonriverine portion of the basin. No other Archaic sites are known in the mountainous areas of the Phase B project area.

The class 3 intensive survey of the preferred Phase B canal route, whether it runs down the Santa Cruz River floodplain or down the eastern side of the Avra Valley, will be a critical step towards identifying the cultural resources that will be directly or indirectly affected by canal construction. Site data must be accurate and as complete as possible in order to make reliable assessments of those sites to be selected for testing. While certain kinds of information— such as stratigraphic data, the presence of datable charcoal or buried features, or the degree of pollen and macrofloral preservation—cannot always be obtained from survey investigations, other kinds of data can be collected. Systematic surface artifact collections and recording, and detailed site mapping, will be important aspects of the survey that can provide data on site function and possibly intra- and intersite relationships. Lithic material is usually present in varying amounts and must not be overlooked. Archaic period sites can be expected to contribute new information on lithic manufacture and use. Even if these kinds of data are not available, descriptive data will aid in better defining Amargosan and Cochise lithic assemblages and possible relationships between these groups.

## Hohokam and Protohistoric Research

### by James D. Mayberry

One problem central to the archaeology of southern Arizona involves the "chaotic state of Hohokam archaeology" (Haury 1978:13). Although one absolute chronology has gained some acceptance (Haury 1976, Kelly 1978), potentially serious reservations about its validity remain (Doyel and Plog 1980; McGuire and Schiffer 1982; Plog 1980; Wilcox and Shenk 1977). The Pioneer period is the main point of contention; interpretations of its length vary from 800 years (Haury 1976) to 200 years or less (Gladwin 1942: 14; Plog 1980). The validity of the assumption of temporally distinct phases during the Pioneer period has also been questioned, with some writers suggesting that each Pioneer period phase overlaps with at least one other (Plog 1980).

The validity of the Salt-Gila Basin's relative and absolute chronologies has direct bearing on the archaeology of the project area as the Tucson Basin chronology has, from its formulation in the 1930s, been totally dependent on the Snaketown chronology (Kelly 1978; McGuire and Schiffer 1982). This assumption of a one-to-one relationship between the Salt-Gila and Tucson Basin chronologies is

contradicted by some data. The Rincon phase, which probably persisted 50 to 75 years *after* the end of the contemporary Sacaton phase of the Salt-Gila Basin, is one example (Greenleaf 1975a: 44; Masse 198 a: 126, 280). The probable existence of a late Sedentary Cortaro phase in the Tucson Basin has no defined counterpart in the Salt-Gila Basin due to a general rejection of its counterpart there, the Santan phase (Haury 1976: 338), there.

Many of the problems with absolute chronologies in the area result from the absence of a standard method in chronometric dating. As discussed elswhere (McGuire and Schiffer 1982), failure to maintain firm contextual control of samples for absolute dating can often result in "anomalous" chronometric dates. Rejection of absolute dates due to discrepancies with ceramically derived chronologies has been a common phenomenon in excavations in the area. Excavators have rejected all or most of their absolute dates at the Gu Achi and the Quijotoa Valley sites in the Papaguería (Masse 1980a: 186ff; Rosenthal and others 1978: 213), at the Baca Float sites in the Santa Cruz Valley (Doyel 1977b: 110) as well as in excavations in the Salt-Gila Basin (Doyel 1977a: 220; Haury 1976: 333). The tautology inherent in rejecting absolute dates not in agreement with preconceived chronologies derived from ceramic seriation is detailed elsewhere (McGuire and Schiffer 1982).

The ceramically derived chronologies devised for the Hohokam area can lead to further confusion in that they segment a cultural continuum, the evolution of decorated Hohokam ceramics, into mutually exclusive types defined by arbitrary criteria. Excavations in the Santa Cruz River Valley south of the project area yielded many ceramics that could not be definitely described as either Rillito Red-on-brown or Rincon Red-on-brown; over 75 percent of the sherds recovered from the Baca Float sites could only be termed "Rillito/Rincon Red-on-brown" (Doyel 1977b: 31). Excavation of the Hodges Site in the Tucson Basin, where the area's ceramic sequence was formulated, was complicated by the principal excavator's frequent inability to distinguish sherds and whole vessels of Rillito Red-on-brown from those of Rincon Red-on-brown (McGuire and Schiffer 1982: 312). A similar situation has been noted for the contemporary wares from the Salt-Gila Basin: Santa Cruz Red-on-buff and Sacaton Red-on-buff (Gladwin 1948: 51).

Supposedly diagnostic Hohokam ceramic types have often proved to be as ambiguous geographically as they are temporally. The late Colonial ware of the Papaguería, Vamori Red-on-brown, is all but identical to Rillito Red-on-brown (McGuire and Schiffer 1982). The diagnostic attributes of the principal Sedentary period decorated wares of the two areas, Topawa Red-on-brown and Rincon Red-on-brown, are also quite indistinct. This has led some (McGuire and Schiffer 1982: 183) to question the validity of the Colonial and Sedentary period Papaguería decorated types as distinct ceramic wares. The

Tucson Basin wares and contemporary Dragoon Red-on-browns of southeastern Arizona have also been termed "indistinguishable" and "too close to call" in many cases (Fulton and Tuthill 1940: 47). Just as the unnamed plain ware of the Tucson Basin would benefit from further study, the formal descriptions of decorated ceramic types from the area need further refinement.

Methodological problems are not the only problematic aspects of the basin's prehistory. Interpretation of the archaeological record itself is often hampered by poorly understood formation and preservation processes. Archaeological clearances and overviews in the area have often relied on surface evidence alone, ignoring the high incidence of buried sites in the Tucson Basin and the Papaguería (Doyel 1979; Masse 1980a). Many Hohokam sites have been recorded at depths ranging from 1 m to 4 m in the floodplains of the project area and elsewhere, often without visible associated surface remains (Doyel 1979: 1; Withers 1973: 5). A high incidence of sites with subsurface features but without surface features has been noted throughout southern Arizona (Teague 1982). Many sites without surface features other than artifact scatters have, upon excavation, yielded extensive subsurface loci, including intact architecture (Masse 1980a: 191; Rosenthal and others 1978).

Differential preservation of artifacts due to weathering or scavenging by later populations has also been a widespread phenomenon in the area (Masse 1980a: 195; Russell 1908). If prehistoric tool assemblages contained high proportions of wooden artifacts as did those of Historic Native American groups, the majority of a site's material culture cannot be expected to have survived archaeological deposition (Masse 1980a: 195; Withers 1973: 70).

Physical impacts to the archaeological record of southern Arizona have long been recognized as posing serious problems in the interpretation of past lifeways (Gladwin and others 1937: 21). In the project area these range from natural processes such as erosion, alluvation, and rodent-mixing (Doyel 1979: 2; Haury 1976) to urbanization (Rozen 1979b; Betancourt 1978b) and agricultural activities (Betancourt 1978b: 51; Schreiber and others 1981: 126). In the heavily urbanized Tucson Basin the majority of recorded sites in several survey areas have been so impacted as to be considered destroyed (Betancourt 1978b: 87; Rozen 1979: 19).

Previous archeological research can also produce biases resulting in unrepresentative site samples. The location of the majority of archaeological investigations, both surveys and excavations, in alluvial floodplains has undoubtedly led to overrepresentation of such areas in terms of recorded sites (McCarthy and Sires 1981: 27). Conversely, bajada and mountain areas are probably seriously underrepresented in the archaeological record.

Future survey along Routes B-1 and B-2, as well as the B-1 and B-2 "Alternate" lines, the B-1, B-2 and B-5 Indian lines, the various feeder lines, and the reservoir and sump

sites has the potential to redress these biases. Detailed mapping, surface collection and excavation of Hohokam sites in the montane and bajada environments in the project area could add significantly to knowledge of Hohokam adaptations to such areas. Such sites include AZ AA:16:16 in the Twin Hills Reservoir area and AZ AA:16:78 and 82 in the Cat Mountain Reservoir area.

Further biases result from differential definitions of sites and 'nonsites", uneven survey crew spacing, and nonsystematic research designs or techniques. A detailed consideration of such potential biases can be found in Wells and Schiffer (1982). Undoubtedly one result of these biases has been an artificial and misleading picture of prehistoric adaptive patterns.

Knowledge of past environments in the area has also been hampered by problems with the data base. The absence of firm dendrochronological data in most of southern Arizona has predicated a reliance on palynological data in most paleoenvironmental reconstructions, evidence open to a variety of potential biases. These include the differential production of pollen by various species (Euler and others 1979: 1095); desert species in particular produce relatively little pollen (Schreiber and others 1981: 250). Potential effects on environmental reconstruction can be gauged by the following example: due to the low pollen production of most desert species, a pollen sample taken in Phoenix during the winter of 1957-1958 contained substantially greater amounts of pine pollen than mesquite pollen, despite the dominance of the latter in local vegetation communities (Martin 1963: 15). Recent work in the Salt-Gila Basin has indicated that desert arboreal species such as desert willow (*Chilopsis linearis*) and blue palo verde (*Cercidium floridum*) may provide dendrochronological data comparable to that obtained from ponderosa pine, juniper and other conifers (Miksicek 1982). Such developments—if they actually work—could provide badly needed chronometric dates for archaeological sites throughout southern Arizona.

Pollen samples from archaeological contexts are also open to sources of potential error. Much of this is due to the fact that samples from archaeological contexts do not necessarily reflect actual vegetation communities of the area during the occupation of a site. Cheno-ams and other vegetation types thriving in disturbed soils are often seriously overrepresented in palynological samples from archaeological sites, a factor often not corrected for in palynological analysis (Grebinger and Adams 1978; Rosenthal and others 1978: 270). Edaphic conditions such as sheetwash or prevailing wind currents can also result in nonrepresentative pollen samples (Rosenthal and others 1978: 264).

Once potential biases and interpretive problems have been recognized, a variety of topics, both general and specific, may be addressed in the Phase B area. Testing of existing archaeological models offers one approach, as conflicting theories exist for a number of concerns current in

Hohokam prehistory. Three general "cultural historical" models exist: the traditional "Gladwinian" model (Gladwin and others 1937; Haury 1976; Masse 1980a); the "Ootam/Hohokam" model (Di Peso 1956, 1974; Hayden 1970) and "systemic" models that reject the association of a single population with Hohokam artifact assemblages (Doyel 1977a; Wilcox 1979a).

Related to these views are divergent models of the origins of the Tucson Basin Hohokam; one would have the area colonized by Salt-Gila Hohokam (Doyel 1977b; Masse 1979, 1980a); others envisage purely local origins for the ceramic agriculturalists of the area (Greenleaf 1975a; Wilcox 1979a; Zahniser 1966). Two Pioneer period sites (AZ AA:12:93 and AA:16:49) may be impacted by Route B-5. Mitigation involving such early sites may provide valuable data on the origins of the Tucson Basin Hohokam as well as data on a possible Archaic-Hohokam continuum.

The subsistence practices of the Hohokam have also been the subject of divergent models; one would have irrigation agriculture as the principal subsistence strategy (Bohrer and others 1969; Grebinger 1971a, b, 1976). Others stress the exploitation of wild resources by the Hohokam (Plog 1980). Many have viewed the Hohokam as pursuing a broad-based subsistence strategy, involving several types of agriculture as well as use of wild plant foods (Doyel 1977b; Haury 1976). Recent work in the Salt-Gila Basin supports this latter view (Crown 1982). Excavations or testing of agricultural features may aid in determining prehistoric agricultural processes.

The transition to the Classic period has inspired probably more models than any other development in the area's prehistory. Most models fall into one of three mutually exclusive groups. One associates changes of the Classic with changing environmental conditions (Grebinger 1971a, 1976; Weaver 1972). Another group would associate the changes of the Classic with ethnic migrations into the area, either by Saladoans from the Globe-Miami area (Haury 1945, 1976; Hayden 1957), or the changing status of native "Ootam" under their Hohokam overlords (Di Peso 1956, 1974; Hayden 1970).

Other models have associated the changes evident in the Classic with internal reorganization of the Hohokam (Doyel 1977a; Grady 1976; Wasley 1966; Wasley and Doyel 1980; Wilcox 1979a). Recent data from the Salt-Gila Basin suggest that many of the changes of the Sedentary to Classic transition are more superficial than substantial; archaeologists, by stressing discontinuities in material culture, have failed to recognize the basic continuity between the Preclassic and Classic Hohokam (Teague 1982). Several sites in the project area with Rincon and Tanque Verde phase components offer opportunities to test assumptions of the Sedentary-Classic transition. Such sites to be impacted by Route B-5 include AZ AA:16:19 and 46, and possibly AZ AA:16:14.

A final general topic receiving differing interpretations involves the relationship of the Hohokam with other precontact groups. Models have ranged from those rejecting a genetic relationship between the Hohokam and the Historic Pima and Papago (Doelle 1981; Fontana and others 1962; Masse 1980a) to those supporting a "Hohokam-Pima Continuum" (Di Peso 1956, 1974; Goodyear 1977; Haury 1976; Rosenthal and others 1978). A third group favors an "Archaic-Hohokam-Piman Continuum" (Grady 1976; Wasley 1966; Wilcox and Shenk 1977). Testing of the various assumptions of these models could employ existing data and collections as well as data gathered in a Class 3 survey and subsequent mitigation in the Phase B area.

A number of more specific topics of archaeological concern might also be addressed during further work in the Phase B area. One of these is the nature of the Hohokam occupation of agriculturally marginal areas such as Avra Valley. Recorded sites within the B-1 and B-2 corridors in Avra Valley include AZ AA:12:71 and AZ AA:16:85. Another site, AZ AA:16:39, is to be directly impacted by the B-1 and B-2 Indian Delivery Line. Detailed surface collection and excavation of these sites could aid understanding of the Hohokam adaptation to the Sonora Desert.

Another topic that may also be addressed at Hohokam sites in the project area is the role of the Tucson Basin in prehistoric interregional exchange systems. One such system that has received particular attention is represented by the spread of marine shell throughout the Southwest. One site immediately outside of the project area, the Hodges site, has been seen as a major center in the manufacture and distribution of marine shell (Kelly 1978: 111). Comparable amounts of marine shell have been recorded at one site within the B-5 alignment, AZ AA:16:25. Further excavation here may clarify the role of the local Hohokam in this far-flung system.

Another research question that may be addressed at Hohokam sites within the project area involves the role of possible integrative mechanisms known as ballcourts. One site to be directly impacted by Route B-5, AZ AA:16:25, contains a ballcourt. As only one ballcourt feature has ever been tested in the Tucson Basin (Kelly 1978), further study may provide valuable information as to the actual role of these enigmatic structures.

Agricultural features associated with dry farming are yet another avenue of research. One site with such features, AZ AA:12:206, is to be directly impacted by Route B-5. Dry farming features have also been recorded within the B-5 corridor to the west of Tumamoc Hill (Masse 1979).

Numerous other topics of archaeological concern may be addressed during further work in the project area. One involves possible temporally and geographically sensitive variables in the unnamed Tucson Basin plain wares. Previous attempts at microanalysis of undecorated ceramics have revealed such variables in the plain wares of both the Papaguería (Masse 1980a; Rosenthal and others 1978) and the Salt-Gila Basin (Rice and others 1979). Given the large number of sites without decorated wares in the project area and the high proportion of plain ware at Hohokam sites, surface collection could provide a diverse sample of plain wares. The majority of plainware sites are within the B-5 corridor but a number of such sites are also in the B-1 and B-2 alignments.

Further work involving ceramics includes a host of other topics. Determination of the effects of different raw materials on brown wares of the Tucson Basin and buff wares of the Salt-Gila Basin could be crucial to the understanding of the Pioneer period and possible relationships between local populations and the Hohokam of the Salt-Gila Basin (see Chapter 4, this volume). Clarification of the relationships between the Tucson Basin brown wares and those of the Papaguería might also be possible. The validity of the Papaguerían types Vamori and Topawa Red-on-brown could also be examined.

The roles of Sells Red and Sells Plain in local ceramic traditions remain problematic; some have associated these wares with intrusive ethnic groups affiliated with the Trincheras and Mogollon cultures (Masse 1980a). Others dispute this, citing the developmental continuity of Sells phase ceramics with local Preclassic traditions of the Papaguería and Tucson Basin (Haury and others 1975; Rosenthal and others 1978). At least one site, AZ AA:16:48, recorded as having Sells Red ceramics, will be impacted by Route B-5. Surface collection from this and possibly other sites could aid in clarifying the position of Sells Red and Sells Plain in local ceramic traditions.

Refinement of current definitions of several prehistoric decorated wares could establish greater chronologial control of many Hohokam sites. Better definition of Rillito and Rincon Red-on-brown could eliminate the tendency to type many samples as Rillito/Rincon Red-on-brown (Doyel 1977b). This could be attempted at sites with components of both phases. Other sites with both late Colonial and Sedentary components to be impacted by Route B-5 include: AZ AA:12:102 and AZ AA:16:45. More precise definition of the latter type could also allow the firm identification of a late Sedentary "Cortaro" Red-on-brown, clarifying conditions in the late Sedentary, a poorly understood period in Tucson Basin prehistory. At least one site with "Cortaro" Red-on-brown (AZ BB:13:126) will be directly impacted by Route B-5.

Analysis of the decorative microtraditions of Tanque Verde Red-on-brown might lead to the definition of temporally distinct variants of that type, allowing for the isolation of late Classic red-on-browns from early Classic wares. This would eliminate reliance on Saladoan polychromes as the primary criteria for identification of late Classic assemblages. This may prove feasible at sites with both early and late Classic components. Several of these (AZ AA:12:36, 46, and 107) are within the B-5 corridor.

Such stylistic studies might also establish the point of origin of Tanque Verde Red-on-brown in either the Papaguería (Masse 1980a; Rosenthal and others 1978) or the Tucson Basin (Kelly 1978). Relationships between the Classic period ceramics of several areas might also be studied, including possible connections between Tanque Verde Red-on-brown, Casa Grande Red-on-buff, and San Carlos Red-on-brown. This may be accomplished at sites with early Classic components. Several such sites may be impacted by Route B-5, including AZ AA:12:118 and 97 and AZ BB:13:48 and 126.

Two areas in dire need of more detailed ceramic analysis are the early Historic and Protohistoric periods. Except for a limited number of studies (Fontana and others 1962; Wilcox and Masse 1981a) the ceramics of the Historic Pima, Sobaipuri, and Papago have been grossly neglected. Better temporal and formal definition of the various Pima wares, and their possible relationships with prehistoric ceramics, offer great potential in furthering current understanding of the post-Hohokam occupations of southern Arizona. Even the most cursory analysis and description of the poorly defined Piman plain ware would be a significant accomplishment. The temporal and cultural associations of Whetstone Plain Ware also need further study, in light of recent reevaluations suggesting that this "Protohistoric" ware may postdate the entry of the Spanish into the area (Wilcox and Masse 1981a). A possible Protohistoric and early Historic occupation is found in the B-5 corridor at AZ AA:12:108.

Another problem domain in the archaeology of the area that may be addressed involves buried sites. Ongoing survey by the Arizona State Museum's Tortolita Area Plan Study indicates differential rates of alluviation in the Tucson Basin. In the project area the floodplain of the Santa Cruz north of the confluences of Rillito Creek and the Cañada del Oro seems to be one area with a much more rapid rate of sedimentation. This could result in a relatively higher incidence of buried sites; given the relative abundance of early Pioneer period sites in this region more early Hohokam sites may be sealed under heavy alluvial overburdens. The potential for further study of the Archaic-Hohokam transition along the northernmost reaches of Routes B-1, B-2, and B-5 may include unique opportunities due to the presence of relatively undisturbed buried Pioneer period sites.

Detailed surface mapping and excavation of Hohokam sites in the Phase B area may provide opportunities to study intrasite structure and site formation processes. Although Hohokam sites are often assumed to be, for the most part, nonnucleated *rancherias* with little or no internal organization, recent work (Wilcox and others 1981) has contradicted this. Careful examination of the changing spatial distributions of architectural and extramural features at the site of Snaketown have revealed a dynamic and surprisingly complex intrasite system. Given the large size of many Class I and II sites within the Phase B area, similar intrasite studies may reveal such patterning at Tucson Basin Hohokam sites as well. Especially promising for such studies are several large sites within the B-5 corridor: AZ

AA:12:46, 96, 118; AZ AA:16:25, 45; and AZ BB:13:126. The division of the Sobaipuri village of Bac into three distinct *barrios* (Doelle 1981: 67) offers evidence that intrasite organization existed in the Tucson Basin as late as the eighteenth century.

Intersite relations may also be addressed in the Phase B area by studying extant trail systems linking prehistoric sites. Such analysis has already been performed in the project area, establishing the association of defensive trincheras systems with several Hohokam village sites (Fontana and others 1959; Hartmann and Hartmann 1979). Similar studies of trail systems linking prehistoric village sites have also been performed elsewhere in southern Arizona (Wilcox and others 1981). Trail systems may exist in the Route B-5 alignment near Tumamoc and Martinez Hills (Hartmann and Hartmann 1979).

Intersite organization may also be addressed through analysis and mapping of canal systems (Haury 1945, 1976) and dry farming features, including agricultural trincheras. Study of ceramic microtraditions also has the potential to demonstrate intersite relationships. Previous work in the area (Grebinger 1971a; Grebinger and Adam 1978) has attempted to show the movement of populations between several sites in the Tucson Basin during the Classic period. One of these sites, AZ AA:12:46, is in the B-5 alignment; others may be found in the project area.

The dynamics of interregional contacts and exchange systems may also be addressed at sites in the Project area by analysis of intrusive ceramics and lithics obtained through surface collections or excavations. The relative abundance of nonlocal ceramics at many sites in the area points to extensive contacts between the Tucson Basin and much of the Southwest. Nonlocal ceramics have been recorded at several sites either directly impacted by or located within Route B-5, including AZ AA:12:46, 93, and 118, and AZ AA:16:25. Intrusive ceramics have also been noted at sites to be directly impacted by the B-1 and B-2 Indian Delivery Line (AZ AA:16:39).

Study of agricultural features in the project area can aid in the understanding of Hohokam subsistence practices. Research already performed (Downum and others 1980; Wallace in press) suggests that many agricultural trincheras and other 'dry farming' features were the loci of a number of subsistences and occupational activities. One site with dry farming features will be directly impacted by the B-5 alignment (AZ AA:12:206); areas in the B-5 corridor west of Tumamoc Hill are also reported to contain extensive dry farming features (Masse 1979). Analysis of floral remains from archaeological contexts in the area have illustrated a diversity of domestic and wild plants used by the Hohokam. Identification of an astronomical sighting system at a Classic period site northeast of the project area (Hewitt and Stephen 1981) with rock alignments apparently used for timing agricultural activities suggests the existence of a sophisticated agricultural scheduling system in the Tucson

Basin, similar to that proposed for other areas in southern Arizona (Wilcox and Sternberg 1981). Since several large Classic period sites will be impacted by Route B-5, further survey and site structure analysis may reveal additional astronomical systems in the Tucson Basin.

Areas where the B-1 and B-2 routes cross alluvial fans emanating from the Tucson Mountains may offer opportunities to study *ak chin* farming systems. Previous survey has indicated a high correlation between such landforms and sites associated with *ak chin* systems (Wilson 1981). The majority of these are dated to the late Sedentary, the period when this highly productive strategy may have been first employed. Evidence for irrigation systems may also be revealed by further survey or excavation in the project area, primarily within the floodplain of the Santa Cruz River.

The B-1 and B-2 routes enter the Santa Cruz floodplain only at the northern end of Phase B; therefore, evidence for irrigation systems will most likely be encountered along the B-5 route, which crosses the Santa Cruz floodplain in several areas. One site which lies in the Route B-5 corridor, AZ AA:12:118, has canals recorded in association with Classic period components (ASM site files). Previous survey in the area has also illustrated a diverse assemblage of dry farming features associated with both the Hohokam (Masse 1979) and Protohistoric groups (Rozen 1979a: 60). Again the B-5 alignment holds the greatest potential for the further recording of dry farming features.

Another topic that may be profitably addressed in the Phase B area involves the end of the Classic period and the processes of abandonment. Different processes seem to have occurred in the abandonment of several Classic sites in the Tucson Basin; some appear to have been abandoned *en masse*, with many structures being burned (Grebinger 1971a; Grebinger and Adam 1978). Other sites give evidence for a reduced remnant population lingering after the majority of the site was no longer occupied (Hayden 1957; Wright and Gerald 1950). Detailed site mapping and excavation of any of the Tucson phase sites in the project area may clarify the demographic events represented by the unfortunately vague term "abandonment." At present all of the recorded late Classic sites in the project area are in the Route B-5 corridor, including AZ AA:12:36, 46 and 107.

The presence of a relatively large sedentary population in the Tucson Basin at the time of initial contact by Europeans in the late seventeenth century (Doelle 1981) is not represented by recorded archaeological data. Further survey, specifically oriented towards identification of Piman components and sites could revolutionize current understanding of the Protohistoric period. As previously discussed, this will be difficult until available descriptions of post-Hohokam material cultural assemblages are refined. The close similarities in the distribution of sites dating to the late Classic and early Historic periods (Betancourt 1978b) suggests that sites spanning both periods may exist within the project area. Recognition and excavation of such a site could prove to be of lasting significance, not only to the prehistory of the Tucson Basin but the entire Southwest. Recorded Protohistoric and early Historic sites in the project area include AZ AA:12:108 along Route B-5.

As may be gathered from this discussion, the variety of potential research topics is greater for sites in the Route B-5 corridor than in either the B-1 or B-2 routes. This is due primarily to the abundance of recorded sites in the Santa Cruz Valley relative to the Avra Valley. However, the archaeology of the latter area is so poorly known that even the limited number of potential research topics that can be investigated at sites in the B-1 and B-2 corridors would be a significant addition to the archaeology of the area. Whichever route is finally selected, the adoption of a systematic, problem-oriented research design, to be implemented in a multidisciplinary approach during the class 3 survey and subsequent mitigation, has great potential in providing new data on the prehistory of both the Tucson Basin and the Avra Valley.

Beyond this, there is great interest with respect to a broader problem area, that of regional integration, and change in the kind and level of this integration, through time. Traditionally one of those areas labelled "peripheral" to a Hohokam core, the Tucson Basin and comparable areas elsewhere can now be understood in terms of differentiated but nevertheless integrated elements in a complex regional system that involved ties of many kinds, as yet poorly understood. Comparison of economy, social organization, and material culture in the Tucson Basin and in other parts of the Hohokam system would permit significant advances in our understanding of this. Even more than some other so-called "peripheral" areas, the Tucson Basin has the potential to produce data useful in addressing the earliest mechanisms of Hohokam development, the roles of basic subsistence economy and trade in shaping the nature of Hohokam groups throughout the sequence, and the changing relationship of the Hohokam to adjacent cultural systems.

## Historic Research

### *James E. Ayres*

In assessing the research potential of historic sites in the study area, it is necessary to consider the archaeological and historical research values or qualities that characterize these sites in relation to National Register of Historic Places eligibility criteria. Specifically, National Register Criterion for Evaluation *d*, relating to resources "that have yielded, or may be likely to yield, information important in prehistory or history" addresses the issue of research potential most directly.

It should be noted, as well, that many of these sites also possess qualities or values (for example, public interpretive potential, religious importance, ethnic importance) that do not relate to their research potential but that are nevertheless important and would in part support their inclusion on the National Register. Fifty sites appear either to be associated with events that have made a significant contribution to the broad patterns of our history, to be associated with the lives of persons significant in our past, or to embody the distinctive characteristics of a type, period, or method of construction (National Register Criteria for Evaluation *a*, *b*, and *c* respectively). These sites, the majority of which consist of buildings or structures that are still in use, include 5 ranch-farm related properties, 5 small communities, 1 transportation feature, 4 properties with religious association, 17 residential-related, and 9 miscellaneous properties.

As this category of historic sites—those that are not primarily important for information pertaining to archaeological and historical research interests that they contain—is considered during subsequent phases of the Central Arizona Project planning process, it will therefore be necessary to consider values *in addition to* those related to research potential, and to apply procedures for impact mitigation as appropriate to the value of each site.

The remaining historic sites in the study area primarily possess qualities that would apply to National Register Criterion for Evaluation *d* above; that is, they have yielded, or may be likely to yield, information important to historical archaeology. Several of these sites manifest, in addition, qualities relevant to criteria *a*, *b*, and *c*.

One primary objective of any research project involving historic cultural resources is to establish and verify the basic cultural history of a site or community of sites. Using documentary sources and the results of an evaluation of archaeological site data, including artifacts and the relationships between the distribution of artifacts and cultural features, an attempt should be made to determine the dates of occupation, site function, and cultural and ethnic affiliation. Once this basic cultural history objective has been achieved, it is then appropriate to consider more specific research oriented goals.

One area of general research interest within the discipline of historical archaeology, the analysis of settlement or community cultural patterning, is applicable to the study area sites and, if properly addressed, is capable of producing meaningful scientific information that would otherwise be unavailable. For example, the process of settlement in the Tucson area might be characterized as one of gradual population increase through time accompanied by a concomitant increase in social, cultural, economic, technological, and religious diversity and complexity. The sites in the study area would be useful for addressing questions pertaining to this hypothetical settlement process; such questions might relate to the dynamics of urbanization, to changing settlement patterns through time, to the ethnic composition of different areas at different times, and to the nature of cultural diversity and complexity.

More specifically, each of the proposed Phase B corridors is briefly examined below in relation to its historical archaeological research potential (from the perspective of site-functional categories represented within the corridor).

Although Corridors B-1, B-2, and B-5 begin and end in approximately the same locations, they diverge through the greater part of their lengths. Corridors B-1 and B-2 are located on the west side of the Tucson Mountains, and Corridor B-5 is situated along the Santa Cruz River on the east side of the Tucson Mountains. Each corridor passes through all three of the major physiographic zones discussed in Chapter 5, and sites from all nine functional categories are found to be in or near each of the corridors.

The siting of a Tucson Aqueduct feature on the east side of the Tucson Mountains (Corridor B-5) would potentially affect a greater number of sites than would its location on the west side (Corridors B-1 and B-2). The more sites involved, the greater the number of research questions that can be addressed and successfully answered.

Sites on the east side, organized from the perspective of functional categories, would have the potential to produce information on a number of research interests in addition to those pertaining to cultural history and settlement patterning, as follows:

Residence and Ranch-Farm
   architectural preferences through time and between
      ethnic groups;
   ethnic composition of occupants;
   economic status of occupants;
   level of homesteading (HE) or stockraising homestead-
      ing (SRHE) activity in the project area;
   food procurement, processing, and dietary behavior;
   interaction with small communities and Tucson urban
      area.

Towns
   layout and location of small communities;
   role of the small community within its economic,
      political, and social sphere;
   reasons for small community development;
      interaction with ranchers, farmers, and the Tucson
      urban area

Mining
   sequence and technology of ore extraction and pro-
      cessing;
   recycling of material culture;
   ethnic composition of miners;
   economics of mining and miners;
   food procurement, processing, and dietary behavior;
   interaction with small communities and the Tucson
      urban area.

Transportation
   development and characteristics of historic road and
      railroad;
   networks (This area of research could best be addressed
      through the use of documentary, rather than ar-
      chaeological, sources).

Water Control
   process of development and use of water resources;
   effect on settlement;
   effect on social stratification;
   effect on, and relationship to, the local economy

Trash Deposition
   trash disposal patterns;
   ethnic and economic aspects of trash disposal behavior

Religion
   Religion is represented by a number of cemeteries and
   isolated burials that would probably not be available
   for archaeological research. The cemeteries are on the
   San Xavier Indian Reservation. If these were available
   for study, information about Papago Indian religion
   and burial practices through time could result.

Miscellaneous
   Nine of the miscellaneous sites are not *primarily* important for the archaeological information they are likely
   to yield but all would have the potential for producing
   some archaeological information. The remainder include the site of a former school, remains of three
   commercial enterprises along the Santa Cruz River,
   and an area of rock and earth ridges or terraces. The
   school site may produce information on the architecture of turn-of-the-century rural schools, on ethnic
   composition, student age and sex, and on the relative
   range of student status within the school. Information
   on the ethnic composition of business owners and cus-
   tomers and on the type of products or services involved
   may be produced from the remains of commercial activities. The site containing the rock and earth ridges
   may have to be tested before meaningful questions
   beyond who constructed the site, when, and for what
   purpose can be asked.

Areas of potential research interest are extensive for the historic resources located on the west side of the Tucson Mountains (Corridors B-1 and B-2), although fewer sites are present than on the east side. It is believed, however, that the research potential of the west side corridor is comparable to the east side on a site-specific basis and in terms of categories of research interest. In particular, the number of small towns, residences, ranches and farms, religious sites, and water control sites are represented by substantially smaller numbers. A less complex transportation network was present historically as well. The miscellaneous functional category is only represented by two sites, the Civilian Conservation Corps camps.

The Civilian Conservation Corps camps can be expected to produce information on the composition and structure of all-male quasi-military camps: the type of architecture utilized, foodways and dietary behavior, ethnic composition, social stratification, and the nature of activities that took place at the sites.

The areas of research interest listed above that may be meaningfully addressed at the sites identified in the project area should not be interpreted as representing an inclusive list.

A class 3 intensive survey along the selected Tucson Aqueduct route (either B-1, B-2, or B-5) is expected to encounter a number of historic sites, both those identified by the class 2 study and additional sites that were not represented on the historical documentation available. Given the level of knowledge about historic sites in the Tucson area, research questions appropriately formulated for an intensive survey might include those listed above. The most meaningful, however, for a linear survey would include those relating to culture history.

Although no Papago Indian sites could be identified be-yond the boundary of the San Xavier Reservation, it is likely that temporary Papago saguaro fruit gathering camps were present historically in and around the Tucson Mountains. Examples of these camps may be discovered during the intensive survey.

The placement of reservoirs in the Twin Hills or Cat Mountain area will affect historic sites. Two sites were recorded during the class 2 survey for the Twin Hills location and only three, CM-30, a well and enclosure, CM-29, the Starr Pass Road, and CM-28, a building, were documented within the Cat Mountain reservoir. A number of mining and other sites located in the mountainous terrain surrounding both reservoirs were discovered in the historical documentation. Given the large number of historic mining sites reported in the Tucson Mountains generally and in the Twin Hills-Cat Mountain area specifically, it can be reasonably predicted that several sites related to mining will be located by an intensive survey within the proposed confines of both reservoirs.

These mining sites would be likely to yield information on the historic sequence and technology of ore extraction and processing, culture history of mining in the southern Tucson Mountains, and on other mining-site-related research topics.

# Appendix A

# PREHISTORIC AND PROTOHISTORIC SITES BY CLASS IN ALTERNATE (ONE MILE WIDE) CORRIDORS

## James D. Mayberry and Jon S. Czaplicki

*1. Route(s) B-1 and B-2*
Class II sites
artifact scatters: AZ AA:12:125, 128; AZ AA:16:85

*2. Route B-2 Alternate*
Class II sites
artifact scatters: AZ AA:12:70, 133
artifact scatter and hearth: AZ AA:12:71
Class III sites
rock art: AZ AA:12:63

*3. Avra Valley Feeder Line*
Class I sites
village: AZ AA:12:57, 58, 87, 88
Class II sites
artifact scatters: AZ AA:12:125, 158, 160, 161
artifact scatters with rock art: AZ AA:12:73
trincheras: AZ AA:16:12

*4. Routes B-1 and B-2 Indian Distribution Line*
Class II sites
artifact scatters: AZ AA:16:39

*5. Route B-1 Alternate*
No recorded prehistoric sites

*6. Route(s) B-1 and B-2 CM and TH Feeder Lines*
Class II sites
quarry: AZ AA:16:78
artifact scatter with stone features: AZ AA:16:81

*7. Route B-5*
Class I sites
village: AZ AA:12:118, AZ AA:16:45, 46, 49, 53; AZ BB:13:16, 41, 45, 48, 50
village with pithouse(s): AZ AA:12:9, 10, 11, 36, 46, 56, 93, 95; AZ AA:16
village with mound(s): AZ AA:12:59
village with ballcourt: AZ AA:16:25; AZ BB:13:18(?)
village with houses: AZ AA:12:107
Class II sites
artifact scatters: AZ AA:12:1, 2, 42, 96, 97, 102, 104, 105, 111, 159, 162, 164, 165, 166, 193; AZ AA:16:4, 14, 15, 18, 19, 21, 60, 67, 68, 86; AZ BB:13:43, 44, 75, 126, 148
artifacts scatters and hearth(s): AZ AA:12:38, 86
artifact scatters with mound(s): AZ AA:12:113
artifact scatters and stone features: AZ AA:12:108, 163, 206; AZ BB:13:42
canals: AZ AA:12:92
pits: AZ AA:12:100
artifact scatters with bedrock mortars: AZ AA:16:48, 54
artifact scatters with cremations: AZ BB:13:14
Class III sites
cremations: AZ AA:16:33

*8. Route B-5 Indian Distribution Line*
Class II sites
artifact scatters and stone features: AZ AA:16:76

9. *Twin Hills Reservoir*
   Class II sites
      *artifact scatter with stone features and rock art:*
      AZ AA:16:16

10. *Cat Mountain Reservoir*
    Class II sites
       *artifact scatters:* AZ AA:16:2, 82 (both are Archaic; 82
       may be a campsite)

11. *B-5 TH and CM Feeder Lines*
    No recorded prehistoric sites

12. *Marana Sump and Feeder Routes to B-1, B-2, and B-5*
    Class I sites recorded prehistoric sites
       *village:* AZ AA:12:368
    Class II sites
       *artifact scatter:* AZ AA:12:208, 209, 211, 212, 354,
          355, 357
       *artifact scatter with horno:* AZ AA:12:358

TABLE A.1

**Prehistoric Sites**

| Routes | Class I | Class II | Class III | Total |
|---|---|---|---|---|
| B-1 and B-2 | 0 | 3 | 0 | 3 |
| B-2 Alternate | 0 | 3 | 1 | 4 |
| Avra Valley Feeder Line | 4 | 6 | 0 | 10 |
| B-1 and B-2 I.D.L. | 0 | 1 | 0 | 1 |
| B-1 Alternate | 0 | 0 | 0 | 0 |
| B-1 and B-2 CM, TH Feeder Lines | 0 | 2 | 0 | 2 |
| B-5 | 23 | 42 | 1 | 66 |
| B-5 I.D.L. | 0 | 1 | 0 | 1 |
| Twin Hills Reservoir | 0 | 1 | 0 | 1 |
| Cat Mt. Reservoir | 0 | 2 | 0 | 2 |
| B-5 CM, TH Feeder Lines | 0 | 0 | 0 | 0 |
| Marana Sump and Feeders to B-1, B-2, B-5 | 1 | 8 | 0 | 9 |
| Totals | 29 | 69 | 2 | 99 |

# Appendix B

# HISTORIC SITE INVENTORY

## James E. Ayres

This appendix contains nine categories of information beginning with Inventory Number. Each of the 11 USGS quadrangle maps covering the study area has its own listing of numbers except the Twin Buttes quadrangle in which no sites were located. The inventory number was assigned consecutively for each quadrangle map in the order in which each site was observed in the documentary and other sources.

A total of 229 historic sites, buildings, and structures were identified during Phase I of the study. An additional 16 previously undocumented sites were located during the course of the Phase II field survey.

Formal site numbers assigned to sites previously recorded by the Arizona State Museum are listed in the next column. Primarily because sufficient data do not exist for those sites currently without site numbers, no new formal designations can be assigned at this stage of the project. Following this is a column giving site location by Township, Range, and quarter-Section.

Information specifically relating to the sites follows in the next four columns. The "Type of Site" column provides a specific name association for many sites (for example, Domingo Valencia Ranch, Menlo Park School, M. C. Shortridge House). Where no name association could be made, the site is listed by probable function; for example, House, Mine, or less specifically Building, when the function is uncertain. "Site Date" provides the information available relating to the time of occupation of each site. In several cases, only a single date appears. This means that the site is shown only on one map; therefore, a range of map derived dates could not be established. For example, most sites shown on the General Land Office (GLO) maps or Roskruge's 1893 map of Pima County appear on no other maps.

Where more than one map includes a particular site, the dates of those maps are presented as a tentative range of dates for site occupation. For a few sites, where historical research has been conducted, the exact dates for site occupation have been provided. The range of dates for buildings or structures still in use are listed, for example as, 1910—P. The "P" indicates that the building or structure is in existence and is still in use at the present time. Data based on surface artifacts are provided for sites in a few cases. Some sites are undated. Regardless of the sources of dates, the best possible dates are given for each site.

Finally, the dates presented do not always correspond to those of the map date, particularly when the GLO maps are involved. Where possible the date of the field work preceding the actual map preparation or approval date is given. This date represents the date that the site, building, or structure was actually observed in the field by the surveyor. The difference between the time of the survey and subsequent map preparation and final approval is as great as six years for some GLO maps.

The status column lists information as to the presence or absence of sites. A "P" indicates the site is assumed present if it was recorded by a recent Arizona State Museum site survey or if it was known from personal knowledge to exist. As a group, mining sites also were assumed to be present given the nature of such sites and their location in generally isolated or mountainous terrain. Seventy-one sites were visited in the field. These are designated "SP" for the sites seen and in existence, and "SD" for the sites searched for but which have been destroyed by agriculture, urbanization, or other forces. A "P" or "SP" preceded by an "N" indicates that the site was discovered during the course of the survey. A "U" indicates that information as to the existence of a site is lacking. Next is the source of information from which site location and dates were obtained. Publications mentioned are listed in the References section of this report and the maps used are presented in Table B.1.

In the following inventories (Table B.2), the list of zones in which a site occurs. follows the source of information column. The major zones of mountain (1), bajada (2a, 2b, 2c), and riverine (3) are explained in detail in Chapter 5. The final column lists the probable function of each site. Sites were assigned to one of nine functional categories: Residential (R), Mining (M), Town or community (TOW), Ranch or Farm (RAN), Trash Deposition (T), Water Control (W), Transportation (TRA), Religion (REL), and Miscellaneous (MIS).

TABLE B.1

**Maps Used for Locating Historic Sites**

| Map No. | Date | Title | Author | Location |
|---------|------|-------|--------|----------|
| HM-1 | 1869 | Military Map of Arizona | Military Division of the Pacific | ASU, Arizona Historical Foundation |
| HM-2 | 1920 | Transcontinental and Named Highways of Arizona | — | ASU, Hayden Library |
| HM-3 | 1919 | Insurance Maps of Tucson, AZ 1919 | Sanborn Map Co., New York | ASU, Arizona Room |
| HM-4 | 1930 | Points of Interest of Tucson and Vicinity | — | ASU, Hayden Library |
| HM-5 | 1893 | Map of Pima County | George Roskruge | Arizona Heritage Center |
| HM-6 | 1905 (reprint 1916) | Tucson, 60' Quadrangle Map | USGS | ASM |
| HM-7 | 1905 reprint 1916) | Tucson, 60' Quadrangle Map | USGS | ASM |
| HM-8 | 1905 (reprint 1920) | Patagonia, 60' Quadrangle Map | USGS | ASM |
| HM-9 | 1925 | San Xavier, 30' Quadrangle Map | Corps of Engineers | ASM |
| HM-10 | 1935 | San Xavier Indian Reservation | USDI | ASM |
| HM-11 | 1882 | Map of North Portion of the Papago Indian Reservation at San Xavier (ASM #093051) | USDI | ASM |
| HM-12 | 1922 | Official Relief Map of Pima County | Pima County Highway Department | U of A Main Library |
| HM-13 | 1874(?) | Map of San Xavier del Bac Reservation for Papago Indians | USDI | ASM |
| HM-14 | 1879 | Map of the Papago Reservation (ASM #093048) | USDI | ASM |
| HM-15 | 1882 | Rancho de Martinez Private Land Claim (ASM#093049) | USDI | ASM |
| HM-16 | 1923(?) | Map of Pima County | Pima County | U of A Main Library |
| HM-17 | 1887 | Map of the Territory of Arizona | USDI-GLO | BLM |

TABLE B.1 (continued)

**Maps Used for Locating Historic Sites**

| Map No. | Date | Title | Author | Location |
|---------|------|-------|--------|----------|
| HM-18 | 1883 | Map of the Territory of Arizona | USDI-GLO | BLM |
| HM-19 | 1897 | Map of the Territory of Arizona | USDI-GLO | BLM |
| HM-20 | 1912 | Map of the Territory of Arizona | USDI-GLO | BLM |
| HM-21 | 1873 | Mineral Claim Survey Map | USDI | BLM |
| HM-22 | 1870 | Mineral Claim Survey Map | USDI | BLM |
| HM-23 | 1882 | Mineral Claim Survey Map | USDI | BLM |
| HM-24 | 1888 | Mineral Claim Survey Map | USDI | BLM |
| HM-25 | 1892 | Mineral Claim Survey Map | USDI | BLM |
| HM-26 | 1898 | Mineral Claim Survey Map | USDI | BLM |
| HM-27 | 1902 | Mineral Claim Survey Map | USDI | BLM |
| HM-28 | 1911 | Mineral Claim Survey Map | USDI | BLM |
| HM-29 | 1928 | Mineral Claim Survey Map | USDI | BLM |
| HM-30 | 1896 | T11S, R11E | USDI-GLO | BLM |
| HM-31 | 1933 | T11S, R12E | USDI-GLO | BLM |
| HM-32 | 1914 | T12S, R11E | USDI-GLO | BLM |
| HM-33 | 1896 | T12S, R12E | USDI-GLO | BLM |
| HM-34 | 1904 | T13S, R11E | USDI-GLO | BLM |
| HM-35 | 1934 | T13S, R12E | USDI-GLO | BLM |
| HM-36 | 1908 | T13S, R12E | USDI-GLO | BLM |
| HM-37 | 1871 | T13S, R13E | USDI-GLO | BLM |
| HM-38 | 1904 | T14S, R11E | USDI-GLO | BLM |
| HM-39 | 1927 | T14S, R12E | USDI-GLO | BLM |
| HM-40 | 1918 | T15S, R12E | USDI-GLO | BLM |
| HM-41 | 1888 | T15S, R13E | USDI-GLO | BLM |
| HM-42 | 1871 | T15S, R13E | USDI-GLO | BLM |
| HM-43 | 1921 | T16S, R13E | USDI-GLO | BLM |
| HM-44 | 1888 | T16S, R13E | USDI-GLO | BLM |
| HM-45 | 1945 | T17S, R14E, | USDI-GLO | BLM |
| HM-46 | 1968 | Jaynes, 7.5′ Quadrangle Map | USDI-GLO | BLM |

Table B.2 (pages 105 through 121) contains sensitive information and has been omitted from some copies of this report.

Table B.2

HISTORIC SITE INVENTORY - AVRA

| Inventory Number | Site Number | Location | Type of Site | Site Date | Site Status | Information Source | Zone | Function |
|---|---|---|---|---|---|---|---|---|
| (Avra) A-1 | | T13S-R11E-S25, West Center | Shaft and Tunnel | 1932 | P | HM-35 | 1 | M |
| A-2 | | T13S-R11E-S25, East Center | Prospect | " | P | " | 1 | M |
| A-3 | | T13S-R11E-S36,NE | Mine Dump | " | P | " | 1 | M |
| A-4 | | T13S-R11E-S28,NW | Shaft | 1903 | P | HM-34 | 1 | M |
| A-5 | | T13S-R12E-S31, West Center | Shafts, Tent and Bldg | 1903-1932 | P | HM-34; HM-35 | 1 | M |
| A-6 | | T13S-R12E-S8,NE | Shaft | 1932 | P | HM-35 | 2c | M |
| A-7 | | T13S-R12E-S8,NE | Shaft | 1932 | P | " | 2c | M |
| A-8 | | T13S-R12E-S17, West Center | Shaft | " | P | " | 1 | M |
| A-9 | | T13S-R12E-S18,SE | Shaft | " | P | " | 2c | M |
| A-10 | | T13S-R12E-S31,NE | Mile Wide Mine | 1918-1932 | P | Leach 1918:38 | 1 | M |
| A-11 | | T12S-R11E-S35,NW | Lime Quarry | 1913 | P | HM-32 | 1 | M |
| A-12 | | T13S-R12E-S29 & 30 | Mining Claims | 1902 | P | HM-26 | 1 | M |
| A-13 | | T13E-R12E-S31 & 32 | Mining Claims | 1880-1888 | P | HM-22; HM-24 | 1 | M |
| A-14 | AZ AA:12:101(ASM) | T13S-R11E-S27,NW | Lime Kilns (2) and Quarry | ? | P | ASM Site Survey Files | 1 | M |
| A-15 | | T13S-R11E-S9,SW | CCC Camp | 1934-1941 | SP | Allen 1979 | 2c | Mis |
| A-16 | | T13S-R12E-S31,NW | Gould Mine | 1918 | P | Leach 1918:38 | 1 | M |
| A-17 | | T13S-R11E-S4, East Center | Avra | 1932 | SP | Granger 1975:259 | 2c | Tow |

Table B.2 (Continued)

HISTORIC SITE INVENTORY - BROWN MOUNTAIN

| Inventory Number | Site Number | Location | Type of Site | Site Date | Site Status | Information Source | Zone | Function |
|---|---|---|---|---|---|---|---|---|
| (Brown Mountain) | | | | | | | | |
| BM-1 | | T14S-R11E-S22,NW | Rodriguez Reservoir | 1903-1922 | U | HM-38; HM-12 | 2c | W |
| BM-2 | | T14S-R12E-S5,SE | Silver Lily Mine | 1925-1926 | P | HM-9; HM-39 | 2c | M |
| BM-3 | | T14S-R11E-S5, East Center | Temanalberes Ranch | 1925 | U | HM-9 | 2c | Ran |
| BM-4 | | T14S-R12E-S5,N½ | Mining Claim | 1882 | P | HM-23 | 1 | M |
| BM-5 | | T14S-R12E-S5,NE | Mining Claim | " | P | " | 1 | M |
| BM-6 | AZ AA:16:64(ASM) | T14S-R12E-S5,NE | Trash Scatter | ? | P | ASM Site Survey Files | 2c | T |
| BM-7 | AZ AA:16:65(ASM) | T14S-R12E-S5,SE | Trash Scatter | ? | P | " | 2c | T |
| BM-8 | | T14S-R12E-R5,NE | Amole Camp | 1893 | P | HM-5 | 1 | M |
| BM-9 | | T14S-R11E-S24,NE | Triple C Ranch | 1930s | NSP | ARS Survey | 2c | Ran |
| BM-10 | | T14S-R12E-S8,SW S17,NW | CCC Camp - Pima Co. Preventorium | 1934-? | U | Allen 1979 | 2c | Mis |
| BM-11 | AZ AA:16:70(ASM) | T14S-R11E-S2,NE | Grave | ? | P | Hartmann 1981:54 | 2c | Rel |

Table B.2 (Continued)

HISTORIC SITE INVENTORY - CAT MOUNTAIN

| Inventory Number | Site Number | Location | Type of Site | Site Date | Site Status | Information Source | Zone | Function |
|---|---|---|---|---|---|---|---|---|
| (Cat Mountain) | | | | | | | | |
| CM-1 | | T14S-R13E-S6,SW S7,NW | Davidson Ranch | 1922-1925 | U | HM-21; HM-9 | 1 | Ran |
| CM-2 | | T15S-R12E-S11 & 12 | Saginaw Hill- Arizona Copper Co. | 1893-1925 | SP | HM-5; HM-9 | 1 | M |
| CM-3 | | T15S-R13E-S7,SW | Arizona Group Mine | 1873-1925 | SP | HM-21; HM-9 | 1 | M |
| CM-4 | | T15S-R13E-S7,NE | Mine | " | SP | " | 1 | M |
| CM-5 | | T14S-R12E-S15,NW S16,NE | Coronado Ranch | 1893-1925 | U | HM-5; HM-9 | 2c | Ran |
| CM-6 | | T14S-R12E-S4,SW | Houses (2) | " | U | " | 2c | R |
| CM-7 | AZ AA:16:28(ASM) | T15S-R13E-S9,NE | Upper Reales (7 Houses) | 1888 | P | HM-41 | 3 | R |
| CM-8 | AZ AA:16:62(ASM) | T15S-R13E-S10,NW | Lime Kiln | 1871 | U | HM-42 | 3 | M |
| CM-9 | | T14S-R12E-S25,NW | Lime Kiln | 1926 | SP | HM-39 | 1 | M |
| CM-10 | | T14S-R13E-S7,NW | House - Goat Ranch | 1926-P | P | " | 1 | Ran |
| CM-11 | | T15S-R12E-S3,NW | F. Cañes & Lime Kiln | 1915 | SP | HM-40 | 2c | R |
| CM-12 | | T15S-R12E-S13,SW | House | 1915 | U | " | 2c | R |
| CM-13 | | T15S-R13E-S15,NW | House | 1871 | U | HM-42 | 3 | R |
| CM-14 | AZ AA:16:61(ASM) | T15S-R13E-S10,SW | J. M. Elias House | 1871-1893 | SP | HM-42; HM-5 | 3 | R |
| CM-15 | | T14S-R13E-S21,SW | Sunshine Mine Claim | 1928 | P | HM-28 | 1 | M |
| CM-16 | | T14S-R13E-S18 & 20 | Old Pueblo Copper Company Claim | 1911 | P | HM-27 | 1 | M |
| CM-17 | | T14S-R13E-S17 & 18 | Copper Queen Claim | 1882 | P | HM-23 | 1 | M |
| CM-18 | AZ AA:16:47(ASM) | T14S-R13E-S27,SE | Trash Scatter | ? | P | Betancourt 1978a:101 | 2b | T |
| CM-19 | | T15S-R13E-S10,NW | Angulo House | 1874-1893 | SP | HM-13; HM-5 | 3 | R |
| CM-20 | | T15S-R13E-S3,SW | Hughes House | " | U | " | 3 | R |

Table B.2 (Continued)

HISTORIC SITE INVENTORY – CAT MOUNTAIN (CONTINUED)

| Inventory Number | Site Number | Location | Type of Site | Site Date | Site Status | Information Source | Zone | Function |
|---|---|---|---|---|---|---|---|---|
| CM-21 | | T15S-R13E-S15,NW | Herrera House | 1874-1893 | U | HM-13; HM-5 | 3 | R |
| CM-22 | | T15S-R13E-S15, Center | Burrel House | " | U | " | 3 | R |
| CM-23 | | T14S-R12E-S36,NE | House | 1920-1935 | NSP | ARS Survey | 2c | R |
| CM-24 | | T14S-R13E-S34,NE | Mission Pool | 1922-1930 | SD | HM-12; HM-4 | 2b | Mis |
| CM-25 | | T14S-R13E-S3,SW | Cortaro House | 1893 | U | HM-5 | 2b | R |
| CM-26 | | T14S-R13E-S3,NW | Leon House | " | U | " | 2b | R |
| CM-27 | | T14S-R12 & 13E | Gates Pass Road | " | SP | " | 1 | Tra |
| CM-28 | AZ AA:16:79(ASM) | T14S-R13E-S25,NE | Building | post-1920 | P | ASM Site Survey File | 1 | R |
| CM-29 | AZ AA:16:83(ASM) | T14S-R13E | Starr Pass Road | 1884-P | P | Hartmann 1981:42; HM-5 | 1 | Tra |
| CM-30 | AZ AA:16:80(ASM) | T14S-R13E-S30,NE | Well & Enclosure | 1908-1920 | P | ASM Site Survey File | 1 | R |
| CM-31 | AZ AA:16:51(ASM) | T14S-R13E-S15 | Desert Lab | 1903-P | P | " | 1 | Mis |
| CM-32 | AZ AA:16:36(ASM) | T14S-R13E-S10,NE | Trash Scatter | 1880s | P | " | 2b | T |
| CM-33 | | T14S-R13E-S10, SE | St. Mary's Hospital | 1893-P | P | HM-5 | 2b | Mis |
| CM-34 | AZ AA:16:75(ASM) | T14S-R12E-S2, NE | Mine Shaft | ? | P | ASM Site Survey File | 1 | M |
| CM-35 | AZ AA:16:32(ASM) | T14S-R12E-S10,SW | Mine & Trash | 1880-1910 | P | " | 2c | M |
| CM-36 | AZ AA:16:73(ASM) | T14S-R12E-S16,NE | Trash Scatter | ? | P | " | 2c | T |
| CM-37 | AZ AA:16:74(ASM) | T14S-R12E-S16,NE | Rock Clusters and Trash | ? | P | " | 2c | T |
| CM-38 | | T14S-R12E-S12,NE | Riddell House | 1928-P | NSP | ARS Survey | 1 | R |

Table B.2 (Continued)

HISTORIC SITE INVENTORY - CAT MOUNTAIN (CONTINUED)

| Inventory Number | Site Number | Location | Type of Site | Site Date | Site Status | Information Source | Zone | Function |
|---|---|---|---|---|---|---|---|---|
| CM-39 | | T14S-R13E-S7,SW | House | Late 1920s | P | ARS Survey | 1 | R |
| CM-40 | | T15S-R12E-S3,NW | Lime Quarry | 1915 | SP | HM-40 | 1 | M |
| CM-41 | | T14S-R12E-S3,SE | House | 1930s | NSP | ARS Survey | 1 | R |
| CM-42 | | T15S-R13E-S10,NE | Midvale Farms | 1923-P | P | HM-16 | 3 | Ran |
| CM-43 | AZ AA:16:68(ASM) | T15S-R13E-S9-10-15-16 | House | 1880-1900 | P | ASM Site Survey File | 3 | R |
| CM-44 | AZ AA:16:60(ASM) | T15S-R13E-53,NW | Trash Scatter | Post 1870s | U | ASM Site Survey File | 3 | T |

Table B.2 (Continued)

HISTORIC SITE INVENTORY - JAYNES

| Inventory Number | Site Number | Location | Type of Site | Site Date | Site Status | Information Source | Zone | Function |
|---|---|---|---|---|---|---|---|---|
| (Jaynes) | | | | | | | | |
| J-1 | | T12S-R12E-S22,SE | Molina House and canal | 1895 | U | HM-33 | 3 | R |
| J-2 | | T12S-R12E-S35,SE | Antonio Cañas House | " | SD | " | 3 | R |
| J-3 | AZ AA:12:122(ASM) | T12S-R12E-S35, west center | Ruiz and Aguirre (5 bldgs) | " | SP | " | 2b | R |
| J-4 | | T13S-R12E | Road to Yuma mine | 1893–1907 | P | HM-5; HM-36 | 2b | Tra |
| J-5 | | T13S-R12E | Road to New State Copper Mine | 1907 | P | HM-36 | 2b | Tra |
| J-6 | | T13S-R12E-S12,NE | Talmadge-Rodríguez House | 1893–1907 | SD | HM-5; HM-36 | 3 | R |
| J-7 | | T13S-R12E-S1,NW | DeBascano House | 1907 | U | HM-36 | 3 | R |
| J-8 | | T13S-R12E-S1,SE | Pumping Plant | " | U | " | 3 | W |
| J-9 | | T13S-R12E-S1,SW | Ranch House | " | SP | " | 2b | Ran |
| J-10 | | T13S-R12E-S2,NE | House | " | SD | " | 3 | R |
| J-11 | | T13S-R13E-S18,NE | Nine Mile Water Hole | 1869–1893 | SD | HM-37; HM-5; Granger 1975:270 | 3 | Tow |
| J-12 | | T13S-R13E | Allison Canal | 1893 | U | HM-5 | 3 | W |
| J-13 | | T13S-R12E-S34,NW | Woffenden Gold Claim | 1892 | P | HM-25 | 1 | M |
| J-14 | | T13S-R12E-S34,NE | Lime Kiln | ? | P | HM-46 | 1 | M |
| J-15 | | T13S-R12E-S28,SE | Woffenden Silver Claim | 1892–1898 | P | HM-25; HM-21 | 1 | M |
| J-16 | AZ AA:12:90(ASM) | T13S-R13E-S28,NW | Bianco House | 1911–1914 | U | Betancourt 1978a:51 | 3 | R |
| J-17 | AZ AA:12:93(ASM) | T13S-R13E-S28,SW | Concrete Foundation | 1930s | SP | Betancourt 1978a:59 | 2b | Mis |
| J-18 | | T13S-R13E-S20,SE | Adobe Ruin | 1880–1910 | NSP | ARS Survey | 2b | R |

Table B.2 (Continued)

HISTORIC SITE INVENTORY - JAYNES (CONTINUED)

| Inventory Number | Site Number | Location | Type of Site | Site Date | Site Status | Information Source | Zone | Function |
|---|---|---|---|---|---|---|---|---|
| J-19 | AZ AA:12:96(ASM) | T13S-R13E-S20,NW | Trash Scatter | post-1900 | P | Betancourt 1978a:53 | 2b | T |
| J-20 | | T12S-R12E-S27, Center | Bojorquez House | 1893 | U | HM-5 | 3 | R |
| J-21 | | T13S-R13E-S7,NW | Rodriguez House | " | U | " | 3 | R |
| J-22 | | T13S-R13E-S7,NE | Martinez House | " | U | " | 3 | R |
| J-23 | | T13S-R13E-S7,SE | Cuevas House | " | U | " | 3 | R |
| J-24 | | T13S-R12E-S9,SE | Yuma Mine | 1893-1907 | P | HM-5; HM-36 | 1 | M |
| J-25 | AZ AA:12:106(ASM) | T13S-R13E-S29,NE | Lime Kiln | ? | SP | ASM Site Survey File | 2b | M |
| J-26 | AZ AA:12:55(ASM) | T13S-R13E-S7,SW | ASM's Laguna and Nine Mile Water Hole | 1869- | P | Granger 1975:270; ASM Site Survey File | 3 | Tow |
| J-27 | AZ AA:12:42(ASM) | T13S-R12E-S1,SW | Building | ? | P | ASM Site Survey File | 2b | R |
| J-28 | AZ AA:12:98(ASM) | T12S-R12E-S1,NE | Isolated Burial | ? | P | " | 3 | Rel |
| J-29 | | T13S-R12E-S35,SW | Quarry | ? | P | Whitney 1957:47 | 1 | M |
| J-30 | AZ AA:12:120(ASM) | T13S-R12E-S21,NW | Building | ? | P | ASM Site Survey File | 3 | R |
| J-31 | AZ AA:12:150(ASM) | T13S-R13E-S7,SW | Lime Kiln | ? | SP | " | 2b | M |
| J-32 | | T13S-R13E-S20,NW | House | early 1930s | NSP | ARS Survey | 2b | R |
| J-33 | | T12S-R12E-S35,NW | House and Tank | 1930s | NSP | " | 3 | R |
| J-34 | | T12S-R12E-S28,NE | House | " | NSP | " | 3 | R |
| J-35 | | T12S-R12E-S24,SE | Hemingway House | ? | P | Brew 1979 | 2a | R |
| J-36 | | T12S-R12E-S33,SE | Sahuaro Vista Ranch | 1928 | NP | ARS Survey | 2b | Mis |
| J-37 | | T13S-R12E-S3,NW | Wild Horse Ranch | early 1930s | NP | " | 2b | Mis |

Table B.2 (Continued)

HISTORIC SITE INVENTORY - JAYNES (CONTINUED)

| Inventory Number | Site Number | Location | Type of Site | Site Date | Site Status | Information Source | Zone | Function |
|---|---|---|---|---|---|---|---|---|
| J-38 | | T13S-R12E-S25,SW | Sweetwater Ranch | early 1930s | NP | ARS Survey | 1 | Mis |
| J-39 | | T13S-R12E-S2,NE | House | ca 1920 | NSP | " | 2b | R |
| J-40 | | T12S-R13E-S30,NE | Terraces | ? | NSP | " | 2b | Mis |
| J-41 | | T12S-R13E-S26,SW | Cortaro | 1920-P | SP | Granger 1975:264; HM-16 | 3 | Tow |
| J-42 | AZ AA:12:40(ASM) | T12S-R13E-S31,SW | Badger Hole Ranch | 1900-P | P | ASM Site Survey File | 2a | Ran |

Table B.2 (Continued)

HISTORIC SITE INVENTORY - MARANA

| Inventory Number | Site Number | Location | Type of Site | Site Date | Site Status | Information Source | Zone | Function |
|---|---|---|---|---|---|---|---|---|
| (Marana) M-1 | | T11S-R11E-S15,SW | Wakefield (fenced area) | 1893-1895 | U | HM-5; HM-30 | 2a | R |
| M-2 | | T11S-R11E | Irrigation canal | 1895 | U | HM-30 | 2a | W |
| M-3 | | T11S-R11E | " | " | U | " | 3 | W |
| M-4 | | T11S-R11E-S25,NW | Enclosure | " | U | " | 2a | Ran |
| M-5 | | T12S-R11E-S12 | Irrigation canal | 1913 | U | HM-32 | 3 | W |
| M-6 | | T12S-R11E-S3,NE | Griffin & Pacheco House | " | U | " | 3 | R |
| M-7 | | T12S-R12E-S6,SE | Rillito Station | 1887-P | P | HM-17; Granger 1975:278 | 3 | Tow |
| M-8 | | T12S-R12E-S5,NW | Flores (3 bldgs) | 1893-1895 | U | HM-5; HM-30 | 2a | R |
| M-9 | | T12S-R12E | Road to Silverbell Mines | 1893-P | SP | " | 3 | Tra |
| M-10 | | T12S-R12E-S17,NE | F. Ruelas (3 bldgs and canal) | 1893-1895 | SD | " | 3 | R |
| M-11 | | T12S-R12E-S17,NE | S. Ruelas House | " | SD | " | 3 | R |
| M-12 | | T12S-R12E-S6, NW | T. Landis House | " | U | " | 3 | R |
| M-13 | | T11S-R11E-S16, SW | Desert Stage Stop | 1850s-1897 | U | HM-18; HM-19; Gregonis & Huckell 1980:27 | 2a | Tow |
| M-14 | | T11S-R11E-S22,SW | Marana | 1890-P | P | HM-2; HM-20; Gregonis & Huckell 1980:27; Granger 1975:271-2 | 3 | Tow |
| M-15 | AZ AA:12:54(ASM) | T12S-R12E-S8, SW | Point of the Mountain | 1869-? | U | HM-1; ASM Site Survey File | 3 | R |
| M-16 | | T11-13.15-18S R11-14E | Southern Pacific Railroad | 1880-P | P | Myrick 1975 | 3 | Tra |

Table B.2 (Continued)

HISTORIC SITE INVENTORY - MARANA (CONTINUED)

| Inventory Number | Site Number | Location | Type of Site | Site Date | Site Status | Information Source | Zone | Function |
|---|---|---|---|---|---|---|---|---|
| M-17 | | T12S-R12E-S17,SW | Prospects | ? | NSP | ARS Survey | 1 | M |
| M-18 | | T11S-R11E- across entire | Road Picacho- Tucson | 1895 | U | HM-30 | 3 | Tra |

Table B.2 (Continued)

HISTORIC SITE INVENTORY - RUELAS CANYON

| Inventory Number | Site Number | Location | Type of Site | Site Date | Site Status | Information Source | Zone | Function |
|---|---|---|---|---|---|---|---|---|
| (Ruelas Canyon) | R-1 | T11S-R12E-S12, center | House | 1932 | U | HM-31 | 1 | R |
| | R-2 | T11S-R12E-S24,NE | T-Bench-Bar Ranch | " | P | " | 2a | Ran |
| | R-3 | T11S-R12E-S24,SE | Clayton Ranch | " | U | " | 2a | Ran |
| | R-4 | T12S-R12E-S16, No. center | Weavers Well | 1895 | U | HM-33 | 3 | Ran |
| | R-5 | T12S-R12E-S15,SW | A. Alvarez | " | U | " | 3 | R |

Table B.2 (Continued)

HISTORIC SITE INVENTORY - SAHUARITA

| Inventory Number | Site Number | Location | Type of Site | Site Date | Site Status | Information Source | Zone | Function |
|---|---|---|---|---|---|---|---|---|
| (Sahuarita) S-1 | | T17S-R14E-S6,SE | Hartt House | 1905-1941 | SD | HM-8; HM-45 | 2a | R |
| S-2 | | T16S-R13E-S36,SE | Houses (2) | 1905 | U | HM-8 | 2c | R |
| S-3 | | T17S-R14E-S7,SW S18,NW | Sahuarita | 1879-P | SP | HM-18; Granger 1975:278 | 2a | Tow |
| S-4 | | T17S-R13E-S12,SE | House | 1905 | SD | HM-8 | 2c | R |
| S-5 | | T17S-R13E-S13,NE | House | " | SD | " | 3 | R |
| S-6 | | T17S-R13E-S24,SE | Durazo or Alfredo's Ranch | 1893-1922 | U | HM-12; HM-5 | 3 | Ran |
| S-7 | | T17S-R13E-S25,NE | Houses (2) | 1905 | SD | HM-8 | 3 | R |
| S-8 | | T17S-R13E-S36,NW | Baga Ranch | " | SD | " | 2c | Ran |
| S-9 | | T17S-R13E-S36,NW | Houses (2) | " | SP | " | 2c | R |
| S-10 | | T18S-R13E-S1,NW | S. E. Brown Ranch | 1893 | SP | HM-5 | 2c | Ran |
| S-11 | | T18S-R13E-S1,SE | Houses (2) | 1905 | SP | HM-8 | 2a | R |
| S-12 | | T17S-R13E-S6 | House and Pump House | 1930s? | SD | HM-45 | 2a | R |
| S-13 | | T17S-R13E-S12,SE | Democrat Mill Site | 1882-1893 | SD | HM-23; HM-5 | 2c | M |
| S-14 | | T16S-R13E-S36,SE | Maish and Driscoll | 1893 | U | HM-5 | 2c | R |
| S-15 | | T17S-R13E-S1,SE | Doyle House | " | U | " | 3 | R |
| S-16 | | T17S-R13E-S12,NE | Buehman House | " | U | " | 3 | R |
| S-17 | | T17S-R14E-S7,SE | Hartt House | " | SD | " | 2a | R |
| S-18 | | T17S-R13E-S13,NE | J. K. Brown House | " | SD | " | 3 | R |
| S-19 | | T17S-R13E-S25,NE | G. Morales House | " | U | " | 3 | R |
| S-20 | | T17S-R13E-S25,SW | S. E. Brown House | " | SD | " | 3 | R |

Table B.2 (Continued)

HISTORIC SITE INVENTORY - SAHUARITA (CONTINUED)

| Inventory Number | Site Number | Location | Type of Site | Site Date | Site Status | Information Source | Zone | Function |
|---|---|---|---|---|---|---|---|---|
| S-21 | | T17S-R13E-S36, Center | Moreno House | 1893 | SD | HM-5 | 3 | R |
| S-22 | | T18S-R13E-S1,NW | A. Morales House | " | SD | " | 3 | R |
| S-23 | | T18S-R13E-S1,SE | New Ranch | " | SP | " | 2a | Ran |
| S-24 | | T16S-R13E | Twin Buttes RR | 1904- | P | Myrick 1975:304 | 2c | Tra |
| S-25 | | T16-17S-R13E | Tucson and Nogales RR | 1910- | P | Myrick 1975:311 | 2a | Tra |
| S-26 | | T17S-R14E-S18, Center | House | 1930s? | U | HM-45 | 2a | R |
| S-27 | | T17S-R14E-S18,SW | House | " | U | " | 3 | R |
| S-28 | | T17S-R14E-S30,SW | House | " | U | " | 3 | R |
| S-29 | | T17S-R13E-S25,SE | House | " | U | " | 3 | R |

Table B.2 (Continued)

HISTORIC SITE INVENTORY - SAN XAVIER MISSION

| Inventory Number | Site Number | Location | Type of Site | Site Date | Site Status | Information Source | Zone | Function |
|---|---|---|---|---|---|---|---|---|
| (San Xavier Mission) | | | | | | | | |
| SXM-1 | | T15S-R13E-S19, Center | Kubits Ranch | 1925 | SP | HM-9 | 2c | Ran |
| SXM-2 | | T15S-R12E-S14,SW S23,NW | Domingo Valencia Ranch | 1880s-P | SP | HM-40; HM-9 | 2c | Ran |
| SXM-3 | | T15S-R13E-S21,NE | Papago Village (29 houses) | 1888 | U | HM-41 | 3 | R |
| SXM-4 | | T15S-R13E-S34,SE | Lime Kiln | " | SP | " | 2c | M |
| SXM-5 | | T15S-R13E-S28,NE | Graveyard | " | U | " | 2c | Rel |
| SXM-6 | AZ AA:16:7,8&9(ASM) AZ AA:16:10(ASM) AZ AA:16:35(ASM) | T15S-R13E-S21,22,27 | San Xavier del Bac | 1700-P | P | Granger 1975:280 | 2c | Rel |
| SXM-7 | | T15S-R13E-S22,SE S27,NE | Berger (3 bldgs) | 1882-1893 | U | HM-15; HM-5 | 3 | R |
| SXM-8 | | T15S-R13E-S22,SE | Brush House | 1882 | U | HM-15 | 3 | R |
| SXM-9 | | T15S-R13E-S27,NE | House | " | U | HM-11 | 3 | R |
| SXM-10 | | T15S-R13E-S15,SW | Bedoya House | 1893 | U | HM-5 | 3 | R |
| SXM-11 | | T15S-R13E-S34,NW | Leopoldo Carillo's Stock Ranch | 1874 | U | HM-13 | 2c | Ran |
| SXM-12 | AZ AA:16:12(ASM) | T15S-R13E-S29,SE | Cemetery | 1800-1900 | P | ASM Site Survey File | 1 | Rel |
| SXM-13 | AZ AA:16:13(ASM) | T15S-R13E-S28,NE | Cemetery | 1850-1930 | P | " | 2c | Rel |
| SXM-14 | AZ AA:16:11(ASM) | T15S-R13E-S34,NE | Trash Scatter | 1750-1900 | P | " | 2c | T |
| SXM-15 | AZ AA:16:69(ASM) | T15S-R13E-S27,NW | Building | ? | P | " | 2c | R |
| SXM-16 | AZ AA:16:55(ASM) | T15S-R13E-S27,SW | Trash Scatter | late 19th Century | P | " | 2c | T |
| SXM-17 | AZ AA:16:56(ASM) | T15S-R13E-S21,NE | Trash Scatter | ? | P | " | 3 | T |
| SXM-18 | | T15S-R13E-S27,SW | Trash Scatter | 1880-1920 | NSP | ARS Survey | 2c | T |

Table B.2 (Continued)

HISTORIC SITE INVENTORY - TUCSON

| Inventory Number | Site Number | Location | Type of Site | Site Date | Site Status | Information Source | Zone | Function |
|---|---|---|---|---|---|---|---|---|
| (Tucson) | | | | | | | | |
| T-1 | | T15S-R13E-S10,SE¼ | Ortega House | 1871-1874 | U | HM-42; HM-13 | 3 | R |
| T-2 | | T15S-R13E-S10, East Center | Castro House | " | U | " | 3 | R |
| T-3 | | T15S-R13E-S10,NE¼ | House | " | U | " | 3 | R |
| T-4 | AZ BB:13:94(ASM) | T14S-R13E-S23,SW¼ | Silverlake Hotel Site | 1881-? | P | HM-5; Betancourt 1978a:84 | 3 | Mis |
| T-5 | AZ BB:13:111(ASM) | T14S-R13E-S23,SW¼ | Flour Mill Site | 1857-? | P | Betancourt 1978a:81 | 3 | Mis |
| T-6 | AZ BB:13:109(ASM) | T14S-R13E-S23,NW¼ | Dam | 1910-? | P | Betancourt 1978a:80 | 3 | W |
| T-7 | AZ BB:13:90(ASM) | T14S-R13E-S23,NW¼ | Farmers Ditch Head | 1870-1920 | P | Betancourt 1978a:76 | 3 | W |
| T-8 | AZ BB13:57(ASM) | T14S-R13E-S14,SW¼ | Warners Mill | 1874-? | P | Betancourt 1978a:70 | 2b | Mis |
| T-9 | AZ BB13:6(ASM) | T14S-R13E-S14,NE¼ | San Agustín Mission | 1790s-? | P | Betancourt 1978a:68 | 3 | Rel |
| T-10 | AZ BB:13:65(ASM) | T14S-R12E-S11,SE¼ | Trash Scatter | 1860-1900 | P | Betancourt 1978a:75 | 3 | T |
| T-11 | AZ BB:13:88(ASM) | T14S-R13E-S11,SE¼ | Trash Scatter | " | P | Betancourt 1978a:76 | 3 | T |
| T-12 | | T15S-R13E-S10,NE¼ | T. Elias House | 1893 | U | HM-5 | 3 | R |
| T-13 | | T15S-R13E-S15,NE¼ | School | " | U | " | 3 | Mis |
| T-14 | | T15S-R13E-S3,NE¼ | Etchells House | " | U | " | 3 | R |
| T-15 | | T14S-R13E-S3,SE¼ | El Rio Golf Course | 1930 | SP | HM-4 | 2b | Mis |
| T-16 | | T14S-R13E-S14,SW¼ | Allison House | 1893 | U | HM-5 | 3 | R |
| T-17 | | T14S-R13E-S27,NE¼ | Corbett House | " | U | " | 3 | R |
| T-18 | AZ BB:13:136(ASM) | T15S-R13E-S15,NE¼ | Trash Scatter | ? | P | ASM Site Survey File | 3 | T |

Table B.2 (Continued)

HISTORIC SITE INVENTORY - TUCSON, SOUTHWEST

| Inventory Number | Site Number | Location | Type of Site | Site Date | Site Status | Information Source | Zone | Function |
|---|---|---|---|---|---|---|---|---|
| (Tucson, Southwest) | | | | | | | | |
| TSW-1 | | T16S-R13E-S2,NW¼ | Pumping Station | 1915 | SD | HM-43 | 3 | W |
| TSW-2 | | T16S-R13E-S12,SW¼ | House | 1888 | U | HM-44 | 3 | R |
| TSW-3 | | T16S-R13E-S25,NE¼ | House | " | U | " | 3 | R |
| TSW-4 | | T16S-R13E-S11,NE¼ | Houses (2) | " | U | " | 2c | R |
| TSW-5 | AZ BB:13:18(ASM) | T16S-R13E-S2,NW¼ | Punta de Agua Ranch | 1855-1877 | P | McGuire 1979 | 2c | Ran |
| TSW-6 | | T15S-R13E-S34,NE¼ | Raglans Ranch | 1871-1879 | U | HM-42; HM-14 | 2c | Ran |
| TSW-7 | | T15S-R13E-S34,SE¼ | "Ruins" | 1888 | U | HM-41 | 2c | R |
| TSW-8 | | T15S-R13E-S36,NW¼ | "Ruins" | " | U | " | 2a | R |
| TSW-9 | AZ BB:13:19(ASM) | T15S-R13E-S15,SE¼ | Trash Scatter | 1880-1900 | P | Betancourt 1978a:93 | 3 | T |
| TSW-10 | | T15S-R13E-S23,SW¼ | House | 1882 | U | HM-11 | 3 | R |
| TSW-11 | | T15S-R13E-S15,SE¼ | Frederico House | 1893 | U | HM-5 | 3 | R. |
| TSW-12 | | T15S-R14E-S31,SW¼ | Sayze House | " | SD | " | 2a | R |
| TSW-13 | | T16S-R14E-S6,NW¼ | Arctic Ice Company | " | SD | " | 2a | Mis |
| TSW-14 | | T16S-R14E-S6,SE¼ | Shortridge House | " | SD | " | 2a | R |
| TSW-15 | | T16S-R14E-S7,SW¼ | M. C. Shortridge House | " | U | " | 3 | R |
| TSW-16 | | T16S-R14E-S18,NE¼ | Carrillo House | " | U | " | 2a | R |
| TSW-17 | | T16S-R14E-S18,NE¼ | Lavorin House | " | U | " | 2a | R |
| TSW-18 | | T16S-R14E-S19,NE¼ | King House | " | P | " | 3 | R |
| TSW-19 | | T16S-R14E-S19,NE¼ | Steinfeld House | " | P | " | 2a | R |
| TSW-20 | | T16S-R14E-S19,SE¼ | Martin House | " | SD | " | 2a | R |
| TSW-21 | | T16S-R14E-S30,NW¼ | Lopez House | " | U | " | 3 | R |
| TSW-22 | | T16S-R14E-S30,SW¼ | Merrill House | " | U | " | 3 | R |
| TSW-23 | | T16S-R14E-S30,SE¼ | Weigel House | " | SD | " | 2a | R |

Table B.2 (Continued)

HISTORIC SITE INVENTORY - TUCSON (CONTINUED)

| Inventory S Number | Site Number | Location | Type of Site | Site Date | Site Status | Information Source | Zone | Function |
|---|---|---|---|---|---|---|---|---|
| T-19 | AZ BB:13:84(ASM) | T14S-R13E-S3,NE¼ | Building | 1900-1910 | P | ASM Site Survey File | 2b | R |
| T-20 | AZ BB:13:22(ASM) | T14S-R13E-S14,SE¼ | Trash Scatter | ? | P | " | 3 | T |
| T-21 | | T14S-R13E-S11,NE¼ | St. Mary's Dump | 1880-1910 | P | James Ayres Personal Information | 3 | T |
| T-22 | AZ BB:13:132(ASM) | T14S-R13E-S11,SE¼ | Manning House | 1907-P | SP | ASM Site Survey File | 2a | R |
| T-23 | AZ BB:13:89(ASM) | T14S-R13E-S14,SE¼ | House and Cistern | ? | P | " | 3 | R |
| T-24 | | T14S-R13E-S14,NE¼ | EP & SW RR Depot | 1913-P | SP | Myrick 1975:236 | 2a | Tra |
| T-25 | | T14S-R13E-S11, Center N½ | Subdivision | pre-1935 | SP | HM-3 | 2b | R |
| T-26 | | T14S-R13E-S11,S½ S14,NW¼ | Menlo Park Subdivision | " | SP | " | 2b | R |
| T-27 | | T14S-R13E-S11,SW¼ | Menlo Park School | 1918-P | SP | Tucson Unified School District Files | 2b | Mis |
| T-28 | AZ AA:13:35;56 (ASM) | T15S-R13E-S14 NE¼,SW¼ | Los Reales Community | late 1800s | | ASM Site Survey Files; Betancourt 1978b | 3 | Tow |

Table B.2 (Continued)

HISTORIC SITE INVENTORY - TUCSON, SOUTHWEST (CONTINUED)

| Inventory Number | Site Number | Location | Type of Site | Site Date | Site Status | Information Source | Zone | Function |
|---|---|---|---|---|---|---|---|---|
| TSW-24 | AZ BB:13:54(ASM) | T16S-R13E-S11,NE¼ | Miguel Moreno House | 1874 | P | HM-13 | 2c | R |
| TSW-25 | AZ BB:13:53(ASM) | T16S-R13E-S11,NE¼ | Manuel Amado House | 1870-1890 | P | ASM Site Survey File | 2c | R |
| TSW-26 | | T16S-R13E-S14,NE¼ | H. Fenalstine(?) House | 1874 | U | " | 2c | R |
| TSW-27 | AZ BBL13:14(ASM) | T15S-R13E-S22,SE¼ S27,NE¼ | Trash Scatter | 1870-1930 | SP | " | 3 | T |
| TSW-28 | AZ BB:13:75(ASM) | T15S-R13E-S23,NW¼ | Trash Scatter | ? | P | " | 2a | T |
| TSW-29 | | T15S-R13E-S23,SE¼ | Indian Health Service Bldgs. | 1931-P | P | HM-10; Jay Stock Personal info | 2a | Mis |
| TSW-30 | | T15S-R13E-S34,NE¼ | Trash Scatter | 1920-1935 | NSP | ARS Survey | 2c | T |
| TSW-31 | | T15S-R13E-S35,NW¼ | Houses (6) | 1904 | U | HM-6; HM-7 | 3 | R |
| TSW-32 | | T15S-R13E-S26,SW¼ | Houses (3) | " | U | " | 3 | R |
| TSW-33 | | T15S-R13E-S26,NW¼ | Houses (4) | " | U | " | 3 | R |
| TSW-34 | | T15S-R13E-S23, North Center | Houses (27) | " | U | " | 3 | R |
| TSW-35 | | T15S-R13E-S23,NW¼ | Houses (4) | " | U | " | 3 | R |

# Appendix C

# CHI-SQUARE STATISTICAL DATA

## James D. Mayberry

As a means of testing the assumption that Class I Hohokam sites were functionally distinct from the majority of Class II sites, a chi-square test was run. Chi-square tests can be used to determine the existence of a systemic relationship between two variables (Nie and others 1970: 223). In this case, the variable were the distributions of two site types among the topographic landforms of the landform-site type model. While some of the deviation in site distributions may be due to nonsystematic variables, large deviations, represented by large values of chi-square, are not likely to result from random chance.

Chi-square tests were performed to establish differences in the distribution of sites dating to the Rillito phase, the Sedentary period, the Classic period, and the Tucson phase. Two tests were performed for each of these: one using only those sites in the project area, one including all sites in or near the project area. The null hypothesis for each test was that there was no significant difference in the distributions of Class I and II sites among the various landforms. After correcting for degrees of freedom, levels of significance were derived. In every case the levels of significance were less than 0.10, supporting functions in the Hohokam system. Results of the tests are presented in Table C.1.

TABLE C.1

**Chi-Square Analysis of Site Function**
A. Rillito Phase Sites within the Project Area

|          | Floodplain | Transition | Bajada | Mountain | Avra Valley | Total |
|----------|------------|------------|--------|----------|-------------|-------|
| Class I  | 9          | 10         | 6      | 1        | 0           | 26    |
| Class II | 21         | 8          | 10     | 3        | 1           | 43    |
| Total    | 30         | 18         | 16     | 4        | 1           | 69    |

df= 4                 chi-square= 9.239
Level of significance — between 0.10 and 0.05

B. Rillito Phase Sites in the General Area

|          | Floodplain | Transition | Bajada | Mountain | Avra Valley | Total |
|----------|------------|------------|--------|----------|-------------|-------|
| Class I  | 14         | 16         | 9      | 2        | 0           | 41    |
| Class II | 34         | 14         | 25     | 7        | 1           | 81    |
| Total    | 48         | 30         | 34     | 9        | 1           | 122   |

df= 4                 chi-square= 7.38
Level of significance — between 0.25 and 0.10

C. Sedentary Period Sites within the Project Area

|          | Floodplain | Transition | Bajada | Mountain | Avra Valley | Total |
|----------|------------|------------|--------|----------|-------------|-------|
| Class I  | 15         | 18         | 8      | 1        | 0           | 42    |
| Class II | 21         | 16         | 21     | 10       | 1           | 69    |
| Total    | 36         | 34         | 29     | 11       | 1           | 111   |

df= 4                 chi-square= 9.21
Level of significance — between 0.10 and 0. 05

D. Sedentary Period Sites in the General Area

|          | Floodplain | Transition | Bajada | Mountain | Avra Valley | Total |
|----------|------------|------------|--------|----------|-------------|-------|
| Class I  | 20         | 27         | 12     | 1        | 1           | 61    |
| Class II | 43         | 20         | 50     | 12       | 8           | 133   |
| Total    | 63         | 47         | 62     | 13       | 9           | 194   |

df= 4                 chi-square= 24.00
Level of significance — less than 0.005 probablity

### E. Classic Period Sites within the Project Area

|          | Floodplain | Transition | Bajada | Mountain | Avra Valley | Total |
|----------|------------|------------|--------|----------|-------------|-------|
| Class I  | 17         | 18         | 9      | 1        | 0           | 45    |
| Class II | 15         | 12         | 14     | 10       | 2           | 53    |
| Total    | 32         | 30         | 23     | 11       | 2           | 98    |

df= 4                    chi-square= 8.09
Level of significance—between 0.10 and 0.05

### G. Tucson Phase Sites in the Project Area

|          | Floodplain | Transition | Bajada | Mountain | Total |
|----------|------------|------------|--------|----------|-------|
| Class I  | 7          | 9          | 3      | 1        | 20    |
| Class II | 1          | 2          | 3      | 3        | 9     |
| Total    | 8          | 11         | 6      | 2        | 29    |

df= 3                    chi-square=6.71
Level of significance—between 0.10 and 0.05

### F. Classic Period Sites in the General Area

|          | Floodplain | Transition | Bajada | Mountain | Avra Valley | Total |
|----------|------------|------------|--------|----------|-------------|-------|
| Class I  | 22         | 27         | 15     | 2        | 1           | 67    |
| Class II | 24         | 16         | 27     | 12       | 5           | 84    |
| Total    | 46         | 43         | 42     | 14       | 6           | 151   |

df= 4                    chi-square= 14.37
Level of significance—between .01 and .005

### H. Tucson Phase Sites in the General Area

|          | Floodplain | Transition | Bajada | Mountain | Total |
|----------|------------|------------|--------|----------|-------|
| Class I  | 12         | 7          | 5      | 1        | 25    |
| Class II | 7          | 2          | 5      | 3        | 17    |
| Total    | 19         | 9          | 10     | 4        | 42    |

df= 3                    chi-square= 6.32
Level of significance— between 0.10 and 0.05

# REFERENCES

Ackerly, Neal, and Ann Rieger
1975 An archaeological overview of southwest Pinal County, Arizona. *Arizona State Museum Archaeological Series* 104. Tucson: Arizona State Museum, University of Arizona.

Agenbroad, Larry D.
1966 Preliminary Report on a Desert Culture Site: San Pedro Valley, Arizona. MS, Arizona State Museum Library, University of Arizona, Tucson.
1967 The distribution of fluted points in Arizona. *The Kiva* 32(4): 113-120.
1970 Culture Implications from the Statistical Analysis of a Prehistoric Lithic Site in Arizona. MS, master's thesis, Department of Anthropology, University of Arizona, Tucson.

Allen, Donna
1979 A Preliminary Survey of Camp Pima. Saguaro National Monument West, Tucson, Arizona. MS, Western Archeological Center, National Park Service, Tucson.

Andrews, David A.
1937 Groundwater in Avra-Altar Valley, Arizona. *USGS Water-Supply Paper 796-E.* Washington: Government Printing Office.

Antevs, Ernst V.
1948 The Great Basin, with emphasis on glacial and postglacial times, III. *University of Utah Bulletin* 38(20): 168-191. Salt Lake City: University of Utah.

Ayres, James E.
1970a Two Clovis fluted points from southern Arizona. *The Kiva* 35(3): 121-124.
1970b An early historic burial from the village of Bac. *The Kiva* 36(2): 44-48.
1970c The crisis of urban archaeology: Problem oriented historical archaeology in Tucson, Arizona. Paper presented at the 35th Annual Meeting of the Society of American Archaeology, Reno. MS, Arizona State Museum Library, University of Arizona, Tucson.

Bahti, Mark
1966 A Cache at Huerfano Butte. *The Kiva* 36(2): 17-22.

Baumhoff, Martin A., and Robert F. Heizer
1965 Postglacial climate and archaeology in the Desert West. In *The Quaternary of the United States*, edited by H.E. Wright and David G. Grey, pp. 697-707. Princeton : Princeton University Press.

Berry, Claudia F., and William S. Marmaduke
1982 *The middle Gila Basin: An archaeological and historical overview.* Flagstaff: Northland Research, Inc.

Betancourt, Julio L.
1978a An archaeological synthesis of the Tucson Basin: Focus on the Santa Cruz and its Riverpark. *Arizona State Museum Archaeological Series* 116. Tucson: Arizona State Museum, University of Arizona.
1978b Cultural resources within the proposed Santa Cruz Riverpark archaeological district. *Arizona State Museum Archaeological Series* 125. Tucson: Arizona State Museum, University of Arizona.

Bohrer, Vorsila L., H. C. Cutler, and J. D. Sauer
1969 Carbonized plant remains from two Hohokam sites. *The Kiva* 35(1): 1-10.

Bolton, Herbert E.
1936 *Rim of Christendom.* New York: The MacMillan Company.
1948 (Translator and editor). *Kino's historical memoir of Pimeria Alta*, Vol. I. Berkeley and Los Angeles: University of California Press.

Bowden, Charles
1981 Death of the Santa Cruz calls for a celebration. Tucson: *Arizona Daily Star* 23 August.

Bowen, Thomas G.
1972 A Survey and Re-evaluation of the Trincheras Culture of Sonora, Mexico. MS, Arizona State Museum Library, University of Arizona, Tucson.

Bradley, Bruce A.
1980 Excavations at AZ:BB:13:74, Santa Cruz Industrial Park. *Complete Archaeological Service Associates* 1. Oracle, Arizona: Complete Archaeological Service Associates.

Breternitz, Cory D.
1978 An archaeological survey of the Continental Copper Company 69 and 115 kV transmission line in the lower San Pedro Valley. *Arizona State*

*Museum Archaeological Series* 121. Tucson: Arizona State Museum, University of Arizona.

Breternitz, David A.

1966   An appraisal of tree-ring dated pottery in the Southwest. *Anthropological Papers of the University of Arizona* 10. Tucson: Unviersity of Arizona.

Brew, Susan

1979   Cella, Barr, Evans and Associates Countryside Development Survey, June 5. MS, Project P:79:09, Cultural Resource Management Division, Arizona State Museum, University of Arizona, Tucson.

Browne, J. Ross

1950   *A Tour Through Arizona.* Tucson: Arizona Silhouettes.

Bryan, Alan L.

1965   Paleo-American prehistory. *Occasional Papers of the Idaho State University Museum,* Number 16. Pocatello: Idaho State University.

Bryan, Kirk

1928   Change in plant associations by change in ground water level. *Ecology* 9: 474-478.

1941   Pre-Columbian agriculture in the Southwest as conditioned by periods of alluviation. *Annals of the Association of American Geographers* 31: 219-242.

Burkham, D. E.

1970   Depletion of streamflow by infiltration in the main channels of the Tucson Basin, southeastern Arizona. *U.S.G.S. Water-Supply Paper 1939-B.* Washington: Government Printing Office.

Chambers, George

1954   The old presidio of Tucson. *The Kiva* 20(2-3): 15-16.

Cheek, Annetta

1974   The Evidence for Acculturation in Artifacts: Indians and Non-Indians at San Xavier del Bac, Arizona. MS, doctoral dissertation, Department of Anthropology, University of Arizona, Tucson.

Clotts, H. V.

1917   *History of the Papago Indians and the History of Irrigation, Papago Indian Reservation, Arizona District No. 4.* Washington: United States Department of Interior.

Coe, Carol A.

1979   Archaeological assessment of the Sells Vicinity, Papago Indian Reservation, Arizona. *Arizona State Museum Archaeological Series* 131. Tucson: Arizona State Museum, University of Arizona.

Cook, Ronald U. and Richard W. Reeves

1976   *Arroyos and Environmental Change in the American Southwest.* Oxford: Oxford Research studies in Geography.

Crown, Patricia L.

1982   Variability in Hohokam agricultural practices as observed from studies along the Salt-Gila Aqueduct, Central Arizona Project. Paper presented to the 47th Annual Meeting of the Society for American Archaeology, Minneapolis, MS, Arizona State Museum Library, University of Arizona, Tucson.

Culbert, T. Patrick, editor

1973   *The Classic Mayan Collapse.* Albuquerque: University of New Mexico.

Davidson, Edward S.

1970   Geohydrology and water resources of the Tucson Basin, Arizona. *U.S.G.S. Water Supply Paper 1939-E.* Washington: Government Printing Office.

Di Peso, Charles C.

1953   The Sobaipuri Indians of the upper San Pedro Valley, southeastern Arizona. *The Amerind Foundation* 6. Dragoon, Arizona: Amerind Foundation.

1956   The Upper Pima of San Cayetano del Tumacacori. *Amerind Foundation* 7. Dragoon, Arizona: Amerind Foundation.

1958   The Reeve Ruin of southeastern Arizona. *Amerind Foundation* 8. Dragoon, Arizona: Amerind Foundation.

1974   *Casas Grandes, A Fallen Trading Center of the Gran Chichimeca,* edited by Gloria Fenner. Dragoon, Arizona: Amerind Foundation.

Dobyns, Henry F.

1963   Indian extinction in the Middle Santa Cruz River Valley, Arizona. *New Mexico Historical Review* 38: 163-181.

1981   From fire to flood: Historic human destruction of Sonoran desert riverine oasis. *Ballena Press Anthropological Papers* 20. Socorro, New Mexico: Ballena Press.

Doelle, William H.

1978   Hohokam use of non-riverine resources. In *Discovering Past Behavior: Experiments in the Archaeology of the American Southwest,* edited by Paul F. Grebinger, pp. 245-273. New York: Academic Press.

1980   Comments on papers by Di Peso and Masse. In "Current Issues in Hohokam Prehistory," edited by David E. Doyel and Fred Plog. *Arizona State University Anthropological Research Papers* 23: 231-235. Tempe: Arizona State University.

1981   The Gila Pima in the late seventeenth century. In "The Protohistoric Period in the North American Southwest A.D. 1450-1700," edited by David R. Wilcox and W. Bruce Masse. *Arizona State University Anthropological Research Papers* 24: 57-70. Tempe: Arizona State University.

Downum, Christian, Paul R. Fish, and Suzanne K. Fish

1981   Hohokam terraces and agricultural production in the Tucson Basin. Paper presented to the 45th

Annual Meeting of the Society for American Archaeology, San Diego. MS, Arizona State Museum Library, University of Arizona, Tucson.

Doyel, David E.

1972 Cultural and Ecological Aspects of Salado Prehistory. MS, master's thesis, Department of Anthropology, California State University at Chico.

1977a Classic Period Hohokam in the Escalante Group. MS, doctoral dissertation, Department of Anthropology, University of Arizona, Tucson.

1977b Excavations in the middle Santa Cruz Valley, southeastern Arizona. *Arizona State Museum Contribution to Highway Salvage Archaeology* 44. Tucson: Arizona State Museum, University of Arizona.

1979 Archaeological investigations at AZ BB:13:14. *Arizona State Museum Contributions to Highway Archaeology* 58. Tucson: Arizona State Museum, University of Arizona.

1980 Hohokam social organization and the Sedentary to Classic Transition. In "Current Issues in Hohokam Prehistory," edited by David E. Doyel and Fred Plog. *Arizona State University Anthropological Research Papers* 23: 23-40. Tempe: Arizona State University.

Doyel, David E., and Fred Plog, editors

1980 Current Issues in Hohokam Prehistory. *Arizona State University Anthropological Research Papers* 23. Tempe: Arizona State University.

Eddy, Frank W.

1958 A Sequence of Cultural and Alluvial Deposits in the Cienega Creek Basin, south-eastern Arizona. MS, master's thesis, Department of Anthropology, University of Arizona, Tucson.

Euler, Robert C., George J. Gumerman, Thor N. V. Karlstrom, Jeffrey S. Dean, and Richard H. Hevly

1979 The Colorado Plateaus: Cultural dynamics and paleoenvironment. *Science* 205: 1089-1101.

Ezell, Paul

1954 An archaeological survey of northwestern Papaguería. *The Kiva* 19(2-4): 1-40.

1955 The archaeological delineation of a cultural boundary in the Papagueria. *American Antiquity* 20: 367-375.

1963 Is there a Hohokam-Pima cultural continuum? *American Antiquity* 29: 61-65.

Ferdon, Edwin N., Jr.

1967 The Hohokam ballcourt: An alternative view of its function. *The Kiva* 33(1): 1-14.

Ferg, Alan

1979 The petroglyphs of Tumamoc Hill. *The Kiva* 45(1-2): 95-119.

Fish, Paul R., Peter Pilles, and Suzanne K. Fish

1980 Colonies, traders and traits: The Hohokam in the North. In "Current Issues in Hohokam Ar-chaeology," edited by David E. Doyel and Fred Plog. *Anthropological Research Papers* 23: 151-175. Tempe: Arizona State University.

Flannery, Kent V.

1968 Archaeological systems theory and early Mesoamerica. In *Anthropological Archaeology of the Americas,* edited by Betty J. Meggars. Washington: Anthropological Society of Washington, D.C.

Fontana, Bernard L.

1956 A Report of Site BB:13:11, the "Joe Ben Site." MS, Arizona State Museum Library, University of Arizona, Tucson.

Fontana, Bernard, L., J. Cameron Greenleaf, and Donnelly Cassidy

1959 A fortified Arizona mountain. *The Kiva* 25(2): 41-52.

Fontana, Bernard L., William J. Robinson, C. W. Cormack, and Ernest E. Leavitt, Jr.

1962 *Papago Indian Pottery.* Tucson: University of Arizona Press.

Franklin, Hayward H.

1978 The Second Canyon Ruin, the San Pedro Valley, Arizona. MS, doctoral dissertation, Department of Anthropology, University of Arizona, Tucson.

Franklin, Hayward H., and W. Bruce Masse.

1976 The San Pedro Salado: A case of prehistoric migration. *The Kiva* 42(1): 47-56.

Frick, Paul. S

1954 An Archaeological Survey in the Central Santa Cruz Valley, Southern Arizona. MS, master's thesis, Department of Anthropology, University of Arizona, Tucson.

Fritz, Gordon L.

1972 On Pioneer Hohokam and San Pedro Cochise Settlement Patterns: A new perspective. MS, Arizona State Museum Library, University of Arizona, Tucson.

1973 Records inventory of the archaeological resources of the Tucson Basin. *Arizona State Museum Archaeological Series* 35. Tucson: Arizona State Museum, University of Arizona.

Fulton, William S., and Carr, Tuthill

1940 An archaeological site near Gleeson, Arizona. *Amerind Foundation* 1. Dragoon, Arizona: The Amerind Foundation.

Gabel, Norman M.

1931 The Martinez Hill Ruins: An Example of the Prehistoric Culture of the Middle Gila. MS, master's thesis, Department of Anthropology, University of Arizona, Tucson.

Gasser, Robert E.

1976 Hohokam subsistance: A 2000 year continuum. *Forest Service Southwest Region Archaeological Report* 11. Albuquerque: United States Forest Service, Department of Agriculture.

1980    Exchange and the Hohokam archaeobotanical record. In "Current issues in Hohokam prehistory," edited by David E. Doyel and Fred Plog. *Arizona State University Anthropological Research Papers* 23: 72-77. Tempe: Arizona State University.

Getty, Harry
1951    People of the old pueblo. *The Kiva* 17(1-2): 1-6.

Gelderman, F. W.
1972    *Soil survey of the Tucson-Avra Valley area, Arizona.* U.S. Department of Agriculture in cooperation with University of Arizona Agricultural Experiment Station. Washington: Government Printing Office.

Gish, Jannifer W.
1979    Palynological research at the Pueblo Grande Ruin. *The Kiva* 44(2-3) 159-172.

Gladwin, Harold S.
1942    Excavations at Snaketown III: Revisions. *Medallion Papers* 30. Globe, Arizona: Gila Pueblo.
1948    Excavations at Snaketown IV: Review. *Medallion Papers* 38. Globe, Arizona: Gila Pueblo.

Gladwin, Harold S., Emil W. Haury, E. B. Sayles, and Nora Gladwin
1937    Excavations at Snaketown: I-Material culture. *Medallion Papers* 25. Globe, Arizona: Gila Pueblo.

Goodyear, Albert C., III
1979    The historical and ecological position of protohistoric sites in the Slate Mountains of south-central Arizona. In *Research Strategies in Historical Archaeology*, edited by Stanely South, pp. 203-240. New York: Academic Press.

Grady, Mark A.
1976    Aboriginal Agrarian Adaptation to the Sonoran Desert: A Regional Synthesis and Research Design. MS, doctoral dissertation, Department of Anthropology, University of Arizona, Tucson.

Granger, Byrd
1975    *Will C. Barnes' Arizona Place Names*. Tucson: University of Arizona Press.

Grebinger, Paul F.
1971a   Hohokam Cultural Development in the Middle Santa Cruz Valley, Arizona. MS, doctoral dissertation, Department of Anthropology, University of Arizona, Tucson.
1971b   The Potrero Creek Site: Activity structure. *The Kiva* 37(1): 30-53.
1976    The Salado: Perspectives from the middle Santa Cruz Valley. *The Kiva* 42(1): 39-46.

Grebinger, Paul F., and David P. Adam
1978    The Santa Cruz Valley Hohokam: Cultural developments in the Classic Period. In *Discovering Past Behavior: Experiments in the Archaeology of the Southwest*, edited by Paul F. Grebinger, pp. 215-244. New York: Gordon and Breach.

Greenleaf, J. Cameron
1975a   Excavations at Punta de Agua. *Anthropological Papers of the University of Arizona*. 26. Tucson: University of Arizona.
1975b   The Fortified Hill Site near Gila Bend, Arizona *The Kiva* 40(4): 213-283.

Gregonis, Linda M., and Lisa W. Huckell
1980    The Tucson urban study. *Arizona State Museum Archaeological Series* 138. Tucson, Arizona State Museum, University of Arizona.

Hammack, Laurens C.
1969    Preliminary report of the excavations at Las Colinas. *The Kiva* 35(1): 11-27.

Hard, Robert, and William Doelle
1978    The San Agustin mission site, Tucson, Arizona. Arizona State Museum Archaeological Series 118. Tucson: Arizona State Museum, University of Arizona.

Hartmann, Gayle H.
1981    Pima County land exchange survey. *Arizona State Museum Archaeological Series* 151. Tucson: Arizona State Museum, University of Arizona.

Hartman, Gayle H., and William K. Hartmann
1979    Prehistoric trail systems and related features on the slopes of Tumamoc Hill. *The Kiva* 45(1-2): 39-70.

Harshbarger, J. W. D. D. Lewis, H. E. Skibitzke, W. L. Heckler, and L. R. Kister
1966    Arizona Water. *U.S.G.S. Geological Survey Water-Supply Paper* 1648. Washington: Government Printing Office.

Hastings, James R.
1958-   Vegetation change and arroyo cutting in south-
1959    eastern Arizona during the past century: An historical review. In *Arid Lands Colloquia* pp. 24-39. Tucson: University of Arizona.

Hastings, James R., and Raymond H. Turner
1965    *The Changing Mile*. Tucson: University of Arizona Press.

Haury, Emil W.
1945    The excavation of Los Muertos and neighboring ruins in the Salt River Valley, southern Arizona. *Papers of the Peabody Museum of American Archaeology and Ethnology, Harvard University* 24(1). Cambridge, MA: Peabody Museum, Harvard University.
1953    Artifacts with mammoth remains, Naco, Arizona, 1. Discovery of the Naco mammoth and associated projectile points. *American Antiquity* 19:1-14.
1957    An alluvial site on the San Carlos Indian Reservation, Arizona. *American Antiquity* 33: 2-27.
1958    Post-Pleistocene human occupation of the southwest. In "Climate and Man in the Southwest." *University of Arizona Bulletin* 28(4): 69-75. Tucson: University of Arizona.

1960 Association of fossil fauna and artifacts of the Sulphur Spring stage, Cochise culture. *American Antiquity* 25: 609-610.

1976 *The Hohokam: Desert Farmers and Craftsmen.* Tucson: University of Arizona Press.

1978 Comments, page 6. In "The Proceedings of the 1973 Hohokam Conference," compiled by Donald E. Weaver, Susan S. Borton, and Minnabell Laughlin. *Contributions to Anthropological Research* 2. Ramona, California: Acoma Press.

Haury, Emil W., E. B. Sayles, and William W. Wasley
1959 The Lehner mammoth site, southeastern Arizona. *American Antiquity* 25(1): 2-30.

Haury, Emil W., Kirk Bryan, Edwin H. Colbert, Norman E. Gabel, Clara Lee Tanner, and T. E. Buehrer
1975 *The Stratigraphy and Archaeology of Ventana Cave.* Tucson: University of Arizona Press.

Hay, O. P.
1927 The Pleistocene of the western region of North America and its vertebrated animals. *Carnegie Institution of North Washington Publication* 322. Washington: Carnegie Institution.

Hayden, Julian D.
1957 Excavations, 1940, at the University Indian Ruin. *Southwestern Monuments Association Technical Series* 5. Globe, Arizona: Southwestern Monuments Association.

1970 Hohokam origins and other matters. *American Antiquity* 35: 87-94.

1976 Pre-altithermal archaeology in the Sierra Pinacate, Sonora, Mexico. *American Antiquity* 40: 274-289.

Haynes, C. Vance, Jr.
1965 The geologists' role in Pleistocene paleoecology and archaeology. In *The Quaternary of the United States*, edited by H. E. Wright, Jr. and David G. Frey, pp. 61-64. Princeton: Princeton University Press.

1966 Geochronology of late Quaternary alluvium. *University of Arizona Geochronology Laboratory Interim Research Report* 10. Tucson: University of Arizona.

1968 Preliminary report on the late Quaternary geology of the San Pedro Valley, Arizona: Southern Arizona Guidebook III. Arizona Geological Society, pp. 79-96.

Haynes, C. Vance, Jr., and Peter J. Mehringer, Jr.
1965 The pollen evidence for the environment of early man and extinct mammals at the Lehner Mammoth Site, southeastern Arizona. *American Antiquity* 31: 17-23.

Hemmings, Ernest Thomas
1969 Salvage excavations in a buried Hohokam site near Tucson, Arizona. *The Kiva* 34(2-3): 201-205.

1970 Early Man in the San Pedro Valley, Arizona. MS, doctoral dissertation, Department of Anthropology, University of Arizona, Tucson.

Hemmings, E. T., M. D. Robinson, and R. N. Rogers
1968 Field Report on the Pantano Site (Arizona EE:2:50). MS, Arizona State Museum Library, University of Arizona, Tucson.

Hewitt, James M., and David Stephen
1981 Archaeologial investigations in the Tortolita Mountains Region, southern Arizona. *Anthropology Series Archaeological Field Report* 10. Tucson: Pima Community College.

Hinton, Richard J.
1970 *The Handbook to Arizona.* Glorieta, New Mexico: Rio Grande Press.

Hole, Frank, Kent V. Flannery, and James A. Neely
1969 The prehistory and human ecology of the Deh Luran Plain. *University of Michigan, Museum of Anthropology Memoirs*, 1. Ann Arbor: University of Michigan.

Huckell, Bruce
1973 The Gold Gulch site: A specialized Cochise site near Bowie, Arizona. *The Kiva* 39(2): 205-230.

1979 The Coronet Real Project: Archaeological investigations on the Luke Range, southwestern Arizona. *Arizona State Museum Archaeological Series* 129. Tucson: Arizona State Museum, University of Arizona.

1980 The Anamax-Rosemont Testing Project. Review draft. MS, Cultural Resource Management Division, Arizona State Museum, University of Arizona, Tucson.

1982a The distribution of fluted points in Arizona. *Arizona State Museum Archaeological Series* 145. Tucson: Arizona State Museum, University of Arizona.

1982b The Paleo-Indian and Archaic occupations of the Tucson Basin: An overview. Paper presented at the 1st Tucson Basin Conference, Tucson. MS, Cultural Resource Management Division, Arizona State Museum, Tucson.

1982c A Research Design for the Investigation of Archaic period Sites in the Anamax-Rosemont Land Exchange Area. MS, Cultural Resource Management Division, Arizona State Museum, Tucson.

Huckell, Lisa W.
1980 An archaeological assessment of the proposed Catalina State Park. *Arizona State Museum Archaeological Series* 141. Tucson: Arizona State Museum, University of Arizona.

Huckell, Lisa W., with Bruce B. Huckell
1981 Archaeological Test Excavations at the U.S. Home Corporation's Saddlewood Ranch Proposed Development Area. MS, Cultural Resource

Management Division, Arizona State Museum, University of Arizona, Tucson.

Humphreys, R. R.
1958    The Desert Grassland. *Agricultural Experiment Station Bulletin* 299. Tucson: University of Arizona.

Huntington, Ellsworth
1914    The climatic factor in arid North America. *Carnegie Institution of Washington, D.C. Bulletin* 192. Washington: Carnegie Institution.

Irwin-Williams, Cynthia
1967    Picosa: The elementary southwestern culture. *American Antiquity* 32: 441-457.

Irwin-Williams, Cynthia, and C. Vance Haynes
1970    Climatic change and early population dynamics in the Southwestern United States. *Quaternary Research* 1: 59-71.

Johnson, Alfred E.
1966    The archaeology of Sonora, Mexico. In *Handbook of Middle American Indians* 4: 26-37. Edited by Robert Wauchope. Austin: University of Texas.

Karns, Harry J.
1954    *Luz de Tierra Incognita, Unknown Arizona and Sonora 1693-1721*. Tucson: Arizona Silhouettes.

Kelley, J. Charles
1966    Mesoamerica and the Southwestern United States. In *Handbook of Middle American Indians* 4: 95-110. Edited by Robert Wauchope. Austin: University of Texas.
1980    Discussion of papers by Plog, Doyel and Riley. In "Current Issues in Hohokam Prehistory," edited by David E. Doyel and Fred Plog. *Arizona State Anthropological Research Papers* 23: 49-66. Tempe: Arizona State University.

Kelly, Isabel T.
1978    The Hodges Ruin. *Anthropological Papers of the University of Arizona* 30. Tucson: University of Arizona Press.

Kottlowski, Frank E., Maurice Cooley, and Robert V. Ruhe
1965    Quaternary geology of the Southwest. In *The Quaternary of the United States* edited by H. E. Wright and David G. Frey, pp. 697-707. Princeton: Princeton University Press.

Leach, R. B.
1918    Pima County in review. *Arizona Mining Journal* 2: 35-39.

Lensink, Stephen C.
1976    An archaeological survey of the West Coast/Mid-Continent Pipeline Project of the El Paso Natural Gas Company. *Arizona State Museum Archaeological Series* 105. Tucson: Arizona State Museum, University of Arizona.

MacNeish, Richard S.
1976    Early man in the new world. *American Scientist* 64: 316-327.

McCarthy, Carol Heathington
1982    An archaeological sample survey of the Middle Santa Cruz River Basin, Picacho Reservoir to Tucson, Arizona: A Class II survey of the proposed Tucson Aqueduct, Phase A, Central Arizona Project. *Arizona State Museum Archaeological Series* 148. Tucson: Arizona State Museum, University of Arizona.

McCarthy, Carol Heathington, and Earl Sires
1981    An archaeological overview of the middle Santa Cruz Basin. A supplemental Class I cultural resource survey for Reach B of the Central Arizona Project-Tucson Division. *Arizona State Museum Archaeological Series* 134. Tucson: Arizona State Museum, University of Arizona.

McGuire, Randall H.
1979    Rancho Punta de Agua. *Contribution to Highway Salvage Archaeology in Arizona* 57. Tucson: Arizona State Museum, University of Arizona.
1980    The Mesoamerican connections in the American Southwest. *The Kiva* 46(1-2): 3-38.
1982    Environmental background. In *Hohokam and Patayan Prehistory of Southwestern Arizona*, edited by Randall H. McGuire and Michael B. Schiffer, pp. 13-56. New York: Academic Press.

McGuire, Randall H., and Michael B. Schiffer
1982    Hohokam and Patayan Prehistory of Southwestern Arizona. New York: Academic Press.

Malde, H. E.
1964    Environment and man in arid America. *Science* 145: 123-127.

Marmaduke, William S., and Claudia F. Berry
1980    Cultural Resources Overview Draft, the Middle Gila Basin, Maricopa and Pinal Counties, southern Arizona. MS, Arizona State Museum Library, University of Arizona, Tucson.

Martin, Paul S.
1963    *The Last 10,000 Years*. Tucson: University of Arizona Press.

Martin, S. Clark, and Raymond M. Turner
1977    Vegetation change in the Sonoran Desert region, Arizona and Sonora. *Journal of the Arizona Academy of Science* 12: 59-69.

Masse, W. Bruce
1974    Prehistoric Southwestern Agricultural and Water Control Features: A Technological Description. MS, Arizona State Museum Library, University of Arizona, Tucson.
1979    An intensive survey of prehistoric dry farming systems near Tumamoc Hill in Tucson, Arizona. *The Kiva* 45(1-2): 141-186.
1980a   Excavations at Gu Achi. *Western Archeological Center Publications in Anthropology*. 12. Tucson: Western Archeological Center, National Park Service.

1980b The Hohokam of the lower San Pedro Valley and the northern Papaguería: Continuity and variability in two regional populations. In "Current Issues in Hohokam Prehistory," edited by David E. Doyel and Fred Plog. *Arizona State University Anthropological Research Papers* 23: 205-223. Tempe: Arizona State University.

1981 A reappraisal of the Proto-Historic Sobaipuri Indians of southeastern Arizona. In "The Proto-Historic Period in the North American Southwest. A.D. 1450-1700," edited by David R. Wilcox and W. Bruce Masse. *Arizona State University Anthropological Research Papers* 24: 28-56. Tempe: Arizona State University.

Midvale, Frank
1968 Prehistoric irrigation in the Salt River Valley, Arizona. *The Kiva* 34(1): 28-34.

Miksicek, Charles H.
1979 Archaeobotany of the St. Mary's Site. *The Kiva* 45(1-2): 130-140.

1982 Prehistoric vegetation change and historic desertification in the Salt Gila Basin. Paper presented at the 47th Annual Meeting of the Society for American Archaeology, Minneapolis, Minnesota. MS, Arizona State Museum, University of Arizona, Tucson.

Morris, Donald
1969 Red Mountain: An early Hohokam Pioneer Period site in the Salt River Valley of central Arizona. *American Antiquity* 34: 40-53.

Myrick, David
1975 *Railroads of Arizona, 1: The Southern Roads.* Berkeley: Howell-North.

Nabhan, Gary P.
1979 The ecology of floodwater farming in arid southwestern North America. *Agro-Ecosystems* 5: 245-255.

Nie, Norman H., C. Hadlai Hull, Jean G. Jenkins, Karin Steinbrenner, and Dale H. Bent
1970 *SPSS: Statistical Package for the Social Sciences.* New York: McGraw-Hill.

Pailes, R. A.
1978 Comments, page 50. In "The Proceedings of the 1973 Hohokam Conference," compiled by Donald E. Weaver, Jr., Susan S. Burton, and Minnabell Laughlin. *Contributions to Anthropological Research* 2. Ramona, California: Acoma Press.

Plog, Fred
1980 Explaining social change in the Hohokam Pre-Classic. In "Current Issues in Hohokam Prehistory," edited by David E. Doyel and Fred Plog. *Arizona State University Anthropological Papers* 23: 4-22. Tempe: Arizona State University.

Rice, Glen, David R. Wilcox, Kevin Rafferty, and James Schoenwetter
1979 An archaeological test of sites in the Gila Butte-Santan Region of south-central Arizona. *Arizona State University Anthropological Research Papers*. 18. Tempe: Arizona State University.

Robinson, William J.
1963 Excavations at San Xavier del Bac, 1958. *The Kiva* 29(2): 35-57.

1978 Comments, page 62. In "Proceedings of the 1973 Hohokam Conference," compiled by Donald E. Weaver, Jr., Susan S. Burton, and Minnabell Laughlin. *Contributions to Anthropological Studies.* 2. Ramona, California: Acoma Books.

Rogers, Malcolm J.
1958 San Dieguito implements from the terraces of the Rincon-Pantano and Rillito Drainage System. *The Kiva* 24(1): 1-23.

1966 *Ancient Hunters of the Far West.* San Diego: Union-Tribune Publishing Company.

Rosenthal, E. Jane, Doug R. Brown, Marc Severson, and John B. Clonts
1978 *The Quijotoa Valley Project.* Tucson: Western Archeological Center, National Park Service.

Rothrock, J. T.
1875 Preliminary and general botanical report: Annual report upon the geographical explorations and surveys west of the 100th meridian. Washington: Government Printing Office.

Rouse, Irving
1958 Inference of migrations from anthropological evidence. In "Migrations in New World Culture History," edited by Raymond H. Thompson, *University of Arizona Bulletin* 29(2); *Social Science Bulletin* 27: 63-68. Tucson: University of Arizona.

Rozen, Kenneth
1979a An archaeological survey of the Northern Tucson 138 kV transmission line system. *Arizona State Museum Archaeological Series* 132. Tucson: Arizona State Museum, University of Arizona.

1979b An archaeological survey of the Transportation Corridor Project, Tucson, Arizona. *Arizona State Museum Archaeological Series* 133. Tucson: Arizona State Museum, University of Arizona.

1981 Patterned associations among lithic technology, site content, and time: Results of the TEP St. Johns Project lithic analysis. In "Prehistory of the St. Johns Area, East-Central Arizona: The TEP St. Johns Project," by Deborah A. Westfall, *Arizona State Museum Archaeological Series* 153, pp. 157-233. Tucson: Arizona State Museum, University of Arizona

Russell, Frank
1908 The Pima Indians. *Twenty-sixth Annual Report of*

*the Bureau of American Ethnology*. Part 1. Washington: Government Printing Office.

Sayles, E. B.

1945    The San Simon Branch. Excavations at Cave Creek and in the San Simon Valley I: Material culture. *Medallion Papers* 34. Globe, Arizona: Gila Pueblo.

1958    The Sayles Papers 1958. MS, Archives folder 301, Arizona State Museum Library, University of Arizona.

Sayles, E. B., and Ernst Antevs

1941    The Cochise culture. *Medallion Papers* 29: Globe, Arizona: Gila Pueblo.

Schoenwetter, James

1970    Archaeological pollen studies of the Colorado Plateau. *American Antiquity* 35: 35-48.

Schreiber, Katharina J., Carol H. McCarthy, and Brian Byrd

1981    Report of the testing of the I-10 corridor: Prehistoric and historic archaeological remains between I-17 and 30th Drive (Group II-Las Colinas). *Arizona State Museum Archaeological Series* 156. Tucson: Arizona State Museum, University of Arizona.

Schroeder, Alfred H.

1952    The bearing of ceramics on developments in the Hohokam Classic period. *The Southwestern Journal of Anthropology* 8: 320-335.

1965    Unregulated diffusion from Mexico into the Southwest prior to A.D. 700. *American Antiquity* 30: 297-309.

1966    Pattern diffusion from Mexico into the Southwest after A.D. 600. *American Antiquity* 31: 683-704.

Schumm, S. A.

1965    Quaternary paleohydrology. In *The Quaternary of the United States*, edited by H. E. Wright, Jr. and David G. Frey, pp. 783-794. Princeton: Princeton University Press.

Sheridan, David

1981    *Desertification of the United States*. Council on Environmental Quality. Washington: Government Printing Office.

Shiner, J. L.

1961    A Room at Gila Pueblo. *The Kiva* 27(2): 1-11.

Simmons, Alan H.

1981    The "other" archaeology of northwestern New Mexico: Perspectives on the Aceramic occupation of the San Juan Basin. In *Contract Abstracts and CRM Archaeology*, 2(2): 12-20.

Sires, Earl

1982    Hohokam architectural variability and site structures in south-central Arizona. Paper presented at the 47th Annual Meeting of the Society for American Archaeology, Minneapolis, Minnesota. MS, Arizona State Museum Library, University of Arizona, Tucson.

Smiley, Terah, Henry F. Dobyns, Bonnie Jones, and James T. Barter

1953    San Jose de Tucson, Its History and Archaeological Exploration. MS, Archives folder A-271, Arizona State Museum Library, University of Arizona, Tucson.

Smith, Fay J., John L. Kessel, and Francis J. Fox

1966    *Father Kino in Arizona*. Phoenix: Arizona Historical Foundation.

Smith, G. E. P.

1938    The physiography of Arizona valleys and the occurrence of groundwater. *College of Agriculture Experiment Station Technical Bulletin* 77. Tucson: University of Arizona.

Smith, Watson, Richard B. Woodbury, and Nathalie F. S. Woodbury

1966    The excavation of Hawikuh by Frederick Webb Hodge. *New York Museum of the American Indian Heye Foundation* 20. New York: Museum of the American Indian.

Spalding, Volney M.

1909    Distribution and movements of desert plants. *Carnegie Institution of Washington Publication* 113. Washington: Carnegie Institution.

Stacy, V. K. Pheriba

1974    *Cerros de Trincheras in the Altar Valley, Arizona*. MS, doctoral dissertation, Department of Anthropology, University of Arizona, Tucson.

Stacy, V. K. Pheriba, and Julian Hayden

1975    *Saguaro National Monument: An archaeological overview*. Tucson: Arizona Archeological Center, National Park Service.

Stein, Pat H.

1981    The Palo Verde archaeological investigations. Part 2, Wintersbury: An archaeological, archival, and folk account of homesteading in Arizona. *Museum of Northern Arizona Research Paper* 21. Flagstaff: Museum of Northern Arizona.

Stephen, David, and James Hewitt

1980    Archaeological resources of Midvale Farms property, Tucson, Arizona. MS, Pima Community College, West Campus, Tucson.

Teague, Lynn S.

1974    The archaeological resources of the Winkleman and Black Hills Units of the Bureau of Land Management. *Arizona State Museum Archaeological Series* 47. Tucson: Arizona State Museum, University of Arizona.

1982    The Preclassic to Classic period transition in Hohokam Society. Paper presented at the 47th Annual Meeting of the Society for American Archaeology, Minneapolis, Minnesota. MS, Arizona State Museum Library, University of Arizona, Tucson.

Teague, Lynn S., and Anne R. Baldwin

1978    Painted Rock Resevoir Project Phase I: Preliminary survey and recommendations. *Arizona State Museum Archaeological Series 126*. Tucson: Arizona State Museum, University of Arizona.

Thornber, J.J.
1910   The grazing ranges of Arizona. *Agricultural Experiment Station Bulletin 65*. Tucson: University of Arizona.

Turner, S. F., and others
1943   *Ground-water resources of the Santa Cruz Basin, Arizona*. Tucson: United States Department of the Interior Geological Survey.

Tuthill, Carr
1947   The Tres Alamos site on the San Pedro River, southern Arizona, *Amerind Foundation 2*. Dragoon, Arizona: The Amerind Foundation.

Underhill, Ruth M.
1939   *Social Organization of the Papago Indians*. New York: Columbia University Press.

United States Senate
1965   Federal census-Territory of New Mexico and Territory of Arizona. Excerpts from the Decennial Federal Census, 1860..., 1864,...and 1870. Washington: Government Printing Office.

Upham, Steadman, and Glen E. Rice
1980   Up the canal without a pattern: Modelling Hohokam interaction and exchange. In "Current Issues in Hohokam Prehistory," edited by David E. Doyel and Fred Plog. *Arizona State University Anthropological Research Papers 23*: 78-105. Tempe: Arizona State University.

Urban, Sharon F.
1981   History of the Altar Valley, Arizona. CRM Draft for the Environmental Assessment of the Southern Arizona Auxiliary Airfield; Aviation Directorate, National Guard Bureau, Washington, D.C. MS, Archaeology Section, Arizona State Museum, University of Arizona.

Van Devender, Thomas R.
1977   Holocene woodlands in the southwestern deserts. *Science 198*: 189-192.

Van Devender, Thomas R., and W. Geoffrey Spaulding
1979   Development of vegetation and climate in the southwestern United States. *Science 204*: 701-710.

Wagoner, Jay
1975   *Early Arizona: Prehistory to Civil War*. Tucson: University of Arizona Press.

Walker, Neal P., and Anne S. Polk
1973   An archaeological survey of the AEPCO-Apache Twin Buttes 230 kV Pantano-Whetstone 155 kV power transmission line. *Arizona State Museum Archaeological Series 27*. Tucson: Arizona State Museum, University of Arizona.

Wallace, Henry
in

press   The mortars, petroglyphs, and trincheras on Rillito Peak. *The Kiva*.

Warren, Claude N.
1967   The San Dieguito complex: A review and hypothesis. *American Antiquity 32*: 168-185.

Wasley, William W.
1966   Classic period Hohokam. Paper presented at the Thirty-first Annual Meeting of the Society for American Archaeology, Reno. MS, Arizona State Museum Library, University of Arizona, Tucson.

Wasley, William W., and David E. Doyel
1980   The Classic period Hohokam. *The Kiva 45*(4): 337-352.

Weaver, Donald E., Jr.
1972   A cultural-ecological model for the Classic period Hohokam in the lower Salt River Valley, Arizona. *The Kiva 38*: 43-52.

Wells, Susan J., and Michael B. Schiffer
1982   Archaeological Surveys: Past and Future. In *Hohokam and Patayan, Prehistory of Southwestern Arizona*, edited by Randall H. McGuire and Michael B. Schiffer, pp. 345-384. New York: Academic Press.

Westfall, Deborah A.
1979   An archaeological overview of the Middle and Lower Santa Cruz Basin. A Class I cultural resources survey for the Central Arizona Project-Tucson Division. *Arizona State Museum Archaeological Series 34*. Tucson: Arizona State Museum, University of Arizona.

Whalen, Norman M.
1971   Cochise Culture Sites in the Central San Pedro Drainage, Arizona. MS, doctoral dissertation, Department of Anthropology, University of Arizona, Tucson.
1973   Agriculture and the Cochise. *The Kiva 39*(1): 89-96.
1975   Cochise site distribution in the San Pedro Valley. *The Kiva 40*(3): 203-211.

Wheat, Joe Ben
1955   The Mogollon Culture prior to A.D. 1000. In *Memoirs for the Society for American Archaeology*, edited by Richard B. Woodbury. Boulder: Society for American Archaeology.

White, Cheryl
1966   The Petroglyphs of Saguaro National Monument, Southern Arizona. MS, Arizona State Museum Library, University of Arizona, Tucson.

Whitney, Richard L.
1957   Stratigraphy and Structure of the Northeastern Part of the Tucson Mountains. MS, master's thesis, Department of Geology, University of Arizona, Tucson.

Wilcox, David R.
1979a  The Hohokam regional system. In "An Ar-

chaeological Test of Sites in the Gila Butte-Santan Region, South-Central Arizona," by Glen Rice, David Wilcox, Kevin Rafferty, and James Schoenwetter. *Arizona State University Anthropological Research Papers* 18: 77-115. Tempe: Arizona State University.

1979b Warfare implications of the dry-laid masonry walls of Tumamoc Hill. *The Kiva* 45(1-2): 15-38.

Wilcox, David R., and Lynette O. Shenk

1977 The architecture of Casa Grande and its interpretation. *Arizona State Museum Archaeological Series* 115. Tucson: Arizona State Museum, University of Arizona.

Wilcox, David R., and W. Bruce Masse, editors

1981a The Proto-historic Period in the North American Southwest, A.D. 1450-1700. *Arizona State University Anthropological Research Papers* 24. Tempe: Arizona State University.

1981b The history of Proto-historic studies in the North American Southwest. In "The Proto-historic Period in the North American Southwest A.D. 1450-1700." *Arizona State University Anthropological Research Papers* 24: 1-27. Tempe: Arizona State University.

Wilcox, David R., T. Randall McGuire, and Charles Sternberg

1981 Snaketown Revisited. *Arizona State Museum Archaeological Series* 155. Tucson: Arizona State Museum, University of Arizona.

Wilcox, David R., and Charles Sternberg

1981 Additional studies of the architecture of the Casa Grande and its interpretation. *Arizona State Museum Archaeological Series* 146. Tucson: Arizona State Museum, University of Arizona.

Wilson, Andrew W.

1963 Tucson: A problem in uses of water. In "Aridity and Man," edited by Carl Hodge. *American Association for the Advancement of Science Publication* 74: 483-490. Washington: American Association for the Advancement of Science.

Wilson, John P.

1980 Cultural resources of the proposed Tucson Electric Tortolita-South utility corridor and alternative routes, Pinal and Pima Counties, Arizona. Report No. 21 prepared for Tucson Electric Power Company. Las Cruces, New Mexico.

1981 Archaeological survey of the proposed Tucson Electric Tortolita-South relocates segment, Pinal and Pima Counties, Arizona. Report No. 26 prepared for Tucson Electric Power Company. Las Cruces, New Mexico.

Windmiller, Ric

1971 Early hunters and gatherers in southeastern Arizona. *The Cochise Quarterly* 1: 3-15.

1973 The late Cochise culture in the Sulphur Springs Valley, southeastern Arizona: Archaeology of the Fairchild site. *The Kiva* 39(2): 131-169.

Winter, Joseph C.

1973 Cultural modifications of the Gila Pima, A.D. 1697-1846. *Ethnohistory* 20: 65-76.

1976 The processes of farming diffusion in the Southwest and the Great Basin. *American Antiquity* 41: 421-429.

Winters, Arnold M.

1973 Excavations at Valshni Village, Arizona. *The Arizona Archaeologist* 7: 1-90.

Woosley, Anne I.

1980 Agricultural diversity in the prehistoric Southwest. *The Kiva* 45(4): 317-336.

Wright, Barton A., and Rex E. Gerald

1950 The Zanardelli Site. *The Kiva* 16(3): 8-15.

Zahniser, Jack L.

1970 The archaeological resources of the Saguaro National Monument. *The Kiva* 35(3): 105-121.

Zaslow, Bert, and Alfred E. Dittert

1977 Pattern mathematics and archaeology: The pattern technology of the Hohokam. *Arizona State University Anthropological Research Paper* 2. Tempe: Arizona State University.

## Appendix A

### CULTURAL RESOURCES LOCATIONAL DATA

| Site Number | UTM ZONE 12 Easting | Northing | T4S, R6W Section | ¼ of the ¼ | | Elevation Feet | Approx. Meters |
|---|---|---|---|---|---|---|---|
| AZ T:13:22 (PRI-1) | 325490 325340 325100 325060 | 3659080 3659200 3658740 3658980 | 27 22 | NW SW | NW SW | 600-620 | 185-190 |
| AZ T:13:23 (PRI-4) | 324730 | 3658800 | 28 | NE | NE | 600 | 185 |
| AZ T:13:24 (PRI-6) | 324500 | 3659820 | 28 | NW | NE | 600 | 185 |
| AZ T:13:25 (PRI-9) | 324540 | 3658970 | 28 | NW | NE | 605 | 185 |
| AZ T:13:26 (PRI-12) | 324425 | 3659440 | 21 | SW | SE | 680 | 205 |
| AZ T:13:29 (PRI-23) | 325470 | 3659350 | 22 | SE | SW | 610 | 185 |
| AZ T:13:28 (PRI-43) | 324945 | 3659375 | 21 | SE | SE | 670 | 205 |
| AZ T:13:29 (PRI-63) | 325180 | 3660200 | 22 | SW | NW | 700 | 215 |
| AZ T:13:30 (PRS-78-22) | 326110 | 3658930 | 27 | NW | NE | 650 | 200 |
| AZ T:13:31 (PRS-78-23) | 325920 | 3658870 | 22 | NW | NE | 640 | 195 |
| PRI-2 | 325065 | 3658850 | 27 | NW | NW | 600 | 185 |
| PRI-3 | 324930 | 3658850 | 28 | NE | NE | 600 | 185 |
| PRI-5 | 324760 | 3658890 | 28 | NE | NE | 600 | 185 |
| PRI-7 | 324340 | 3658960 | 28 | NW | NE | 600 | 185 |
| PRI-8 | 324370 | 3659020 | 28 | NW | NE | 610 | 185 |
| PRI-10 | 324615 | 3659150 | 21 | SW | SE | 615 | 185 |
| PRI-11 | 324670 | 3659310 | 21 | SE | SE | 630 | 190 |

113

| Site Number | UTM ZONE 12 | | T4S, R6W | | | Elevation | |
| --- | --- | --- | --- | --- | --- | --- | --- |
| | Easting | Northing | Section | ¼ of the ¼ | | Feet | Approx. Meters |
| PRI-13 | 324460 | 3659620 | 21 | NW | SE | 680 | 205 |
| PRI-14 | 324540 | 3659830 | 21 | NW | SE | 680 | 205 |
| PRI-15 | 324600 | 3659890 | 21 | SW | NE | 680 | 205 |
| PRI-16 | 324030 | 3659180 | 22 | SW | SW | 615 | 185 |
| PRI-17 | 325065 | 3659220 | 22 | SW | SW | 615 | 185 |
| PRI-18 | 325270 | 3659280 | 22 | SW | SW | 630 | 190 |
| PRI-19 | 325400 | 3659310 | 22 | SW | SW | 615 | 185 |
| PRI-20 | 325345 | 3659360 | 22 | SW | SW | 620 | 190 |
| PRI-21 | 325295 | 3659435 | 22 | SW | SW | 650 | 195 |
| PRI-22 | 325690 | 3659510 | 22 | NE | SW | 610 | 185 |
| PRI-24 | 325415 | 3659240 | 22 | SW | SW | 610 | 185 |
| PRI-25 | 325725 | 3658730 | 27 | NE | NW | 620 | 190 |
| PRI-26 | 325605 | 3658640 | 27 | NE SE | NW NW | 610 | 185 |
| PRI-27 | 325620 | 3658840 | 27 | NE | NW | 610 | 185 |
| PRI-28 | 325695 | 3658845 | 27 | NE | NW | 610 | 185 |
| PRI-29 | 325650 | 3658850 | 27 | NE | NW | 610 | 185 |
| PRI-30 | 325745 | 3659150 | 22 | SE | SW | 610 | 185 |
| PRI-31 | 325630 | 3658995 | 27 | NE | SW | 610 | 185 |
| PRI-32 | 325750 | 3658830 | 27 | NE | NW | 610 | 185 |
| PRI-33 | 325745 | 3658770 | 27 | NE | NW | 610 | 185 |
| PRI-34 | 325635 | 3659375 | 22 | SE | SW | 610 | 185 |
| PRI-35 | 325930 | 3659535 | 22 | NW | SE | 625 | 190 |

| Site Number | UTM ZONE 12 | | T4S, R6W | | | Elevation | |
|---|---|---|---|---|---|---|---|
| | Easting | Northing | Section | ¼ of the ¼ | | Feet | Approx. Meters |
| PRI-36 | 325980 | 3660180 | 22 | SW | NE | 720 | 220 |
| PRI-37 | 325940 | 3660180 | 22 | SW | NE | 640-720 | 195-220 |
| PRI-38 | 325265 | 3659505 | 22 | NW | SW | 670 | 205 |
| PRI-39 | 325200 | 3659745 | 22 | NW | SW | 680 | 205 |
| PRI-40 | 324900 | 3659590 | 21 | NE | SE | 680 | 205 |
| PRI-41 | 324995 | 3659450 | 21 | SE | SE | 680 | 205 |
| PRI-42 | 324950 | 3659405 | 21 | SE | SE | 680 | 205 |
| PRI-44 | 324880 | 3659375 | 21 | SE | SE | 670 | 205 |
| PRI-45 | 324850 | 3659435 | 21 | SE | SE | 670 | 205 |
| PRI-46 | 325380 | 3659225 | 22 | SW | SW | 615 | 185 |
| PRI-47 | 325780 | 3659945 | 22 | SE | NW | 620 | 190 |
| PRI-48 | 325680 | 3660280 | 22 | NE | NW | 680 | 205 |
| PRI-49 | 325145 | 3659920 | 22 | SW | NW | 680 | 205 |
| PRI-50 | 325275 | 3659545 | 22 | NW | SW | 680 | 205 |
| PRI-51 | 324445 | 3659005 | 28 | NW | NE | 605 | 185 |
| PRI-52 | 324465 | 3659080 | 21 | SW | SE | 605 | 185 |
| PRI-53 | 324440 | 3659520 | 21 | NW | SE | 680 | 205 |
| PRI-54 | 324435 | 3659560 | 21 | NW | SE | 680 | 205 |
| PRI-55 | 324515 | 3659640 | 21 | NW | SE | 680 | 205 |
| PRI-56 | 324560 | 3659725 | 21 | NW | SE | 680 | 205 |
| PRI-57 | 324590 | 3659845 | 21 | NW | SE | 680 | 205 |
| PRI-58 | 324670 | 3659755 | 21 | NE | SE | 680 | 205 |
| PRI-59 | 324700 | 3659695 | 21 | NE | SE | 680 | 205 |

| Site Number | UTM ZONE 12 | | T4S, R6W | | | Elevation | |
| | Easting | Northing | Section | ¼ of the ¼ | | Feet | Approx. Meters |
|---|---|---|---|---|---|---|---|
| PRI-60 | 325000 | 3660140 | 21 | SE | NE | 700 | 215 |
| PRI-61 | 325070 | 3660130 | 22 | SW | NW | 700 | 215 |
| PRI-62 | 325115 | 3660085 | 22 | SW | NW | 680 | 205 |
| PRI-64 | 325010 | 3660285 | 21 | NE | NE | 710 | 215 |
| PRI-65 | 324970 | 3659620 | 21 | NE | SE | 685 | 210 |
| PRI-66 | 324970 | 3659670 | 21 | NE | SE | 685 | 210 |
| PRI-67 | 325080 | 3659755 | 22 | SW | SE | 685 | 210 |
| PRI-68 | 324830 | 3659845 | 21 | NE | SE | 680 | 205 |
| PRI-69 | 324915 | 3659915 | 21 | SW | NE | 685 | 210 |
| PRI-70 | 325000 | 3659990 | 21 | SW | NE | 695 | 210 |
| PRI-71 | 324965 | 3660045 | 21 | SW | NE | 700 | 215 |
| PRI-72 | 325030 | 3660090 | 21 | SW | NE | 700 | 215 |
| PRI-73 | 324470 | 3659475 | 21 | NW | SE | 660 | 200 |
| PRI-74 | 324595 | 3659730 | 21 | NW | SE | 660 | 200 |
| PRI-75 | 324570 | 3659660 | 21 | NW | SE | 670 | 205 |
| PRI-76 | 324960 | 3659350 | 21 | SW | SW | 660 | 200 |
| PRI-77 | 325030 | 3659580 | 22 | NW | SW | 670 | 205 |
| PRI-78 | 325100 | 3659230 | 22 | SW | SW | 620 | 190 |
| PRI-79 | 325100 | 3659170 | 22 | SW | SW | 620 | 190 |
| PRI-80 | 324780 | 3659360 | 21 | SE | SE | 676 | 206 |

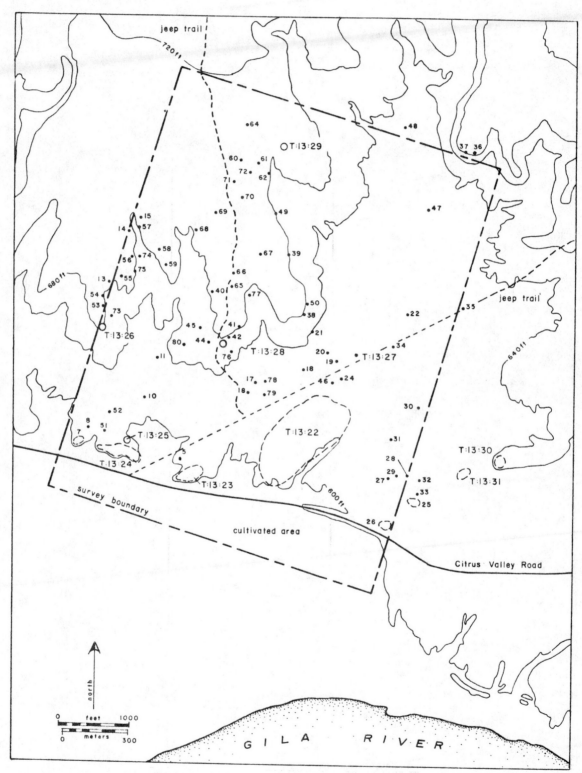

Figure A.1.   Location of sites.

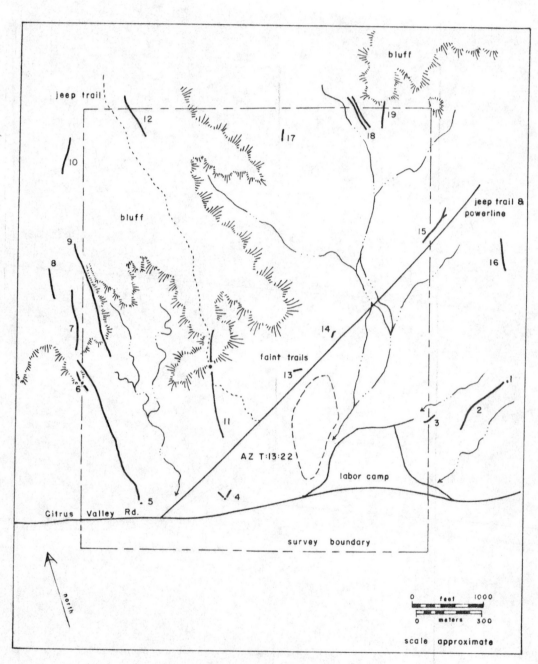

Figure A.2.    Trails in the study area.

Appendix B

STANDARD ASM SITE FORM AND SHORT FORM

ARIZONA STATE MUSEUM
Site Survey Form

Recorded by                                        (080) ASM Number:_____

(137)   Recorder(s)_____

        Date_____

        Site Reference

(143)   Project_____    Site Field Number_____

(105)   Site Name_____    (150) Ownership_____

(130)   Previous Refs. to Site_____

(145)   Photographs: B/W No(s)._____    Color No(s)._____

        Components

(090)   Number Recorded_____    (160) Present Use_____
                                                     (historic sites only)

        Location

(010)   State_____    (020) County_____

(025)   Quad Name and Series_____

(027)   Year Quad. Published_____    Map Number_____

(030)   T._____R._____ Sec._____,_____1/4 of the_____1/4

(070)   UTM Zone |_,_| Easting |_,_|_,_|_,_| Northing |_,_|_,_|_,_| -

        Other Project References_____

        Description of how to get to site:

121

Environment

(110)  Elevation (ft.)_____

(115)  Nearest Primary Drainage (give name)

Permanent_____

Semipermanent_____

Impermanent (runoff only)_____

(200)  Physiographic Province

____Desert

____Mountain

____Plateau

____Transition          Other (Specify)_____

Vegetation (refer to Brown and Lowe, 1974, for definitions)

(210)  Biotic Communities (Formation):     (215)  Biotic Communities (Community):

____Tundra                      ____Pine

____Forest                      ____Mixed Broadleaf

____Woodland                    ____Cottonwood-Willow

____Scrubland                   ____Pinyon-Juniper

____Grassland                   ____Mesquite Bosque

____Desertscrub                 ____Mixed Paloverde-Cacti

____Marshland                   ____Creosote-Bursage

                                ____Other (specify, using
                                          Brown and Lowe, 1974)

                                _____

                                _____

(220)  Contemporary Floral Observations:

| Name | On site | Near site | On and near site |
|------|---------|-----------|------------------|
| _____ | ____ | ____ | ____ |
| _____ | ____ | ____ | ____ |
| _____ | ____ | ____ | ____ |
| _____ | ____ | ____ | ____ |
| _____ | ____ | ____ | ____ |
| _____ | ____ | ____ | ____ |
| _____ | ____ | ____ | ____ |
| _____ | ____ | ____ | ____ |

(250)  Topographic Setting (See <u>Dictionary of Geological Terms</u>, American Geol. Inst.)

____alluvial fan       ____cave          ____mesa          ____rock shelter

____arroyo             ____cliff         ____mountain      ____sand bar

____bajada             ____delta         ____pediment      ____slope

____beach              ____dunes         ____plain         ____talus

____bluff              ____floodplain    ____plateau       ____terrace

____canyon (floor)     ____hill          ____playa         ____valley

____canyon (side)      ____meadow        ____ridge         ____Other (specify)

_____

(270)  Dominant Substrate

Consolidated:        ____Igneous      Type_____

                     ____Metamorphic  Type_____

                     ____Sedimentary  Type_____

Unconsolidated:      ____clay

                     ____silt

                     ____sand

                     ____gravel

                     ____cobble

                     ____boulder

(280)  Soil Type

____clay              ____gravel

____silt              ____loam

____sand              ____other (Specify, using class names.
                              Refer to Brady 1974:48)

_____

(900)   Comments on Site Environment

      Give any relevant additional information concerning the environmental
setting of the site, including observed relationships between environmental features or site and environmental features.

<u>Component</u>

(500)  Type

| | |
|---|---|
| \_\_\_\_Agricultural | \_\_\_\_Habitation |
| \_\_\_\_Ceremonial | \_\_\_\_Resource Exploitation |
| \_\_\_\_Communication | \_\_\_\_Historic/Commercial |
| \_\_\_\_Defensive | |

(501)  Features (indicate estimated number; additional information can be provided
on p. 9).

| | |
|---|---|
| \_\_\_\_Agricultural terrace | \_\_\_\_Field |
| \_\_\_\_Artifact (isolated) | \_\_\_\_Fieldhouse |
| \_\_\_\_Artifact scatter | \_\_\_\_Fire circle |
| | \_\_\_\_Firepit |
| \_\_\_\_Ballcourt | \_\_\_\_Fortification |
| \_\_\_\_Barn | \_\_\_\_Fort |
| \_\_\_\_Battlefield | |
| \_\_\_\_Bedrock metates | \_\_\_\_Garden |
| \_\_\_\_Bedrock mortars | \_\_\_\_Gate |
| \_\_\_\_Borrow pit | \_\_\_\_Granary |
| \_\_\_\_Building/specify | \_\_\_\_Gridded fields |
| \_\_\_\_Burial | \_\_\_\_Hearth (lined) |
| \_\_\_\_Cache | \_\_\_\_Hearth (unlined) |
| \_\_\_\_Campsite | \_\_\_\_Hogan |
| \_\_\_\_Canal | \_\_\_\_Hotel |
| \_\_\_\_Cave | \_\_\_\_House |
| \_\_\_\_Cemetery | \_\_\_\_House mound |
| \_\_\_\_Checkdam | \_\_\_\_House ring |
| \_\_\_\_Chipping station | \_\_\_\_Isolated room |
| \_\_\_\_Church | \_\_\_\_Inscription |
| \_\_\_\_Clay source | |
| \_\_\_\_Cliff dwelling | \_\_\_\_Kiva D-shaped |
| \_\_\_\_Compound | \_\_\_\_Kiva rectangular |
| \_\_\_\_Cremation | \_\_\_\_Kiva round |
| | \_\_\_\_Kiva Great |
| \_\_\_\_Dam | \_\_\_\_Latrine |
| \_\_\_\_Enclosure | \_\_\_\_Lithic concentration |
| | \_\_\_\_Lithic scatter |

_____ Mescal pit

_____ Midden

_____ Mine

_____ Mining Camp

_____ Mining Town

_____ Mission

_____ Mound

_____ Object/specify (to be used only for register sites)

_____ Petroglyph

_____ Pictograph

_____ Pit

_____ Pithouse

_____ Platform mound

_____ Pueblo (general)

_____ Pueblo adobe

_____ Pueblo cobble

_____ Pueblo dressed masonry

_____ Presidio

_____ Quarry

_____ Ramada

_____ Ranch

_____ Reservoir

_____ Roasting pit

_____ Rock art

_____ Rock pile

_____ Rock shelter

_____ Road

_____ Sheet trash

_____ Sherd concentration

_____ Sherd scatter

_____ Shrine

_____ Sleeping circle

_____ Stage station

_____ Stone alignment

_____ Stone circle

_____ Storage area

_____ Storage pit

_____ Storage room

_____ Structure/specify

_____ Terrace

_____ Tinaja

_____ Trading post

_____ Trail

_____ Trash (general)

_____ Trash mound

_____ Tower (round)

_____ Tower (square)

_____ Town

_____ Village

_____ Waffle garden

_____ Wall

_____ Wall (segment)

_____ Water control devices

_____ Water tank

_____ Wickiup

_____ Windbreak

_____ Workshop

_____ Other (specify)_____

_____

(505) Component identification (basis for)

_____ Functional        _____ Spatial

_____ Temporal          _____ Archival

(510) Area of Component in square meters _____

(515) Greatest Depth (in meters)

    _____ Unknown

    _____ Surface

    _____ Stratified (Estimated minimum depth_____)

    _____ Structures (Estimated minimum depth_____)

(525) Time

    _____ Prehistoric

    _____ Transitional

    _____ Historic

    _____ Unknown

(535) Cultural Affiliation

| | | | |
|---|---|---|---|
| _____ Anasazi | _____ Halchidhoma | _____ Navajo | _____ Sinagua |
| _____ Anglo | _____ Havasupai | _____ Ootam | _____ Sobaipuri |
| _____ Apache | _____ Hohokam | _____ Oriental | _____ Spanish |
| _____ Amargosan | _____ Hopi | _____ Pai | _____ Trincheras |
| _____ Cerbat | _____ Hualapai | _____ Paiute | _____ Yavapai |
| _____ Cochise | _____ Maricopa | _____ Paleo-Indian | _____ Yuma |
| _____ Cocopah | _____ Mexican | _____ Papago | _____ Zuni |
| _____ Desert Culture | _____ Mogollon | _____ Patayan | _____ Ute |
| _____ Hakataya | _____ Mojave | _____ Pima | _____ Other (Specify) |
| | _____ Mormon | _____ Salado | _____ |
| | | | _____ Unknown |

(540) Period_____

(545) Phase_____

(530) Dates_____

Artifacts

(630, 631) Ceramics

    Estimated percentage of total artifact assemblage_____

    Collections made_____ Sampling Procedure_____

    Sample Numbers_____

    Identification (list only most specific level known)

        Ware_____ Type_____

        Ware_____ Type_____

        Ware_____ Type_____

        Ware_____ Type_____

(650, 651, 660, 661, 670, 671)

Lithics

Estimated percentage of total artifact assemblage _____

Collections made _____ Sampling Procedure _____

Sample Numbers _____

Material: Indicate by placing appropriate letters after artifact types present.

A. Igneous     a. fine

B. Sedimentary     b. medium

C. Metamorphic     c. coarse

Flaked

Chopper _____     Knife _____

Core _____     Point _____

Cobble tools _____     Preform _____

Flake (Primary, unused) _____     Scraper _____

Flake (Secondary, unused) _____     Other (Specify) _____

Flake (Utilized) _____     _____

Ground

Abrader _____     Metate trough _____

Full grooved axe _____     Mortar _____

3/4 grooved axe _____     Ornament _____

Double bit axe _____     Palette _____

Mano _____     Pestle _____

Maul _____     Polishing stone _____

Metate (unspecified) _____     Preform _____

Metate basin _____     Shaft straightener _____

Metate slab _____     Other (Specify) _____

(680) Other Material Items

Estimated percentage of total artifact assemblage_____

Collections made_____ Sampling Procedure_____

Sample Numbers_____

Material:                                    Type:

_____         _____

_____         _____

_____         _____

_____         _____

_____         _____

_____         _____

_____         _____

_____

(690) Non-Artifact Collections

Kind:                                        Sample Numbers:

_____         _____

_____         _____

_____         _____

_____         _____

_____         _____

(900) Additional information concerning cultural features and artifacts: Note
relationships between features, and between artifacts and features.
Include any relevant additional information concerning the physical
characteristics and possible function of features, artifacts, and
component as a whole, and concerning relationships between components.

(520)   Integrity of Component

\_\_\_\_\_No disturbance

\_\_\_\_\_Natural disturbance

\_\_\_\_\_erosion

\_\_\_\_\_deposition

\_\_\_\_\_Human disturbance

\_\_\_\_\_vandalized                    \_\_\_\_\_grazed

\_\_\_\_\_excavated                     \_\_\_\_\_logged

\_\_\_\_\_cultivated                    \_\_\_\_\_chained

\_\_\_\_\_damaged by construction

Describe degree of disturbance and note present use of area. (Locate disturbed areas on site map.)_____

_____

_____

_____

(900)   Research Potential (Include reference to any characteristics which might make this site especially useful for specific research problems).

(900)  Surveyor Recommendations

       Further work_____

      _____

      _____

      _____

      _____

      Estimates for total data recovery

         man days_____

         heavy equipment
            (type and hours)_____

(550)  National Register Status        (560)  State Register Status

      ____listed                          ____listed

      ____should be nominated*           ____should be nominated*

      ____should not be nominated*      ____should not be nominated*

      ____status indeterminate           ____status indeterminate

      *If checked, explain reason:

## Sketch of Site Setting

Note location with respect to access roads, drainages, trails, buildings,
natural landmarks, and other important reference points. Include north
arrow, key and scale.

Plan View

Cross-section

## SHORT FORM

Recorded by _____

Date _____ Other Map Reference _____

Project _____ Site Field Number _____

Photographs B/W no(s)_____ Color no(s)_____

State_____ County_____

Quad and Series _____

T_____R_____S_____,_____1/4 of the _____ 1/4.

UTM Zone _____ Easting_____Northing_____

Description of how to get to site:

Elevation_____Dimensions of site_____

Boundaries: Natural_____ Arbitrary_____

Vegetation:

Topography:

Components:

Material Culture:

Disturbance:

Comments:

Appendix C

MITIGATION PROGRAM FOR STUDY AREA


        Two budgets follow that are based on recommendations in Chapter
6. The first budget is for relocating selected features or sites,
preparing records, and setting datums as the initial step in a
monitoring program. Once this has been done, additional work will be
required only after each major episode of flooding, to check the
condition of the remains. This subsequent work can be done on a daily
rate basis, with fieldwork at $330.00 per person per day and letter
report preparation at $180.00 per person per day.

        The second budget is for testing and mitigation work. All
figures in this appendix are based on September 1981 rates and must be
considered tentative estimates.

# BUDGET

Painted Rock Reservoir Initial Monitoring
Corps of Engineers

## Direct Costs

### Personnel Services

| | |
|---|---:|
| Project Director - 12 days @ $81.00/day | $ 972.00 |
| Archaeological Specialist III | |
|     Field - 1 person for 6 days @ $75.36/day | 452.16 |
|     Report - 1 person for 12 days @ $75.36/day | 904.32 |
| Archaeological Specialist I | |
|     Field - 1 person for 6 days @ $55.84/day | 335.04 |
|     Report - 1 person for 5 days @ $55.84/day | 279.20 |
| Report Draftsman | |
|     1 person for 5 days @ $55.84/day | 279.20 |
| Editor | |
|     1 person for 5 days @ $55.84/day | 279.20 |
| Typing and Clerical | |
|     1 person for 3 days @ $42.00/day | 126.00 |
| CRMD Administrative Assistant - 3 days @ $49.92/day | 149.76 |
| Division Bookkeeping - 3 days @ $43.84/day | 131.52 |
| Wage Subtotal | $ 3,908.40 |
| Vacation/Sickleave Accrual, 5% of Wage Subtotal | 195.42 |
| Total Wages and Accruals | $ 4,103.82 |
| Employee Benefits, 21.6% of Total Wages and Accruals | 886.42 |
| Total Personnel Services | $ 4,990.24 |

### Travel

| | |
|---|---:|
| Subsistence | |
|     2 people for 6 days each = 12 days @ $40.00/day | $ 480.00 |

Vehicles
   1 4 X 4 Carryall, 6 days @ $10.00/day dispatch fee     $ 60.00
   1000 miles @ $0.30/mile     300.00

Operations

Supplies
   Research     $ 75.00
   Office     20.00
   Report     100.00

Repair and Maintenance
   Equipment     100.00
   Vehicles     100.00

Reproduction
   Field Notes     10.00
   Report     200.00

Total Travel & Operations $ 1,445.00

Total Direct Costs    $ 6,435.24

Indirect Cost

43% of Total Direct Cost    $ 2,767.15

Total Cost    $ 9,202.39

Rounded to:    $ 9,202.00

# BUDGET

## Testing at Painted Rock Dam
## Corps of Engineers

### Direct Costs

#### Personnel Services

| | |
|---|---:|
| Project Director - 55 days @ $81.00/day | $ 4,293.00 |
| **Archaeological Specialist III** | |
| Preparation - 1 person for 2 days @ $75.36/day | 150.72 |
| Field - 1 person for 15 days @ $75.36/day | 1,130.40 |
| Report - 1 person for 45 days @ $75.36/day | 3,391.20 |
| **Archaeological Specialist I** | |
| Field - 1 person for 15 days @ $55.84/day | 837.60 |
| Report - 1 person for 45 days @ $55.84/day | 2,512.80 |
| **Archaeological Aide II** | |
| Field - 2 people for 15 days = 30 days @ $48.96/day | 1,468.80 |
| **Report Draftsman** | |
| 1 person for 10 days @ $55.84/day | 558.40 |
| **Editor** | |
| 1 person for 12 days @ $55.84/day | 670.08 |
| **Typing and Clerical** | |
| 1 person for 15 days @ $42.00/day | 630.00 |
| CRMD Administrative Assistant - 13 days @ $49.92/day | 648.96 |
| Division bookkeeping - 13 days @ $43.84/day | 469.92 |
| Wage Subtotal | $ 16,861.88 |
| Vacation/Sickleave Accrual, 5% of Wage Subtotal | 843.09 |
| Total Wages and Accruals | $ 17,704.97 |
| Employee Benefits, 21.6% of Total Wages and Accruals | 3,824.27 |
| Total Personnel Services | $ 21,529.24 |

### Travel

| | |
|---|---:|
| **Subsistence** | |
| 4 people for 15 days each = 60 days @ $40.00/day | $ 2,400.00 |

Vehicles
   1 4 X 4 Carryall, 20 days @ $10.00/day dispatch fee        $ 200.00
   1700 miles @ $0.30/mile                                            510.00

## Operations

Supplies
   Research
   Office                                         $ 150.00
   Report                                         30.00
                                               150.00

Repair and Maintenance
   Equipment
   Vehicles                                      100.00
                                               100.00

Reproduction
   Field Notes
   Report                                         15.00
                                           3,000.00

                        Total Travel & Operations $ 6,655.00

                        Total Direct Costs        $ 28,184.24

## Indirect Cost

43% of Total Direct Cost

                                             $12,119.22

Total Cost                          $40,303.46

Rounded to:                      $40,303.00

Appendix D

COLLECTIONS

Collections were limited to a few sherds, which are stored
at the Arizona State Museum. A complete list of collections
follows:

AZ T:13:28 (PRI-43)

Feature 1: 1 sherd, Gila Plain, Gila Bend var.

Feature 2: 2 sherds, probably Salt Red.

Isolated Sherd: Lower Colorado Buff Ware (possibly
        Palomas Buff).

AZ T:13:30 (PRS-78-22)

2 sherds, unidentified Papaguerian brown ware.

PRI-18

1 sherd, Lower Colorado Buff Ware, possibly Patayan II

PRI-66

1 sherd, Lower Colorado Buff Ware, possibly Colorado Beige